FANATICS AND FOOLS

The Game Plan for
Winning Back America

ARIANNA HUFFINGTON

miramax books

HYPERION

NEW YORK

ISBN 1-4013-5213-8

First Edition
10 9 8 7 6 5 4 3

For my daughters
Christina and Isabella

CONTENTS

SECTION II:
A BUSH REPUBLICAN TAKES CALIFORNIA

ADVENTURES ON THE CAMPAIGN TRAIL

SECTION III:
THE FOOLS

SECTION IV:
THE OTHER SIDE OF THE MOUNTAIN

FANATICS
AND FOOLS

INTRODUCTION

This book should be dedicated to an unfailing source of inspiration for me: the California recall race. If it had not happened and if I had not run for governor, this would simply be a book of criticism and outrage. These are perfectly legitimate responses to our current political landscape. But my temporary transformation from pundit to candidate brought me face-to-face with the inadequacy of criticism and outrage, no matter how witty, quotable, or justified.

Don't get me wrong: in the pages ahead there will be plenty of criticism of the fanatics who now run the Republican Party and the fools guiding the Democratic Party who have enabled the fanatics to prevail. But the heart of the book is my newfound conviction that to win in November, the Democratic nominee will have to propose a return to the idealism, boldness, and generosity of spirit that marked the presidencies of FDR and JFK and the short-lived presidential campaign of Bobby Kennedy.

The 2004 presidential election will be a political event with unprecedented significance for our lives and the lives of our children. Bush Republicans have offered a messianic vision of a new world built on tax cuts. This call has proven incredibly alluring: it's clear, it's broad, and it's accessible. Democrats need to present a vision that is equally clear, broad, and accessible, and that answers the fundamental question: what sort of America do we want to live in? Do we want an America that's fair and generous and demands the best of its citizens, an

Bush Republicans have offered a messianic vision of a new world built on tax cuts. This call has proven incredibly alluring: it's clear, it's broad, and it's accessible. Democrats need to present a vision that is equally clear, broad, and accessible, and that answers the fundamental question: what sort of America do we want to live in?

America where equal opportunity is a reality, not an empty slogan, an America that is respected around the world for its commitment to freedom and justice, an America that takes on the mantle of superpower in order to confront repression, relieve suffering, and preserve world peace? Can we aspire again to creating a country where full-time work yields a living wage and where good schools and good health care forge a stronger America in which every citizen is better off?

If the question is accurately framed, the Bush Republicans' one-note answer doesn't even have the virtue of self-interest. An America where the gulf between rich and poor is not so grotesque, where hard work is rewarded, where every child can get a decent education, and where health care is available to everyone is a stronger America for us all—including Bush Republicans.

These are long-standing American ideals, not inventions of the left. But an indication of how successful the Republican machine has been at framing the overarching political debate is that even in times of dire emergency, when a state like California is facing the prospect of bankruptcy, tax increases, which should be a viable fiscal lifeline, are instead seen as a suicide pill. We've gotten to the point in this country where you can't raise taxes to repel an invasion from Mars unless you are able to disguise them as an economic stimulus package.

So here we are, watching the social contract go up in flames, not just in California, but in the entire country. It's a blaze ignited by the fanatics and watched helplessly by the fools. But ushering Bush and his band of fanatics out of the White House in 2004 is going to take more than just a critique, however masterful, of what they've done to our country. It's going to take a moral vision that replaces the dark grasping of the Bush administration. And given the stakes, and the way our political system is currently structured, it's going to have to be the Democratic presidential candidate who provides it.

There you have it. This is my endorsement for president in 2004: The Democrat. Although the story I'm about to tell you of fanatics and fools, of evil villains and even one or two heroes, is very much a political thriller, I'm violating one of Tom Clancy's golden rules: I'm starting with a surprise beginning rather than concluding with a surprise ending. That I should pick a side for 2004, especially one I've been criticizing as tired, intellectually bankrupt, and complicit in the current crisis, rather than advocate some new progressive coalition, is a big turnaround for me. In the years that have passed since my Republican interlude, I've been more comfortable on the outside of the two-party system because only from the outside, I believe, is the true geography of our national crisis visible. But from that perspective I have seen the crisis deepen alarmingly in recent times. We can't wait any longer for some sort of tectonic change. So while keeping the fires of reform burning, I'm sticking my nose in the Democratic tent, hoping that the Democratic nominee will offer the progressive transformation this country so desperately needs.

I suppose my optimism about the future comes down to what I think about human nature. If I thought that we were just material beings, driven purely by self-interest, then I would have to concede that we have no hope of rallying people around a noble alternative to the rescue fantasy offered by Rummy, Cheney, Cowboy George, or Arnold the "Terminator." If on the other hand I believed—and I do—that we are capable of both good and evil, then it's time to appeal to what is best in us, to summon "the better angels of our nature." Only then are we likely to build a nation where community and caring and compassion are not just throat-clearing openings to commencement addresses.

I've always believed this should be the goal of a healthy democracy. But I've had quite a journey when it comes to deciding the best means for getting there.

One stop along the way was on January 24, 1993, at a "Conservative Summit," in Washington, D.C., sponsored by the *National Review*. I gave a speech entitled "Can Conservatives Have a Social Conscience?" The event was kicked off in bombastic style by Master of Ceremonies Charlton Heston, who smugly announced that he was "one of the most politically incorrect people" because "I am heterosexual, Anglo-Saxon, married to the same woman for forty-nine years, and not the recipient of any entitlement of any kind."

That type of statement tends to set a certain tone. Sitting on the dais, scanning my notes, I listened with mounting horror to the speaker who preceded me, Brent Bozell, who had been the national finance chairman of the legendarily inclusive '92 Buchanan for President campaign. As Bozell's hard-right homilies were paraded in front of what, in the interest of fairness, can only be described as an adoring crowd, I asked myself two questions: "How can he and I both call ourselves Republicans?" and "Where is the nearest exit?"

Approaching the podium with trepidation, I wondered what the audience that applauded the previous speakers' harsh brand of conservatism would do with mine, which challenged the audience to rise to what I considered the core of true conservatism—the biblical admonition that we shall be judged by what we do for the least among us.

In its article on the event, the *New York Times* reported that "Mrs. Huffington's goal is the redemption of the Republican Party. If she had her way, greed and selfishness will be banished forever, to be replaced by altruism, compassion, and the 'kinder, gentler' world that George Bush talked about but failed to deliver." The *Times* reporter, Karen De Witt, went on to express the opinion, "It is an odd notion to link altruism and compassion with conservatives, considering last year's Republican convention."

I too had been appalled by the 1992 Republican convention—particularly Pat Buchanan's divisive speech (the one Molly Ivins memorably nailed as probably sounding better in the original German). But I believed at the time—wrongly, as it turned out—that I could challenge the Republican Party by harking back to the nobler traditions of its past.

The problem is not with rank-and-file Republicans but with the party's leaders. The same conservative audience that gave a standing ovation to Bozell gave a standing ovation to me. We just appealed to different parts of their brains and their psyches. I reached out to classic conservatism that sees individuals as the spiritual center of society, and expects them to obey the Golden Rule: "Do unto others as you would have them do unto you." Indeed, they are expected to follow the biblical precept, "To whom much is given, from him that much more shall be expected." Individuals, not government, have the responsibility to form communities, to weave a social fabric that sustains the weak, cares for the young, and nurtures those who have grown old. Without this component of social conscience, the potent doctrine of individual responsibility is reduced to an exclusively material self-interest. And individuals are reduced to little more than economic entities: producing and consuming units.

I believed just as deeply in the need for social responsibility during my Republican days as I believe in it now. But these days I draw very different conclusions from that basic principle. The reason is very simple. The social challenge I issued that morning during my speech, a gauntlet I kept throwing down until my final disillusionment with the Grand Old Party, was never taken up. The hope and expectation that people would roll up their sleeves and get their hands dirty to solve social problems at the local level was never fully realized. There were never enough volunteers, never enough donations, never enough model partnerships and pilot projects set up to prove what we conservatives claimed: that we could solve America's ills without "big government."

Feeling that the whole system had to be shaken up, I cast my vote in 2000 for neither Bush nor Gore. Instead I marked my ballot for "none of the above" as a protest against the broken status quo. But that wasn't enough. So I helped organize the Shadow Conventions to coincide with the Republican convention in Philadelphia and the Democratic convention in Los Angeles and put the media spotlight on the fact that neither major party was addressing three key issues facing us: 1) the painful truth that we've become two nations, separated by an ever-widening economic gulf—not just in income but in educational opportunities, access to health care, even in the quality of the air we breathe and our statistical chances of living to an old age; 2) the way money is corrupting our politics and campaign contributors are buying public policy; and 3) the nation's failed $40-billion-a-year war on drugs, which has turned into a war on the poor and minorities.

Then came the Bush White House—and all it has brought with it, including Iraq, multitrillion-dollar tax cuts, corporate scandals, the gutting of environmental regulations, a record-breaking number of lost jobs, and the neglect of millions of struggling Americans. Despite this abysmal performance, there was no "loyal opposition." There was some bickering, a little partisanship, a bit of token jockeying from the other side of the aisle, but no clear alternative vision to rally around.

Last year, during the course of a thirteen-city college speaking tour, I came to a realization: it wasn't just me. To put it bluntly, Americans young and old, northerner and southerner, city slicker and country cousin, rich and poor (OK, maybe not the Bush rich) are all royally pissed off. But the pain, rage, and anxiety that came pouring out as soon as I opened the floor to questions and comments signaled that indignation had risen to a whole new level. This was not the dry, intellectual harrumphing found on the op-ed page. This was the cry of people who were ready to stop just talking and start acting.

I knew how they felt. I've always had a hard time just identifying wrongs and leaving it at that. I too wanted to take action, to move beyond the confines of jousting punditry. Which brings us to January 2003. That's when the *Oregonian* newspaper abruptly decided to stop carrying my syndicated column, giving as a reason: "She has dragged herself across the line from being a commentator to being an activist." The truth is that I have always seen myself as a crusading journalist in the tradition of my heroes Upton Sinclair, Lincoln Steffens, and Ida Tarbell. I have always wanted to walk my talk, which is why, two years after I helped organize the Shadow Conventions, I cofounded the Detroit Project with my friends and fellow activists, Lawrence Bender, Laurie David, and Ari Emmanuel. It's a grassroots campaign to prod Detroit to stop building gas-guzzling SUVs and start producing cleaner, more fuel-efficient cars that will allow us to break our addiction to foreign oil. That was what constituted crossing the line, in the *Oregonian*'s memorable phrase.

Two months after the Detroit Project, I helped create the Bermuda Project to expose corporate America's growing use of shady offshore tax havens to avoid paying its fair share.

While the Shadow Conventions, the anti-SUV campaign, and the anti-tax-haven campaign were actually extensions of what I had been doing for my whole life, my next campaign definitely broke new personal ground. I ran for governor.

Though I didn't support the recall effort, once it was set in motion—once it was definitely going to happen—I felt it was foolish to assume it would be defeated. And I was drawn by the unprecedented opportunity it offered to elect a truly progressive governor to the world's fifth-largest economy. And to give a voice to all the people of California, not just those who could afford to buy public policy.

I also wanted to connect the dots between California's plight and the reckless economic policies of the Bush administration. And, as I ended up saying again and again and again over the course of the campaign, there was nothing more laughable than hearing Bush Republicans prattling on self-righteously about the fiscal irresponsibility of Gray Davis while ignoring the orgy of fiscal irresponsibility that the White House and the Republican Congress are hosting.

But I learned on the campaign trail that laying out clearly articulated policies and a clear critique of your opponent is not enough. And it will definitely not be enough to beat Bush in 2004. The Democratic nominee will have to have a powerful narrative to counter the very simple but very compelling "tax cuts, more tax cuts, and further tax cuts" fairy tale being put forth by the Bush White House. What I have realized is that the narrative must be exceptionally bold—transcending not just what passes for the current Democratic vision but even the vision of the politically successful Clinton

You cannot have a strong America if one third of eighth graders can't read. You cannot have a strong America if millions of our citizens don't have the basic resources to take care of their health. You cannot have a strong America without strong families. And you cannot have strong families when you have two parents each working two-and-a-half jobs just to make ends meet. This is not a left-wing vision. The common good encompasses a lot of common ground.

years. It has to go back to the founding of our country, to the spiritual absolute the Founding Fathers grounded America in when they declared "all men are created equal"—a premise Abraham Lincoln called "the father of all moral principle."

It's the same moral principle FDR gave expression to when he said that "the test of our progress is not whether we add more to the abundance of those who have much; it is whether we provide enough for those who have too little." It's the same moral principle Bobby Kennedy echoed amid the social upheaval of the 1960s: "I believe that as long as there is plenty, poverty is evil."

Not only have we become unmoored from those principles, we've drifted tragically far from them. Which is why, as I learned on the campaign trail, stopping any more Republican takeovers has an urgency that supersedes the larger imperative of breaking the stranglehold of two party politics in order to challenge the broken status quo.

This difference between the urgent and the important is exactly what prompted me to drop out of the recall race when it became clear that I wouldn't win. If I had not, and Arnold Schwarzenegger had eked into the governor's office, I would not have been able to forgive myself. And even though my withdrawal ultimately proved futile, the sense of foreboding that motivated it was validated when, in his first budget, the new governor proposed cutting $4.6 billion from health care, education, and welfare programs. He had already repealed the car tax without having alternative funding for the essential local government services—things like police and fire departments—that the $4 billion from the car tax was earmarked for.

It's clear that the damage being done by the Republican fanatics—whether in Washington or Sacramento—is such that we cannot afford the kind of protest votes that are geared toward long-term reform. I didn't have a problem with Ralph Nader's running in 2000. But that was then and this is now. Now we have seen George Bush's true colors. We have seen what has happened in Iraq. We have seen what has happened to the goodwill we once enjoyed around the world. We have seen the results of his regressive economic policies. We have seen who benefits and who loses in the world according to George Bush. It's folly to pretend that it doesn't make a difference whether Bush or his Democratic opponent is in the White House. It's like trying to unring the last three years' carillon of alarms.

It's all well and good to dream about how wonderful it would be to remodel your home, but when your house is going up in flames, your first priority must be putting the fire out. Our collective priority for the near term must be to evict the Crawford squatter from the White House. Only then can we set about remodeling our democratic home. We simply can't do it in reverse.

In a very real way, the California recall race was a microcosm of everything that is going on in the country today, a showcase for the strengths and weaknesses of the two political parties. The Bush Republicans' greatest strength was the simplicity of their antitax, anti-regulation message, hand-delivered by a charismatic messenger. The Democrats' greatest failing was a partywide lack of insight, courage, and strategic acumen.

So this book is divided into four parts. The first is a chapter-and-verse diagnosis of the fanaticism that drives the Bush White House. It also offers a clear-eyed prescription: Bush cannot be treated, let alone cured. He has to be surgically removed. The second part is a close-up look at a remarkable breakthrough in Bush Republican cloning—the rise of the charming antitax fanatic Arnold Schwarzenegger. The third part recounts and examines the Democratic Party leadership's congenital inability to stop shooting itself in the foot. It comes with a prescription: the Democrats need more than Bushwhacking and a better Medicare drug plan to regain the White House in November. Precisely what this "more" is will be found in the fourth part of the book—my hard-earned-in-the-trenches political donation to the Democratic presidential nominee.

It's the secret weapon for beating Bush.

A president once said: "You are the generation that must decide. Will you ratify poverty and division with your apathy—or will you build the common good with your idealism? Will you be the spectator in the renewal of your country—or a citizen?" That president, believe it or not, was George W. Bush. He said it at a commencement address at Notre Dame in May 2001. (The transcript does not note whether he had a straight face or not.)

But he's actually getting good at saying things like this. For George W. Bush, this rhetoric is designed to mask the reality of how he governs. It's a spoken word Potemkin village. If he were speaking the truth, he would have said, "I have ratified poverty by increasing it by 3 million people. Increased poverty and growing middle-class casualties have in turn enlarged the divisions between us. Even though I never speak about apathy except in commencement addresses, I understand it because my actions can only produce a certain grinding hopelessness after a time. So do me a favor and stay on the sidelines: The last thing I need at this point is a bunch of concerned citizens in my way. And by the way, let's win one for the Gipper!"

Security isn't just about protecting America from terrorists. It's also about protecting America's families from poverty and a bleak future for their children. True strength will come from a vision of New Responsibility that extends beyond caring for your own family to caring for your fellow man.

According to Catholic teachings, "the corruption of the best is the worst." George Bush's corrupt use of the concept of "the common good" muddies the water to such a shameful degree that the idea loses all meaning. The point of government is to provide for the common good, but on George Bush's lips it is transformed into an empty platitude. The Democratic nominee has the difficult task, made harder by the clever cynicism of Bush's message mavens, of resurrecting the idea of our common good and breathing real meaning into it.

And as Bush demonstrated at Notre Dame, you cannot talk about the common good without talking about lifting people from poverty. But notice how, in the course of a single presidential pronouncement, poverty suddenly became the responsibility of apathetic college students. It's subtle trickery to equate concern and caring with a cure. Sure, a cure starts there. But, as Bush points out in the same speech, "a determined assault on poverty will require both an active government and active citizens."

This book will show how those sentiments are exactly what the Democratic nominee has to express—and mean—as the foundation of a vision that will defeat Bush in November. This vision must link the compelling mission of the moment—to strengthen our country so that it can stand up to the assaults of this new millennium—with the pursuit of the common good. A truly strong America is one that can help the less fortunate, can admit mistakes, can once again excite the admiration of people around the world, regardless of their prejudices, by its fine example.

If you accept the inherent link between the common good and a strong America, then the list of what needs to be done becomes obvious. You cannot have a strong America if one-third of eighth graders can't read. You cannot have a strong America if millions of our citizens don't have the basic resources to take care of their health. You cannot have a strong America without strong families. And you cannot have strong families with two parents each working two-and-a-half jobs just to make ends meet.

This is not a left-wing vision. People of good faith, regardless of party, understand that fairness—rules of the game that all must abide by—is essential to the public welfare. But fairness and nurturing and a strong safety net do not mean babying our citizens and removing life's inevitable obstacles. The common good is achieved, in large measure, through the incentives that come from competition—as long as competition takes place on a level playing field.

Here's the message President Bush offered his audience of idealistic college grads: "The methods of the past may have been flawed, but the idealism of the past was not an illusion. Your calling is not easy, because you must do the acting and the caring. But there is fulfillment in that sacrifice, which creates hope for the rest of us. Every life you help proves that every life might be helped. The actual proves the possible. And hope is always the beginning of change."

If you closed your eyes, you would think you were listening to the ideal Democratic nominee—not the words of a zealous right-wing ideologue who used "compassion" as a campaign slogan, then tossed it aside like a soiled tissue as soon as he stepped into the Oval Office. But when the Democratic candidate uses the same rhetoric it will have to be matched with action.

Different times require different leaders and different strategies. This book is about the coming presidential election, and an alternative moral vision of strength. Without this vision, the public will be fooled again by the Republican fanatics selling strength but meting out punishment and weakness. Ultimately, this book will argue, the Democratic nominee will have to counter the White House's culture of fear and disunity with a bold vision that acknowledges uncertainty and evil in the world without being intimidated by them. Security isn't just about protecting America from terrorists. Security is also about protecting America's families from poverty and a bleak future for their children. True strength will emerge from a vision of New Responsibility that extends beyond caring for your own family to caring for your fellow man.

SECTION I

THE FANATICS

THE FANATICS' MATRIX

Remember how the Bush administration ambled unassumingly into office, downing Texas-sized helpings of humble pie at every meal? "I hope I'm viewed as a humble person," the president said just before moving into the White House. On his first day on the job, he counseled his senior staff members to "be an example of humility and decency and fairness." White House Chief of Staff Andy Card echoed the sentiment, setting a low bar by telling would-be staffers, "Be among the most humble people in Washington."

Well, those days didn't last long. Forget tiptoeing. Before its first year in office was out, Team Bush was stomping through the halls of power like Godzilla trampling the streets of Tokyo. Humble pie was no longer being served at the White House; instead it was being shoved in everyone else's face.

As the tidal wave of misinformation leading up to the war in Iraq and the $1.3 trillion tax cut was followed by a tidal wave of misinformation following the war in Iraq and the passage of an additional $800 billion tax cut, I found myself racking my brain trying to reconcile the ever-widening chasm between what the White House claims to be true and what is actually true. After all, despite his jus' folks image, we know the president and his men are not stupid, and I don't believe their wanton behavior is merely a case of compulsive lying.

The only explanation for the growing gap between their delusional rhetoric and our not-so-rosy reality is that we are being governed by a gang of out-and-out fanatics. The defining trait of the fanatic—be it a Marxist, a fascist or, gulp, a Wolfowitz—is an utter refusal to allow anything as piddling as evidence to get in the way of an unshakable belief. Bush and his fellow fanatics are the political equivalent of those yogis who can hold their breath and go without air for hours. Such is their mental control, they can go without truth for, well, years. Because, in their minds, they're always right. Oopso facto. Words mean nothing. They're just tools to get what you want. That pretty much sums up the White House MO on everything, from the status of Al Qaeda to the condition of postwar Iraq to the job-producing virtues of the latest round of tax cuts.

WHEN PAUL O'NEILL SOUNDS LIKE TIP O'NEILL—AND OTHER FANATICAL ABERRATIONS

In January 2004, former Treasury Secretary Paul O'Neill offered a concurring second opinion to my diagnosis, backed by some 19,000 pages of lab results: the country is being governed not by the genial figurehead now pretending to run toward the center in hopes of reelection, but by a band of out-and-out fanatics.

According to O'Neill, invading Iraq was a Bush goal before he had even learned where the Oval Office supply closet was. It came up just ten days after the inauguration, at the new president's first National Security Council meeting. "It was all about finding a way to do it," he says. "That was the tone of it. The president saying, 'Go find me a way to do this.'"

Of course, All the President's Men (and Condi, too!) did just that, gathering a collection of dubious facts, half-truths, quarter-truths, and—the House Specialty—no-truths (what "unpatriotic" people would call lies) to match the desired outcome. A slice of Nigerien yellowcake, anyone?

The picture of a White House teeming with fanatics gets even clearer with O'Neill's depiction of the Bush brain trust's dogged devotion to cutting taxes for the wealthy.

And, before I go any further, one word of advice to the White House attack dogs immediately unleashed on O'Neill: If you want to belittle his bona fides, you've got to come up with something better than saying, "We didn't listen to him when he was here. Why should we now?" Let's get real. Is there anyone more central to developing economic policy than the Treasury Secretary?

Now, of course, the Bushies are painting him out to be a cross between Jerry Garcia, Karl Marx, and the disgruntled former employee who just shot up the local post office. Yeah, what an anti-establishment wack-job: former CEO of Alcoa, and a friend of Don Rumsfeld's since the sixties.

Anyway, whether or not the high priests of the church of tax cuts listened to him, O'Neill certainly listened to them, and did what this administration makes a fetish of not doing: telling the American people what their government is really up to. To hear O'Neill tell it, the true believers surrounding the president, headed by Karl Rove and O'Neill's one-time patron Dick Cheney, are all devout disciples of the first commandment of Bush Republicans: thou shalt cut taxes for the wealthy, no matter what the cost to the greater good. They have all drunk the supply-side Kool-Aid—and simply don't care to hear any debate on this subject. Or on any other for that matter. As O'Neill puts it, "That store is closed." To disagree with the Bush clan is, according to their vast, self-serving, post–9/11 definition of patriotism, to hate America.

What's more, in classic fanatical fashion, the inner circle in the Oval Office displays an utter intolerance of dissent.

When O'Neill, who had the gall to be concerned about the looming fiscal crisis triggered by the growing budget deficit, argued against a second round of tax cuts, he was quickly put in his place by Cheney. "Reagan proved that deficits don't matter," growled the vice president, blithely ignoring the nearly twenty years it took to undo the fiscal damage Reagan's budget-busting had wrought. Besides, added Cheney, sounding less like the most powerful #2 in history than a kid cajoling his parents into giving him ice cream because he has cleaned his plate, "We won the mid-term elections, this is our due." An over-stuffed gift bag for the president's prosperous donor corps is "our due?" Is it actually possible to so badly misread what this country—or, indeed, democracy—is about?

It's a measure of how effectively the GOP radicals have framed the political debate, with taxes as the root of all evil, that Paul O'Neill, a bedrock-ribbed establishment Republican, comes across among the Bush Republicans like Tip O'Neill.

Hell, it turns out even President Bush had his doubts about the virtue of following his first round of serve-the-rich tax cuts with a heaping second helping. "Haven't we already given money to rich people?" Bush asks at a 2002 meeting of his economic team. "Shouldn't we be giving money to the middle?" Quick, ring security! How did that man get in here?

This momentary bout of presidential scruples was quickly

cured by Karl Rove. "Stick to principle. Stick to principle. Don't waver," he urged Bush repeatedly. The principle, I suppose, being: "If we wanna win in 2004 we gotta keep our Pioneers and Rangers happy!" Boy Genius, indeed.

The most alarming thing that emerges from O'Neill's revelations is the total lack of leadership on Bush's part. Just as the president was finally outgrowing the long-standing rumors that he was a cheerful pawn in a game he was too dumb to understand, O'Neill applies the paddles to the "Bush as clown" theory, turns on the juice, and yells, "Clear!"

At the very moment that Rove and the Bush reelection team are gearing up to sell us the president as the macho, heroic cowboy from Crawford who is going to keep us all safe from terrorists, despots, and Mad Cow meat, here comes his former Treasury Secretary with his devastating assessment of Bush as "a blind man in a roomful of deaf people."

So here we have one more wakeup call to open the American public's eyes to the deadly consequences of being governed by a disengaged dolt in the hands of a gang of brazen fanatics.

PROOF? WE DON'T NEED NO STINKING PROOF

Who else but a fanatic would have made the outrageous claim, as the president did in September 2002, that "you can't distinguish between Al Qaeda and Saddam when you talk about the war on terror?" Really? He couldn't differentiate between a group of evil ultraradical Islamic fundamentalists who carried out the September 11 attacks and an evil secular nationalist who, despite the frantic efforts of the Bush administration, has in no way been directly linked to 9/11? When every expert who knows anything about the Mideast can distinguish between the two, was it too much to ask that a president ready to go to war and commit the lives of American troops examine the universally accepted facts a bit more closely? Is our bar for the presidency set *that* low?

Another distinguishing behavior of fanatics is to regress to earlier stages of development. Bush Administration fanatics were so intent on toppling Saddam, so tightly gripped by a need to succeed where the president's war hero dad failed, so determined to lay the murderous 9/11 assault at Baghdad's door that they regressed to that level of childhood development where fantasy, reality, and wish fulfillment become one. They've discovered that wild obsessions can be a fountain of youth of sorts: if you are truly determined to believe what you want to believe, abracadabra, suddenly you're three years old again. Except this time, you're playing with the safety of the world for the next few decades, not blocks and fingerpaint.

I believe there's a clinical term for this condition: going off the deep end. How else to explain the president's bizarre response to a reporter's straightforward query back in the fall of 2002 about who poses a bigger threat to America, Saddam or Al Qaeda. "That's an interesting question," he replied. "I'm trying to think of something humorous to say, but I can't when I think about Al Qaeda and Saddam Hussein."

When did the president take over the *Tonight Show*? Why would the idea that he should make a joke about such a deadly serious subject even cross his mind? During that same press conference, instead of bothering to give any semblance of a defense of his sudden mental merging of Saddam and Osama, the president launched into a fantasy-fueled diatribe: "The danger is, is that they work in concert. The danger is, is that Al Qaeda becomes an extension of Saddam's madness and his hatred and his capacity to extend weapons of mass destruction around the world."

The president's condition spread like the West Nile virus throughout the West Wing and beyond. Witness the symptomatic blurring of fact and fantasy exhibited by Defense Secretary Donald Rumsfeld. When asked at a Senate Armed Services Committee hearing in September 2002 what was compelling us to "take precipitous actions" against Iraq, Rumsfeld barked, "What's different? What's different is three thousand people were killed." Yeah, by Mohammed Atta and company—not Saddam Hussein. But why quibble over details when there is a propaganda war to be won? In this latest rewrite of history, Osama lost his beard and grew a mustache, morphing into the Butcher of Baghdad, or one of the lookalike stand-ins Saddam was using for public appearances.

National Security Advisor Condoleezza Rice continued the assault on reality when she vaguely yet ominously claimed, "There clearly are contacts between Al Qaeda and Iraq that can be documented." Well, then why not document them? We've documented contacts between Al Qaeda and our oil dealers in Saudi Arabia and Al Qaeda and our new best friends in Pakistan. But I don't see any B-2s powering up for raids over Riyadh or Karachi.

As is the White House custom, Rice simply refused to back up her claims. So did Rumsfeld, who memorably rebuffed a reporter by saying, "That happens to be a piece of intelligence that either we don't have or we don't want to talk about." In other words: Proof? We don't need no stinking proof! And just because I'm asking your sons and daughters to sacrifice their lives, doesn't mean you deserve to know whether proof even exists. At the time, Senator Bob Graham, who as chairman of the Senate Intelligence Committee was privy to the inside scoop, told the nation he had seen no evidence of any link between Al Qaeda and Saddam Hussein. So we were left with the fevered, infantile imaginings of the president and his pals. "We had dots before," Anna Perez, Rice's spokeswoman, told us helpfully. "Now we have a higher density of dots. Have we connected those dots? No." Wouldn't it have been nice if the president had put down his saber-rattle, picked up his crayons, and connected the dots before drawing us into a bloody war?

A FIELD GUIDE TO FANATICS

By all accounts, the behind-the-scenes battle within the Bush administration over just what information should be used, or spun, or hidden to make the case that Saddam Hussein posed an imminent threat was a knockdown, drag-out fight between the facts and a zealous, highly politicized, who-needs-proof? mind-set. At the end of the day, the truth was left writhing on the floor.

Hey, why let the facts get in the way of a perfectly good war?

This pathological pattern of disregarding inconvenient reality is not just troubling, it's deadly. And it's threatening to drag us into a Sisyphean struggle against evildoers around the globe, or in whatever locale Karl Rove thinks would best advance Operation Avoid 41's Fate.

Since I'm not a psychiatrist, I have been consulting the work of various experts in the field in order to get a better understanding of the fanatical mind-set that is driving the Bush administration's agenda—and scaring the living daylights out of an enormous number of observers. Dr. Norman Doidge, professor of psychiatry at the University of Toronto, has identified the telltale symptoms of fanaticism. Among them are an intolerance of dissent, a doctrine that is riddled with contradictions, the belief that one's cause has been blessed or even commanded by God, and the use of reinforcement techniques such as repetition to spread one's message. Sound like anyone you know? George W. Bush, Dick Cheney, Don Rumsfeld, Karl Rove, Paul Wolfowitz, and Richard Perle . . . come on down! According to Doidge, one of the essential features of fanatics is their unshakable certainty that not only is their cause good "but that it is the only good, an absolute good." Or as President Bush famously declared, "There is no in-between, as far as I'm concerned. Either you're with us, or you're against us."

This absolute intolerance of dissent, says Doidge, often extends beyond the fanatics' enemies, frequently leading to a "campaign of terror" against those within their own ranks. If you're wondering what this has to do with the GOP, you might want to give a call to Republican Senators Olympia Snowe and George Voinovich. After having the temerity to question the wisdom of the president's massive tax-cut plan, the senatorial pair became the targets of withering TV attack ads in May 2003, sponsored by the tax-slashing acolytes at the Club for Growth, that portrayed them as "so-called Republicans" and compared their opposition to the latest round of tax cuts to France's opposition to the war in Iraq. It was a Night of the Long Knives, GOP-style.

Another crucial element of a fanatic's faith, according to Professor Dixon Sutherland, who teaches religion at Stetson University, is that he "sees himself as acting for God. . . . You have a circular logic that is very powerful that combines God's authority—through the Bible—with a messenger who carries out that authority." Majority Leader Tom DeLay, for example, saw the 2000 election as a choice between a "biblical worldview" and the worldview of "humanism, materialism, sexism, naturalism, postmodernism, or any of the other isms." The Republican Party, of course, represented the biblical worldview, God, and all the goodisms.

The president himself seems to have shared a messianic delusion with, of all people, now-deposed Palestinian Prime Minister Mahmoud Abbas. According to the Israeli newspaper *Haaretz*, Bush told Abbas, "God told me to strike at Al Qaeda and I struck them, and then he instructed me to strike at Saddam, which I did, and now I am determined to solve the problem in the Middle East. If you help me I will act, and if not, the elections will come and I will have to focus on them." It's too bad that God didn't tell Bush that solving the problems in the Middle East is more important than reelection.

Bush seems like an agnostic, however, when compared with Bible-thumping Lieutenant General Jerry Boykin, the deputy undersecretary of defense for intelligence. Among Boykin's zany claims is that a smudge that appeared on a photograph he took during the American debacle in Mogadishu, Somalia, was a miraculous manifestation of the "enemy . . . the principalities of darkness. . . . It is a demonic presence in that city that God revealed to me as the enemy." Either that or a little special sauce from a Big Mac. Or maybe Boykin's chemical warfare gear wasn't zipped up all the way.

Breathing fire from the pulpit of the Good Shepherd Community Church in Sandy, Oregon, in June 2003, Boykin opined that they're after us "because we're a Christian nation. . . . We are hated because we are a nation of believers." In another guest sermon in Florida, he shared the parable of Osman Atto with the congregation. "There was a man in Mogadishu named Osman Atto," the story began. Managing to evade Boykin's troops, Atto "went on CNN and he laughed at us, and he said, 'They'll never get me because Allah will protect me. Allah will protect me.' Well, you know what?" Boykin asked. "I knew that my God was bigger than his. I knew that my God was a real God and his was an idol." The happy ending was that Atto was eventually caught. Praise God!

Bush and Boykin share more than just their belief in the extremely direct hand God takes in American affairs abroad. Specifically, they agree on God's involvement in voter fraud in Florida. "Why is this man in the White House?" Boykin asks on a widely circulated videotape. "The majority of Americans did not vote for him. Why is he there? And I tell you this morning that he's in the White House because God put him there for a time such as this." Through his loyal disciple Justice Scalia.

While Bush may have shaken the general's faith in him by mildly disavowing his comments after they raised an understandable ruckus in the Muslim world, the general was neither forced to resign, demoted, nor disciplined in any way. Boykin's immediate superior, Defense Secretary Rumsfeld, showed a characteristically brusque lack of concern. As many began to wonder whether having a general officer with such a charming confidence in the miraculous, the supernatural, and God's active hand in human affairs in charge of cold, hard intelligence gathering was a really good idea, Rumsfeld was vague and dismissive. "I've not seen the videos, which I understand are pieces of a speech or speeches that he made and, therefore, I not only have not seen that, but I have not seen the full context of what it was he said. We do know that he is an officer that has an outstanding record in the United States armed forces," he said. Then he threw up a smokescreen about base closings and concluded with a highly original non sequitur. "I'm going to go to Iceland. I'm going to go to Iceland." Exit chuckling.

Bush, Boykin, and Rumsfeld's blithe unconcern merely confirmed the worst fears of Muslims. Ibrahim Hooper, a spokesman for the Council on American Islamic Relations, said, "Again we see a disconnect. We hear pleasing words about Islam but then we see complete inaction. He's not re-assigned. He's not removed. Nothing."

WHITE HOUSE BRIEFING,
WEDNESDAY, OCTOBER 29, 2003, 12:15 PM

Russell Mokhiber (editor of the *Corporate Crime Reporter*): Earlier this year, General Boykin said the following: "George Bush was not elected by a majority of voters in the United States. He was appointed by God." Does the president believe that God played any role in getting him to the White House?

Scott McClellan: Again, the president has addressed that matter.

Russell Mokhiber: Not whether God played any role in getting him to the White House.

Scott McClellan: The president has addressed that matter and I'm not going to go back through it.

Gustave le Bon, a social scientist known for his theories about the psychology of crowds, has stressed the importance of repetition as a weapon in the fanatic's arsenal. Repetition breeds blind acceptance and contagion. "Ideas, sentiments, emotions and beliefs," writes le Bon, "possess in crowds a contagious power as intense as that of microbes." As James C. Moore, coauthor of *Bush's Brain: How Karl Rove Made George W. Bush Presidential,* says, "If the president says it over and over enough, people will believe it, just as Karl Rove got him to say over and over that Saddam Hussein was involved in 9/11." The technique was so successful that a poll taken by the Pew Center in October 2002 showed that 66 percent of Americans believed that Hussein and bin Laden were both behind the attacks.

Wonder why Iraq's WMD are MIA? The answer may lie in the *DSM*—the *Diagnostic and Statistical Manual of Mental Disorders.* I know it can sound a bit cheap to call people you disagree with nuts, which is why I refer you to the psychiatric literature. And to be extra fair, I'll ask you to keep an open mind, something the Bushies stopped doing a long time ago.

GEORGE BUSH TAKES THE BLUE PILL

If you think the president only acts like a fanatic overseas, think again. His dogged devotion to selling his tax cuts for the wealthy as a "jobs creation plan"—despite all the evidence that they are nothing of the sort—proves that he can be just as fervent in the good ol' USA. "Jobs are on the line," said Bush after the Senate passed its version of the tax cut. "I call on Congress to resolve their differences quickly so I can sign a bill that will help create jobs, boost take-home pay, and spur economic growth." And for those with "—illionaire" as part of their economic description, it was a homerun.

It obviously made no difference to the president that ten Nobel Prize–winning economists condemned his tax cuts as "not the answer" to high unemployment. Not interested. Not listening. The 1.4 million jobs the White House repeatedly predicted the tax cuts would create were more a matter of a fanatic's faith than of dispassionate forecasting.

We are told again and again that jobs are a "lagging indicator." You want lagging? Last December, economists forecast an increase of 150,000 jobs. They came up only 149,000 short. And bad as this was, it was also an indicator of an even bigger problem. There cannot be a real recovery driven by consumers carrying record-breaking personal debt, while productivity increases are not matched by wage increases, companies are turning more and more to offshore workers, savings rates are hitting new lows, and trade and budget deficits are skyrocketing.

All this is happening on the watch of our conservative leaders. Conservatism is supposed to stand in clear counterpoint to the excesses of the counterculture—with responsibility, self-discipline, and living within one's means replacing the "if it feels good, do it" ethos. But George Bush and his corporate cronies have sacrificed these values on the altar of consumption: "If it feels good, buy it!"

The fact is there are now 3 million more Americans unemployed than when Bush took office—the vast majority of them having lost their jobs after the president's initial $1.3 trillion tax cut was passed in 2001. Difficult evidence to ignore, unless "Ignore the evidence" is your eleventh commandment. A popular definition of insanity is doing the same thing over and over again while expecting a different result. Well, that seems to be the White House theory on the power of tax cuts to produce new jobs: it didn't work before; let's try it again.

FANATICS IN ACTION, PART ONE: THE FOXES GUARDING THE HENHOUSE

When describing the Bush administration, terms like *arrogant, cocky, galling,* and *drunk with power* spring to mind.

Almost every day of his presidency brings fresh evidence that Bush and his crew believe that they can get away with just about anything—no matter how shocking, offensive, corrupt, underhanded, or in-your-face the transgression. The prevailing motto seems to be "Our way or the highway. If you don't like it, move to Canada."

Want a good example of Bush's screw-you mind-set? How about the stunning appointment of cover-up cover boy Henry Kissinger to head the 9/11 Commission? I mean, what was the president thinking? Was he deliberately trying to select the one person in the world least likely to get to the bottom of the foul-ups that preceded September 11? Was Prince Bandar too busy reining in his wife's charitable impulses to take the job?

The only thing more ludicrous than naming Kissinger to head this inquiry would be picking somebody who thinks "pollution is a right" to head the Department of the Interior or selecting a guy who made his name fighting to undercut the authority of the Securities and Exchange Commission as its chairman. Oh, wait a minute, that's right, Bush already did both of those things when he named Gale Norton and Harvey Pitt, respectively, to those posts. It can only be a matter of time before Rush Limbaugh is tapped to be the new drug czar.

AMERICA VS. THE HATERS

We were told again and again by the proponents of invading
Iraq that it was a bold step necessary to prevent future casualties. But how many present casualties will we have to suffer
in order to avoid those future ones?

The loopy justification for what *New York Times* columnist
William Safire calls "Iraq War III," the bloody occupation,
was given by George Bush at a news conference with U.S. Administrator Paul Bremer in late October: "Again . . . I repeat
myself that the more progress we make on the ground, the
more free the Iraqis become, the more electricity is available,
the more jobs are available, the more kids that are going to
school, the more desperate these killers . . . become, because
they can't stand the thought of a free society. They hate freedom. They love terror. They—they love to try to create fear
and chaos."

Yup, there it is. It's us against the haters again. Yes, they
hate us all right, but admitting that the whole truth is deeper
and more complicated should be the first step in making
"progress on the ground," not the last.

The steady drumbeat of the American death toll in Iraq
proceeded unabated even after Saddam's capture. Elusive terrorist bands had imported the vicious method of suicide
bombing and employed it toward new goals: to kill not only
Americans but also Iraqis who cooperate with them and independent aid groups trying to pick up the pieces. The UN administration building was attacked and the chief envoy, Sergio
Vieira de Mello, was killed on August 19, 2003. On the first
day of Ramadan, forty-three people were killed and over two
hundred wounded in four coordinated suicide attacks on five
police stations and the headquarters of the International Red

Cross. And then came the horror of the helicopter shot down in Fallujah. Throughout, the Bush drones kept up the happy talk. Those who sought an end or a solution or even a discussion of what the hell we should be doing next were shouted down as defeatists and traitors.

But even the intellectually and emotionally isolated administration could not resist the urge to tinker with public opinion. And they weren't the only ones.

In one of the most cynical public relations campaigns since Willie Horton walked through that revolving door and murdered Michael Dukakis, some bright eyes (an Army battalion commander, Lieutenant Colonel Dominic Caraccilo, claims to be the guy) came up with the brilliant idea of composing heartfelt letters from average American servicemen and women. The letters presented the authors' situations as tough but promising, the occupation as winnable, and the troops themselves as tired but motivated and optimistic, which many undoubtedly are.

There was only one small problem with the clever scheme: the same letter was sent to their hometown paper by hundreds of soldiers. The form letters informed the home front that "the quality of life and security for the citizens has been largely restored, and we are a large part of why that has happened. . . . The majority of the city [in this case Kirkuk] has welcomed our presence with open arms." Everyone appreciates the importance of discipline in the armed forces, but the odds that dozens of soldiers would have exactly the same thing to say about their situation in Iraq proved too great a coincidence for some alert readers. Red-faced editors, unfortunately, were not quite as alert, so the letters ran in at least eleven newspapers including the *Boston Globe*. Colonel Caraccilo, as soon as you retire from the army, there's a high-paying job just waiting at the RNC for an innovative thinker like you.

An incriminating document of a different sort came to light in mid-October. It was an unusually gloomy assessment of our progress in the Global War on Terror. The author was not Michael Moore but Don Rumsfeld. Here are some of the things Rummy wanted to know: "Are we winning or losing the Global War on Terror? . . . Have we fashioned the right mix of rewards, amnesty, protection and confidence in the U.S.? . . . Are we capturing, killing or deterring and dissuading more terrorists every day than the madrassas and the radical clerics are recruiting, training and deploying against us? . . . Is our current situation such that 'the harder we work, the behinder we get'? . . . Do we need a new organization?"

He forgot one question: do we need a new secretary of defense? The most damning thing about the memo was that Rumsfeld was asking his top flunkies the very same questions that he and the rest of the administration bitterly derided when they were asked by others, including a few reporters who had not yet given up on reporting. The war in Iraq has also become a war on the media. In widely publicized comments, President Bush spoke of the press as a "filter" that was darkening the message on Iraq through its own pessimistic lens.

But while Rumsfeld's team may or may not have discussed these questions at its next meeting, the answers were not forthcoming. Rumsfeld, who has a notorious affection for rhetorical questions, seemed to want to turn the whole thing into a benign and airy thought experiment: "Are we thinking about interesting things sometimes?"

Meanwhile, Rummy's "long, hard slog" continues.

There seems to be plenty of money for new cops to patrol the streets of Baghdad, but very little for those protecting America's inner cities.

PORTRAITS IN FANATICISM:
DON RUMSFELD, NO HOLDS BARRED

It is impossible to do one's homework on Don Rumsfeld
without learning far more about 1950s Ivy League athletics
than any sane person would ever care to know. No journalist digging for insight into the famously flinty Rummy
seems able to resist pointing out that he captained the
Princeton varsity wrestling team in 1954 and was a runner-
up at the NCAA championships. It's just too juicy a biographical morsel; it seems to say so much. That is, if you
believe that life endlessly recapitulates college—or high
school.

In the Bush administration senior class photo, Rummy is
the gritty, never-say-die scrapper, always ready to go to the
mat with any opponent, even those far above his fighting
weight. Contrast Colin Powell, the earnest, unassuming
head of the social service organization—you know, that ex-
tracurricular activity that looks so good on a college application but is, well, frankly a bit boring? Colin's nice and all,
you gotta like him, but Rummy, well, he's the kid whose
high-testosterone school spirit really brings the boys in the
bleachers to their feet!

(In this scenario George Bush, of course, would assume
the same role he played at Andover: head cheerleader. Class
president? Er, that would be Dick Cheney, quietly making
the key decisions about whether the fall dance should have a
Hawaiian theme or '50s sock hop motif from his secure and
undisclosed location in the second-floor boys' room.)

Rummy's grudging admirers in the media, and their number is legion—after all, good copy is king and Rummy is consistently quotable—love to tell you that, when wrestling for

Princeton, Rumsfeld was famous for his use of the "fireman's carry," literally picking his opponents up and hurling them to the mat. Who knows, if the WWF had come along forty years earlier, Don Rumsfeld might have become Hulk Hogan or The Rock of his era, rather than both the youngest (in 1975 under Ford) and oldest (in 2001 under George W.) secretary of defense in American history. And America would be the better for it.

As Pentagon supremo, Rumsfeld still employs the fireman's carry from time to time, twirling an inquisitive reporter or uppity Congressman over his head before, whammo, lights out. But he has also perfected a number of moves that enable him to emerge repeatedly on top of the heap in the internecine warfare that always seems to break out in his immediate vicinity.

Here are a few of Rummy's favorite maneuvers:

The "Ginger Rogers": In this crowd-pleaser, you don't just vanquish your opponent, you do a little dance around his unconscious body just so everyone else on the team gets the message. You may have noticed the little jig that Don did when he forced Army Secretary Thomas White to appear alongside him at a press conference announcing the cancellation of White's pet project—the Army's $11 billion Crusader artillery system. White, dazed and confused, turned out to be no Fred Astaire.

The "Come and Get Me": Another powerful tool for illustrating exactly who's the boss (hint: it's Rumsfeld). This baffling but effective tactic involves avoiding away matches and making your opponents follow you to your home turf. After an initial unsatisfactory meeting with the Joint Chiefs in their sanctum sanctorum, the so-called Tank, deep within the recesses of the Pentagon, Rumsfeld has refused to make a return visit. The service chiefs have been forced to come to the secretary's office whenever they need his help. You can be sure that the politically astute generals make a point of dropping by often.

The "Army of One": Teammates! What a pain! Rumsfeld has shown little patience for the play-nice necessary to build a functional team. (Rumsfeld has shown little patience for anything, actually.) Just ask our jittery allies in Europe.

The "Weight Class Mismatch": There aren't a lot of worthy opponents in the superpower class, but that doesn't mean there's no one left for us to fight. Since some smaller wrestlers still seem capable of inflicting some superficial damage, however—a battle with North Korea, for instance, could cause us to lose our Seoul—Rumsfeld has been careful to fight only guaranteed losers. Lucky Iraq seems to have gotten the nod not because the scrawny adversary actually had any weapons of mass destruction hidden under its uniform but because the other candidates all presented knotty complexities.

The "A Little Blood Never Hurt Anybody": On the other hand, nobody ever won any important contest without suffering a little damage. American toll in Iraq as of February 2004: over 500 dead and over 3,000 wounded, and climbing.

The "Soccer Team Could Use a Little Help Too": Rumsfeld, who suffers from acute memorandum diarrhea, sending out missives to, among other things, correct an underling's grammar, has been known to infuriate officials at the State Department and elsewhere with abrasive rebukes and unhelpful suggestions. And while Rumsfeld's stock may have declined lately, few people have the guts to consign his messages to the shredder—if they know what's good for them.

The "Rules Are for Losers": Time was, back during the Cold War, when human rights conventions and international law served American purposes. The Soviet Union's long rap sheet of brutal repression could be waved in the face of any country having trouble making up its mind whose side it was on. But in today's world, the Geneva Convention is as intimidating as a squirt gun to players with the will to win. After collecting suspicious persons by the planeload in Afghanistan and Iraq, Rummy put an illegal hold on hundreds of prisoners in Guantánamo Bay, some as young as fifteen.

All of these tricks and strategies, gambits and gambles are employed by Don Rumsfeld in order to crush any enemy. But what happens when the match is over? Who cleans up the mess? Turns out there is more to life than just competition. Winning the immediate battle isn't everything and it isn't the only thing. Rummy may learn that the hard way in Iraq, but more likely he won't learn a damn thing. He's a fanatic, remember?

DOING THE IRAQ MATH

Everyone knew from the beginning that public opinion on Iraq would hinge on the number of casualties. Even back in the belligerent days of the fall of 2002, when over 70 percent of Americans supported an invasion of Iraq, support for the war plummeted—down to only 39 percent in a Zogby poll—when the prospect of "thousands of American casualties" was added to the question. Given that the purported groundswell of public opinion in favor of the war was being dropped like an old-fashioned "dumb bomb" to kill dissent on both sides of the political aisle, it's not surprising that no one in the Bush administration was talking about the Pentagon's estimates of how many of our soldiers would be sent home in body bags.

In fact these vital figures were the only numbers that never seriously became part of the war debate. We had estimates of how much the war was going to cost, how many troops would be deployed, how much the price of oil might go up, and how long our forces would have to remain in Iraq. We had been given head counts of Iraq's fractious Kurds and Shiites, reference numbers for Security Council resolutions defied; we had been frequently reminded that Saddam had been in power for thirty-four years, eleven of them since the last time we tried to send him and his mustache packing. But no one in the Bush administration was talking casualty numbers. Indeed, the more the postwar casualty numbers increased, the less they were talked about. Except in a dismissive way.

On November 2, 2003, an Army Chinook helicopter was shot down. Sixteen American soldiers died—at the time, the most significant loss of American life since the president's now obviously idiotic announcement of the end of "major combat." As the early reports came in, Rumsfeld, splitting hairs with Tim Russert on *Meet the Press* over the number of casualties, offered these words of hope: "As time goes on, some of the wounded may very well have been moved over to killed in action." Thanks, Don. This cavalier attitude toward the pain of the children, parents, and friends left behind was in keeping with the administration's decision to allow no photographs of coffins and to have the president attend no funerals and no memorials for fallen soldiers.

LIBERATION BLUES

At the time, the fall of Baghdad was treated as the ultimate vindication of the Bushie brigades. The Bible tells us that pride goeth before a fall. In Iraq, it cameth right after. As soon as that statue of Saddam hit the ground, the mood around the Rumsfeld campfire was all high fives, I-told-you-sos, and endless smug prattling about how the speedy fall of Baghdad was proof positive that those who opposed the invasion of Iraq were dead wrong.

What utter nonsense. In fact, the speedy fall of Baghdad proved that the antiwar movement was dead right.

The whole pretext for our unilateral charge into Iraq was that the American people were in imminent danger from Saddam and his mighty war machine. After David Kay, the former chief weapons inspector in Iraq, told the world in January 2004 that Iraq did not have any weapons of mass destruction at the time the war began, the president downgraded the threat Iraq had posed to "grave and gathering."

But back in the spring of 2003, he was hyping the danger as so clear and present that we couldn't even give inspectors searching for weapons of mass destruction another thirty days, as France and other spurned allies had wanted. It turned out that, far from being on the verge of destroying Western civilization, Saddam and his twenty-first-century Gestapo couldn't even muster a halfhearted defense of their own capital. The hawks' cakewalk disproved their own dire warnings of imminent biological and chemical attacks by battle-hardened loyalists. You can't have it both ways, especially since the invasion proved wildly successful in one other regard: it unified most of the world—especially the Muslim world—against us.

Back in 1991, more than half a dozen Arab nations were part of our Desert Storm coalition. In 2003, Operation Iraqi Freedom's "Coalition of the Willing" had zero. Not even the polygamous potentates of Kuwait—whose butts we saved last time out and who were most threatened by whatever threat Iraq still presented—would join us. And I'm sorry, but substituting Bulgaria and the island of Tonga for Egypt and Oman just doesn't cut it when it comes to winning hearts and minds on the Arab street.

In fact, almost everything about the invasion—from the go-it-alone buildup to the mayhem that followed the fall of Saddam—played right into the hands of those intent on demonizing our country. Islamic extremists are having a field day signing up recruits for the holy war they're waging against us. Instead of "Uncle Sam wants you," their recruiting posters might as well feature a different kind of patriotic image: an American soldier ill-advisedly draping the American flag over Saddam's face.

The antiwar movement never opposed the war out of fear that America would lose. It was the Bush administration's pathological and frantic obsession with an immediate, damn-the-consequences invasion that fueled the protests. And please don't point to a few jubilant Iraqis dancing in the streets to validate the case for "preemptive liberation." You'd be doing the Baghdad boogaloo too if the murderous tyrant who'd been eating off golden plates while your family starved finally got what was coming to him. It in no way proves that running roughshod over international law and pouring Iraqi oil—now brought to you at ultrapremium prices by the good folks at Halliburton—onto the flames of anti-American hatred was a good idea. It wasn't before the war, and it still isn't, as became pretty obvious once the unintended consequences began to unfold.

The idea that our slam dunk of Saddam actually proves the White House was right is particularly dangerous. It encourages the Wolfowitzes and the Perles and the Cheneys to argue that we should be invading Syria or Iran or North Korea or Cuba as soon as we catch our breath. They've tasted blood, and the quagmire that followed the collapse of the Saddam regime may not be deep enough to assuage their fanaticism.

It's important to remember that the Arab world saw a very different war than we did, and a very different occupation. During the war they were seeing babies with limbs blown off, children wailing beside their dead mothers, and Arab journalists killed by American tanks and bombers. They were seeing American forces leaving behind a vast wake of destruction, looting, hunger, humiliation, and chaos. And after the "liberation" they were seeing violent religious factions waging war, including one instance in late August when seventy-nine people in the Shiite holy city of Najaf were killed in a bomb explosion, and ongoing attacks on Iraqis collaborating with Americans. New Iraqi police officers were killed inside a police station on payday, as were Iraqi security guards and a member of the Iraqi Governing Council. And in the middle of January 2004, for the first time a truck bomb exploded in the heavily guarded American headquarters—one of the worst suicide bombings in Iraq, killing eighteen Iraqi civilians and wounding at least sixty others.

Both during the war and after, it was as if Osama bin Laden were handling our PR. The language and imagery were all wrong. During the war, Tom DeLay was gushing about our "army of virtue" at the same time that we were blowing up mosques. After the war, with 150,000 U.S. troops on Iraqi soil, Lieutenant General Boykin asserted that our "spiritual enemy will only be defeated if we come against them in the name of Jesus." What a message to send to a Muslim world already convinced that we're waging a war on Islam.

Equally undiplomatic was the White House's claim that the administration couldn't do anything to keep Christian missionaries—including some who have described the Islamic prophet Mohammad as a "demon-possessed pedophile" and a "terrorist"—from going on a holy crusade to Baghdad. Gee, you think the Arab world might take that the wrong way? If there is one thing that could bring Sunnis and Shiites together, it's the common hatred of evangelical zealots who denigrate their Prophet. And it certainly didn't help to have the American media referring to Jay Garner, the retired general Don Rumsfeld picked to oversee the rebuilding of Iraq for five minutes, as "viceroy." I suppose it could have been worse; they could have called him "head bwana." Or "Garner of Arabia."

The administration's tin ear for local sensitivities was brightly showcased, in fact, by the choice of the fat-headed Garner. Like the president, the demoted viceroy never cared what the facts indicated; to him even a shattered glass could be half full. "We ought to be beating our chests every day," he said, dismissing the problems besetting Iraq. "We ought to look in a mirror and get proud. We ought to stick out our chests and suck in our bellies and say, 'Damn, we're Americans.'" That's sure to win us some more goodwill around the world. Hoo-rah, and pass the Kool-Aid, General Jay!

Any student of world history knows that shame and humiliation are forces every bit as powerful as aggression and greed. The American occupation has been a case study in the politics of shame, with humiliated mobs emerging from the rubble to dance ring-around-the-burning-Humvee. But the fanatics on the Bush team remain in denial.

The first warning sign that self-delusion was going to be the order of the day came in May 2003, hours after the deadly reemergence of Al Qaeda in Riyadh. "America," the president

said, "is now more secure, the world will be more peaceful."
More peaceful than what? The West Bank? He clearly wasn't
going to let a little fact like twenty-three dead civilians, including nine Americans—the result of three closely coordinated suicide bomb attacks—change what he had said again
and again before the bombing in Riyadh. He had assured us
that "we are winning the war on terror" and that Al Qaeda
was "on the run . . . slowly, but surely, being decimated." And
shortly after forty people died and two hundred were injured
in simultaneous car bombings throughout Baghdad, Bush actually said that the violence escalates "the more progress we
make on the ground."

He was similarly unperturbed by a troubling report from
the International Institute for Strategic Studies, an influential
nonpartisan British think tank. Released on May 13, 2003,
the day after the Riyadh bombings and three days before the
president repeated his claim that "the United States people
are more secure," the report found that Al Qaeda was "just
as dangerous" and "even harder to identify and neutralize"
than it had been prior to 9/11. And just four hours after the
president strapped on his trusty blinders and delivered his
rosy vision of a more peaceful world, the tranquility was shattered by five simultaneous suicide blasts in Casablanca, Mo-
rocco, that killed forty-four. Oh well, at least we still had that
Jessica Lynch TV movie to make us feel good about our preemptive war.

The president's evidence-be-damned fanaticism has been
equally apparent when it comes to the state of postwar Iraq.
"Life is returning to normal," he proclaimed just two weeks
after the fall of Baghdad. "Things have settled down inside
the country."

Just who is preparing his morning briefing papers? Polly-andy Card? Little Condoleezza Sunshine? Did he bother consulting any Iraqis about "normal life" there? Probably not. One of the keys to being a flourishing fanatic is to surround yourself with those of a similar—and equally deluded—mindset. According to that mind-set, the definition of "settling down" can be expanded to include rampant looting, sporadic water and electrical service, disastrous hospital conditions, outbreaks of cholera and dysentery, uncollected garbage and raw sewage in the streets, the ransacking of half a dozen nuclear facilities, missing barrels of radioactive material, increasing anti-American sentiment, and disparate ethnic and religious groups arming themselves. And, most tragically, the ever-growing body count of American soldiers. No wonder Don Rumsfeld called the media's reporting of all this "an overstatement."

HAWK NEARLY DOWN:
WOLFOWITZ IN BAGHDAD

I don't know if the movie rights to Deputy Secretary of Defense Paul Wolfowitz's October visit to Iraq are still available, but if they are, I dearly hope that some director with an eye for the absurd will take this unique opportunity to make the black comedy of the decade.

Hawkowitz arrived in Baghdad feeling chipper and determined to hand out a pair of rose-colored goggles (RCGs) to anyone he met—this despite some truly depressing polling data released just a few days before. Conducted by the Iraq Center for Research and Strategic Studies, the poll asked 1,620 Iraqis in seven cities a series of questions about their attitude toward the coalition troops. Sixty-six percent said they viewed the troops as occupiers, and only 14 percent saw them as liberators. Six months before, when the soldiers first arrived, those numbers had been close to even: 45 percent saw us as an occupying force while 42 percent believed we were there to liberate Iraq. In terms of the outlook for the future, twice as many Iraqis (46 to 23 percent) thought the situation had gotten worse rather than better, and half opposed the presence of coalition troops; only a third supported them.

Clearly the coalition forces were facing a situation that was sharply deteriorating. But Wolfowitz remained fanatically determined to look on the bright side. American troops are "taking the fight to the enemy," he blustered. In Tikrit he lauded the local security forces: "These young Iraqis are stepping forward to fight for their country along with us. . . . It's a wonderful success story that speaks volumes." But a different story was about to speak volumes. And it was a story not of success but of the appalling impotence of the Tikriti security forces.

Just after Wolfowitz left Tikrit, a Black Hawk helicopter had to crash-land after being shot down with a rocket-propelled grenade: the same tactic that would result a week later in the crash of an Army Chinook in which sixteen soldiers would die. After his triumph in Tikrit, the Wolf retreated to Baghdad's supposedly invulnerable Green Zone, where he continued to accentuate imaginary positives—that is, until he was chased out of the country by six rockets that smashed into his hotel, killing a U.S. colonel. The closest anyone came to acknowledging what was really going on was when Paul Bremer admitted that it was possible the forces opposed to the occupation were "getting better organized."

As one of the most fanatical of the fanatics, Wolfowitz faced a real test of his faith in Iraq. What he believed was so

clearly contradicted by what he saw that it would not have
been surprising if his brain had exploded like a car bomb. But
Wolfowitz is one of that special breed with the capacity to al-
ter personal reality. It's hard to imagine how many further
disasters could have befallen him on his trip before he would
have conceded that perhaps something was amiss. If his hotel had been razed around him, one can easily imagine Wolfowitz emerging from the rubble, dusting himself off, and
declaring that the demolition phase of the rebuilding of
Baghdad was proceeding right on schedule.

PORTRAITS IN FANATICISM: RICHARD PERLE, PRINCE OF DARKNESS

For years now, political reformers have been railing against
the unseemly—and rampant—practice of former government
officials pouring out of Washington's golden revolving door
only to return a short time later as well-paid lobbyists, auc-
tioning off their access and influence. Well, it turns out those
were the good old days. Today's new breed of public servant
prefers to cash in while still stalking the halls of power and still
creating public policy.

As chairman of the Pentagon's influential Defense Policy
Board—a position that is unpaid but still subject to government ethics rules—Richard Perle was the frothing pit bull of
the Bush administration's dogs of war. At the same time, he is
the managing partner of Trireme Partners, a firm that special-
izes in homeland security and defense, and he serves on the
board of directors of Autonomy, a software company whose
clients include the Defense and Homeland Security departments. He is also on the board of Hollinger International, a

media conglomerate whose chairman, Conrad Black, was fired in January and sued for $200 million following the disclosure that $32 million in unauthorized payments had been made to him and other executives. Perle himself is being investigated for, among other things, a payment of $2.5 million by Hollinger to Trireme Partners, Perle's company.

Talk about having your cake and eating it too. On second thought, better make that "eating your soufflé," because Richard Perle—whose side obsession, he once told me, has been to open a nationwide chain of soufflé restaurants—has taken double-dipping to a whole new level.

One of Perle's deals put him in the pay of Global Crossing. The bankrupt telecommunications company was then struggling to win government approval for its proposed sale to Hong Kong–based Hutchison Whampoa and Singapore Technologies Telemedia. The sale had come under scrutiny by the Defense Department and the FBI because it would place Global's fiber-optic network—which is used by the U.S. government—under the control of a firm with close ties to those freedom-loving folks in Beijing.

Enter Richard Perle. Global Crossing was hoping Perle could convince his good buddies in the Defense Department to put aside their national security concerns and let the dicey deal go through. And Perle was clearly confident that he could deliver: he signed an affidavit claiming to be uniquely qualified to advise Global, and in a highly unusual arrangement for a Washington gun for hire, agreed to make $600,000 of his $725,000 fee contingent on his bringing home the bacon.

I guess he figured, "Hey, I convinced the president to toss aside two hundred years of historical precedent and launch a preemptive war despite the trepidation of the majority of the world. How hard can it be to persuade a few government bureaucrats—including my old pal Rummy—to look the other way while I do an end run around the public interest and bank a quick 725 grand?" After all, you know what they say about casting Perles before swine.

During his years in the Reagan administration, Perle was dubbed the "Prince of Darkness" because of his hard-line stance on national security issues. But I suppose when you toss nearly three quarters of a million dollars into the mix, the gloomy prince is more than happy to click on his night-light and refashion his hard line into a squiggle.

This sleazy state of affairs caught the eye—and turned the stomach—of Representative John Conyers, Jr., the ranking Democrat on the House Judiciary Committee, who called on the Defense Department to investigate whether Perle's business dealings constituted a conflict of interest. Adding insult to injury is the fact that Perle's deal was with a disgraced company that was among the worst of the corporate crooks. He was lining his pockets at the expense of the 10,000 laid-off Global employees who saw $32 million in severance pay wiped out—and the shareholders who lost $57 billion in equity—when the company declared bankruptcy.

The hubris is unfathomable. In legal documents drafted in connection with the proposed Global Crossing sale, Perle couldn't have been clearer about what the telecom company would be buying with its fat fee. "As chairman of the Defense Policy Board," declared Perle in the affidavit, "I have a unique perspective on and intimate knowledge of the national defense and security issues" likely to be raised by the governmental review of the sale. Knowledge, he pointed out, "that is not and could not be available" to the other lobbyists trying to get the deal approved. In other words, "I've got Rumsfeld's ear and access to all sorts of super–top-secret information that none of these other jokers on your payroll do. I know more. I can do more. So I'm worth more." And he had the unmitigated chutzpah to put this sales pitch in writing. And sign it. I guess this is what the Bush administration means by "transparency."

But of course when reporters began sniffing around the deal, Perle's power plumage shriveled up faster than George in the "shrinkage" episode of *Seinfeld*. First he tried the classic Bush administration Plan A—the simple, 180-degree lie. He just told reporters that he never signed the statement. That didn't work, so on to Plan B—claiming ignorance: he had signed it but never read it. Finally, no doubt realizing this all sounded a bit too much like "the dog ate my affidavit," Perle declared that none of it mattered anyway, since his position on the Defense Policy Board actually, now that you mention it, had "nothing to do" with the Global deal, so how could he possibly be using his public office for private gain?

So when there's money to be had, Perle's position at the Defense Policy Board affords him "a unique perspective" on advising Global Crossing, but when ethical questions are raised, his Defense Policy Board post has "nothing to do" with his work for the telecom company.

And this is the guy our president put his trust in when it came to waging war on Iraq?

The Pentagon's inspector general reached the conclusion in November that Perle violated no ethics rules, even though "on its face, the affidavit would appear to violate D.O.D. ethics regulations that prohibit the use of official position for personal gain." Apparently, the fact that Perle and his lawyers revised the affidavit after questions were raised by the press made it all OK in the eyes of the inspector general. If only all of us were given a chance to retrace our steps after getting caught, our jails would not be so overcrowded. But in the cozy Washington world of Richard Perle and his fellow fanatics, all's well that ends well. The president sent a letter to Congressional leaders in the middle of September indicating that he would "take no action to suspend or prohibit the proposed 61.5% investment by Singapore Technologies Telemedia." The withdrawal of Hong Kong's Hutchison Whampoa greased the tracks. While Perle eventually resigned as chairman, he remains a member of the influential Defense Policy Board. And the war in Iraq, which he was so instrumental in advocating, smolders on.

ARE WE FEELING SAFER YET?

"Either you are with us or you are with the terrorists," said Bush a week after 9/11. Six months later, he reiterated the importance of sending an unambiguous message to the world: "I said that if you harbor a terrorist, you're just as guilty as the terrorist; if you feed one or hide one, you're just as guilty as those who came and murdered thousands of innocent Americans." Unless of course you're Saudi Arabia.

Much has been made of the new Bush Doctrine, that marvel of philosophical precision that has been amended, parsed, redacted, and clarified so many times that it now has more footnotes than an annotated version of *Remembrance of Things Past*, more clauses than a Donald Trump prenup, more exceptions than a desperate girl's edition of *The Rules*.

Bush hit the public with the new Bush Doctrine in his 2002 State of the Union address. "I will not wait on events, while dangers gather," he said moments after labeling North Korea, Iran, and Iraq an "Axis of Evil." "I will not stand by, as peril draws closer and closer." This new concept of attack-before-they-might-attack-us was a lethal departure from a century-long tradition of defense, rather than offense, of being on the side of victims, rather than aggressors.

When the Bush fanatics rolled out their public relations campaign in support of invading Iraq, they were relying on a document called the "National Security Strategy of the United States of America." It spelled the new doctrine out in full: "The greater the threat, the greater is the risk of inaction—and the more compelling the case for taking anticipatory action to defend ourselves, even if uncertainty remains as to the time and place of the enemy's attack. To forestall or prevent such hostile acts by our adversaries, the United States will, if necessary, act preemptively. . . . The purpose of our actions will always be to eliminate a specific threat to the United States or our allies and friends. The reasons for our actions will be clear, the force measured, and the cause just."

The melodramatic nature of Bush's aggressive posture has meant that when he whips out something as powerful as his famed "dead or alive" vow, he raises certain expectations. His muscular language made it clear that winning the war on terror included the capture or killing of Osama bin Laden. Instead we were asked to settle for the arrests of John Walker Lindh and Zacarias Moussaoui. We've gone from the original Broadway cast to the community theater production.

And while the president has repeatedly promised "to make sure Americans are more secure and more safe than ever before," you have to wonder, when you look around, if we are really safer than we were on September 10. Are our borders and seaports more secure? Are we more prepared to face biological warfare or dirty nukes?

Two years after 9/11, Nathaniel Heatwole, a twenty-year-old college student, hid box cutters, modeling clay, matches, and sunscreen bottles filled with bleach on four airplanes to highlight weaknesses in airport security. He sent an e-mail to the Transportation Security Administration describing where the bags were hidden, including dates and flight numbers—and added his name and phone number. A month later TSA notified the FBI, which interviewed Heatwole and charged him with a federal crime carrying a ten-year maximum sentence. "Amateur testing of our systems does not show us in any way our flaws," Stephen McHale, TSA deputy administrator explained. "We know where the vulnerabilities are and we are testing them. . . . This does not help."

Even though the basic assumptions behind the Bush Doctrine—that we're living in a post-containment, post-deterrence, post–Cold War world—are correct, there was no new thinking applied to the new realities. It quickly became Us vs. the Evil Empire all over again, only this time with a Middle Eastern accent. This worldview is mustier than the plot lines of "Yes, Dear"—and about as realistic. In fact, our new enemies are shadowy, lurking in sleeper terrorist cells in more than sixty countries—including the good ol' USA—and armed with dirty nukes, anthrax-laced letters, smallpox spores, and box cutters as weapons of mass destruction. Yet the fanatics in the White House stuck to a simpleminded, binary approach to our national security.

His reduction of the protean challenge of eradicating terrorism down to simple regime change in Iraq is another sign of the president's limited ability to handle complexity. Here's how bad it is: even shrinking the worldwide terrorist threat to an Axis of Evil that included only three of the plethora of countries with terrorist ties proved too complicated for him,

The only explanation for the growing gap between the Bush administration's delusional rhetoric and our not-so-rosy reality is that we are being governed by a gang of out-and-out fanatics. The defining trait of the fanatic—be it a Marxist, a fascist or, gulp, a Wolfowitz—is an utter refusal to allow anything as piddling as evidence get in the way of an unshakable belief. That pretty much sums up the White House MO.

so he crossed North Korea and Iran off the list and indicted—
and convicted—Saddam's Iraq as the source of all evil.

Such sledgehammer reductionism is not only intellectually
lazy, it's extremely dangerous. As post–9/11 arrests in Pakistan, Indonesia, and Malaysia have shown, our ability to
fight—let alone win—the war on terrorism depends on the cooperation of countries that are not exactly our natural allies.
We need a network of far-flung informants to obtain the splin-
ters of information that will allow us to take the kind of "preemptive action" that truly will protect us from terrorist
attacks. But taking unilateral action against Iraq only solidified
the fragmented opposition, pushing our enemies together
(and many of our friends away) and leaving us to go it alone.

And please don't tell me that the world is with us because
we got some loans and grants at the Madrid conference and
a few soldiers from Azerbaijan and Latvia. This is our war and
our very expensive—in both lives and dollars—quagmire.
September 11 proved that, in the war against terror, information is the ultimate weapon. Effective preemption is no
longer about who's the strongest; it's about who's the most
clued in. Our safety depends on arming those entrusted with
defending our lives and liberty not with the most powerful
nuclear warheads but with the most potent information. And
we are not going to get that from the Latvians.

PORTRAITS IN FANATICISM:
JOHN ASHCROFT, THE FANATICS' FANATIC

When you tell people that you are writing a book about fanatics in the Bush administration, many, perhaps most, assume
that it will consist of 350 pages about John Ashcroft inter-

spersed with a few gibes at Karl Rove and Richard Perle. Many people know one or more facts about the attorney general that seem at odds, to put it mildly, with our secular age and the idea of a tolerant and inclusive governing structure. To put it another way, he absolutely puts the fear of God—an angry, vengeful one at that—into a hell of a lot of people.

John Ashcroft is a devout member of the Assemblies of God, a strict Pentacostal sect, which forbids its members from drinking, dancing, or gambling. The attorney general observes all of these rules to such an extent that Phyllis Schlafly reported that he was grossly offended when someone tried to sell him a raffle ticket to win a signed copy of a Rush Limbaugh book at a conservative fund-raiser. Anyone who thinks conservatism is monolithic and uniform has only to contrast John Ashcroft and Bill Bennett.

Although he doesn't dance, Ashcroft, as many fans of late-night television know, does sing. As a senator, he held down the baritone section of The Singing Senators, a foursome that broke up, like the Beatles, when Ashcroft went off to do a solo project and member Jim Jeffords decided he liked a different sort of music. Ashcroft's cornball patriotic tune "Let the Eagle Soar" became an Internet hit and then aired repeatedly on *The Late Show with David Letterman,* until finally the AG himself turned up to sing it:

> Let the mighty eagle soar.
> Soar with healing in her wings,
> As the land beneath her sings:
> "Only God, no other kings."

Just to show how fair I can be, I will say that John Ashcroft has a very pleasant singing voice.

Ashcroft's unlikely rise through life may be the clearest proof yet that prayer actually works. In 2000, after six years in the Senate from conservative Missouri, Ashcroft found himself locked in an unusually venomous neck-and-neck race with another former governor, Democrat Mel Carnahan. Two weeks before the election, Carnahan was killed in a plane crash, too late to have his name taken off the ballot. Ashcroft went on to campaign against and eventually lose to a dead man in one of the most embarrassing defeats in recent memory.

Ashcroft's dirty little secret was not, of course, his religion, which he wears on his sleeve, but his incompetence. This is how *Reason* magazine described his term as Missouri's governor: "Ashcroft's political tenure in Missouri seems more comic-gothic than inspiring or statesmanlike. . . . Events just didn't give him any occasions to rise to. Instead we see Ashcroft signing the papers to disincorporate the city of Times Beach, victim of a notorious dioxin scare; urging tourists to avoid his state lest they interfere with an ongoing FBI manhunt for neo-Nazis; petulantly refusing for a time to return a commemorative silver dinner set to its rightful owner, the USS *Missouri*. . . . legalizing rape due to a clerical error; begging constantly for federal aid as his hapless state was battered by floods and crop failures; and unsuccessfully bowing and scraping on *Donahue* to General Motors execs in the hopes they would site new auto plants in his state."

You've got to admit, it's funny stuff.

When Bush handed the now-unemployed former senator the Justice brief, many viewed it as an inevitable concession to the party's right wing, especially conservative Christians. Ashcroft, after all, was ranked higher than Jesse Helms by the John Birch Society while a senator. He had been outspoken on the issues that matter most to the party's base, what Howard Dean has called "God, gays, and guns."

Ensconced at Justice, Ashcroft initiated morning prayer meetings (now rarely held because the attorney general begins his days in the White House), anointed himself with holy oil before taking the oath of office (he used Crisco before his swearing in to the Senate), and, famously, draped a cloth over the unclothed breast of a statue inconveniently placed in one of Justice's standard photo op sites. Otherwise, in the early days Ashcroft must have been a disappointment to those hoping and praying for fire and brimstone from the attorney general's office.

After a bruising confirmation hearing and squeaking into office with the support of only fifty-eight senators, he seemed to be sulking or maybe just keeping his head down during his first year-and-a-half as attorney general. Besides the prayer meetings, his greatest innovation as an administrator seemed to be a sharply curtailed workweek. Ashcroft would leave for Missouri on Thursday afternoon and reappear Tuesday morning. Conservatives grumbled; liberals relaxed.

Then came September 11, and as it did for so many others in the Bush administration, something snapped for John Ashcroft. Two months later, with testosterone all but visibly oozing from his pores, a combative Ashcroft faced a Senate panel that would, he expected, have the temerity to ask him some impertinent questions about his department's emerging draconian policies. Preempting any criticisms phrased as questions, Ashcroft memorably declared, "To those who scare peace-loving people with phantoms of lost liberty, my message is this: your tactics only aid terrorists, for they erode our national unity and diminish our resolve. They give ammunition to America's enemies, and pause to America's friends.

They encourage people of good will to remain silent in the face of evil."

OK, and who wants to ask the first question?

This was a declaration of war, not on terrorists—the president had taken care of that already—but on doubt and dissent. In light of what we now know about the flimsy case for war in Iraq, Ashcroft's forward action in mowing down the skeptics served the Iraq hawks brilliantly. To the everlasting shame of those who were cowed by fear of being branded traitors under Ashcroft's new definition of the term, the administration waltzed off to war with barely a peep from the opposition that really should have mattered: Democratic senators and congressmen.

Barred by his religion from celebrating his victory over the Senate with a vigorous dance, Ashcroft began instead to craft his masterpiece, the USA PATRIOT Act—"Uniting and Strengthening America by Providing Appropriate Tools Required to Intercept and Obstruct Terrorism." Yes, it is a forced acronym. The act, which erodes essential civil liberties and rights that countless Americans have fought and died for, expands the capacity of government to do pretty much whatever the hell it feels like as long as it can link its actions, no matter how tenuously, to the fight against terrorism. It allows searches, seizures of people and evidence, wiretaps, and e-mail taps without probable cause. Through a revision of grand jury rules, it erodes the Great Wall that bars the CIA from domestic spying. It allows the FBI unimpeded access to financial and medical records and even, though this provision has not been used (yet), to information from public libraries about suspicious book borrowing. And it clarifies the status of noncitizens detained on national security matters: they have no status. With the Senate quivering in fear of Ashcroft's basilisk eye, the PATRIOT Act passed almost unanimously. Only Russ Feingold voted against it.

The war that John Ashcroft has declared is, like Bush's Iraq adventure, a preemptive one, preemptively investigating people for crimes that they might be thinking about committing and imprisoning them indefinitely, without access to a lawyer, to make sure that they don't commit them. The thought police of science fiction has become a reality, not peeking in our windows to see if we are downloading pornography—not yet, at any rate—but into our minds to divine our intentions. I'd consider sending Ashcroft my DVD of *Minority Report* for his birthday, if I didn't think he'd have me investigated for it.

No Bush-era initiative would seem legit without the hallmark of hypocrisy; Ashcroft finds his in the one aspect of the lives of suspected terrorists he has forbidden his G-men to investigate: namely, whether or not the suspects have ever tried to buy a gun. During a Senate hearing, Senator Dick Durbin read from an Al Qaeda training manual to the stone-faced attorney general. "In countries like the United States, it's perfectly legal for members of the public to own certain types of firearms. If you live in such a country, obtain an assault rifle legally, preferably an AK-47 or variations." Ashcroft is determined to defend Americans' Second Amendment right to bear arms while trampling on the guarantees set forth in the rest of the Bill of Rights.

With the prison camp at Guantánamo Bay bursting at the seams (although, at this writing, only a single person, Zacarias Moussaoui, has been charged with direct involvement in the atrocities of September 11), Ashcroft has used the PATRIOT Act as an excuse to go trawling in other waters. It's exactly the sort of authoritarian abuse of power that the September 10

John Ashcroft would have legitimately feared. Using PA-
TRIOT's liberal provisions for access to financial records,
Ashcroft's FBI has pursued a Vegas strip club owner suspected of bribing local officials. Michael Galardi, who allegedly paid off one county commissioner with $400 worth
of free lap dances, may not be the most savory character on
the Strip, but he's hardly a threat to national security. More
ominously still, Ashcroft seems to have followed the vi-
ciously authoritarian spirit of PATRIOT rather than the letter of other laws in a number of cases that sit close to the
heart of his fellow social conservatives. Since 9/11, Iron
John has abandoned his states' rights stance, and cracked
down on medical marijuana clinics in California and Oregon, ignoring local, voter-mandated laws allowing the clinics to operate.

He also has ordered a slowdown on Freedom of Information Act requests. And the Justice Department, which has
gone from the nation's "good cop" to its "crazy cop" in the
frenzied PATRIOT atmosphere, has tossed a Texas journalist, Vanessa Leggett, in jail for six months on civil contempt
charges (and threatened her with criminal charges, which
could lead to years in jail) for not turning over her notes in a
murder case. Perhaps if Ashcroft were not so selective in his
targets, we could all be treated to the amusing spectacle of
Robert Novak pacing in a D.C. lockup, writing his column in
solitary confinement until he gives up the name of the administration official who leaked him the information that ex-
posed Valerie Plame as a covert CIA operative.

Like Bush, John Ashcroft is one of those people for whom
September 11 proved to be a defining moment. While Bush
has made the startling, and startlingly unremarked upon,
transformation from a humble critic of nation building to the

biggest nation builder since Stalin and FDR faced off across the smoldering European ruins of World War II, Ashcroft has slipped off into the deep end.

BUSH'S OUTRAGES:
THE DIRTY LAUNDRY LIST

The White House has shown its disdain for public opinion— and indeed the public interest—in an exceptionally wide variety of areas. Here are just a few of the more blood-boiling cases:

- On the environment: Not satisfied with just gutting the Clean Air Act, the White House chose to announce this polluter-friendly decision in the most dismissive, least accountable way possible, delivered not by the president or then EPA head Christie Todd Whitman but by a low-level administrator, on a Friday afternoon leading into a holiday week, and with no cameras allowed. In your face, people who like fresh air!

- On stealing from the poor to give to the rich: In an act of reverse Robin Hood effrontery, the president helped defray some of the cost of his nonstop campaigning with an accounting trick that allowed him to dip into the coffers of the Office of Family Assistance by piggybacking campaign appearances onto trips ostensibly made to talk about welfare reform. That's right, money meant to assist poor families was used to help elect politicians who believe that, even with all the problems facing this country, cutting taxes for the rich should be job number one. These, of course, are the same Scrooges who did nothing to stop the unemployment benefits of 800,000 workers from expiring during the midst of the 2002 holiday season. And a year later, Congress put an end to extended unemployment benefits, which means that every week 90,000 workers stop receiving any assistance. Ho, ho, ho, jobless people! Happy Recovery!

• On sucking up to special interests: I guess that the back channel passage of a tailor-made—and White House approved—amendment to the Homeland Security Bill protecting Eli Lilly, maker of the questionable vaccine preservative Thimerosal, from billions in potential lawsuits just wasn't enough of an insult to democracy. To pour salt in that fresh wound, the administration asked a federal claims court to block public access to documents unearthed in over a thousand Thimerosal-related claims. (It later withdrew the request in the uncomfortable spotlight of embarrassing publicity.) Take that, suffering parents of autistic children!

• On political patronage: At the same time the White House was moving to scale back pay increases for career federal employees, it was also secretly doling out big-buck bonuses to political appointees—a practice banned during the Clinton presidency because of abuses during the previous Bush administration. Who was it again who was going to restore integrity to the White House?

• On fighting the war on terror: A majority of Americans have a negative view of Saudi Arabia. But not the president. The White House continues to treat

If the Democrats want to reclaim the White House, they must first reclaim the language of patriotism and the language of responsibility. They have to wrestle the flag from the hands of the Republicans who have desecrated it by using it to advance their own tribal interests. And they have to take back "responsibility" from the grossly irresponsible GOP that has saddled our children with a national debt that will reach $12 trillion over the next ten years.

the spoiled princes of the House of Saud as bosom brothers, welcome at the Crawford ranch anytime they're in the mood for a little down-home cookin'. Indeed, during a speech the president gave last fall at the American Enterprise Institute, he actually patted his Saudi Arabian buddies on the back, saying, "The Saudi government is taking first steps toward reform. By giving the Saudi people a greater role in their own society, the Saudi government can demonstrate true leadership in the region." True leadership? What about the desert kingdom's two-faced attitude, the money that ended up in the pockets of 9/11 hijackers, its telethons for suicide bombers, its refusal to let U.S. planes targeting the Taliban take off from Saudi soil, and the not-insignificant fact that most of the 9/11 hijackers were Saudi, as are most of the suspects being held in Guantánamo?

In your eye, America!

THE BUSH RECORD: MISSION ACCOMPLISHED

If you still need to be convinced just why it is morally imperative to remove Bush from the White House in 2004, here is a quick overview of his record.

Since George W. Bush took office, three million people in America have lost their jobs, bringing the total to 9 million out of work.

Since George W. Bush took office, the number of poor Americans has increased by 3 million—500,000 of them children.

Since George W. Bush took office, there has been an increase of 10% in the number of families struggling to put food on the table—now up to 12.1 million people.

Since George W. Bush took office, 3.8 million Americans have been added to the list of those with no health insurance. The total now stands at over 43 million.

Real median family income has fallen $1,439 in the last two years.

The wages of most workers are now falling behind inflation.

In 2002, 38 percent of adults requesting emergency food assistance were employed; 48 percent of those seeking emergency food assistance were families with children.

Of the 3.5 million people who were homeless at some point last year, 40 percent were families with children.

Average tuition for college has risen by 28 percent since George W. Bush took office while 64 percent of high school seniors are reading below the level considered appropriate by the National Assessment for Educational Progress.

Since George W. Bush took office, there has been dramatically less regulatory activity than during previous administrations, including his father's. George W. Bush's EPA finalized only two significant new rules, and both were court-ordered. Bush's father finalized fourteen in his first two years, and Clinton finalized twenty-three. Not surprisingly, Bush's 2005 budget cuts the funding for the EPA by 7.3 percent.

Since George W. Bush took office, personal indebtedness has increased by 14 percent and personal bankruptcies by 12 percent, while business bankruptcies have dropped by over 15 percent. This shift is not by accident but by design. The Bush administration has consistently treated corporations with the compassion it has denied to individuals. In 2003 more people ended up in bankruptcies than suffered a heart attack or were diagnosed with cancer or graduated from college.

The richest 20 percent of Americans earn more than 50 percent of the nation's income—the highest level since the 1920s—while the poorest 20 percent earn only 3.5 percent.

Asthma and other environmental respiratory diseases are at an all-time high: 20 million people suffer from asthma, and six million of these are children. The president's preposterously titled "Clear Skies" legislation actually lowers the emissions standards for power plants, just as new technology is coming on line that would make a higher standard attainable and affordable. In yet another sellout to the politically astute and environmentally psychopathic energy industry, Bush has also given a bye to dirty power plants on their responsibility to clean up the messes they make by postponing the cleanup deadline by a decade.

Where is the political leader who will put flesh and blood on these statistics, capture the public imagination, and provoke enough public outrage to lead to change? Where is the storyteller who will gather us around as a nation and tell us real-life tales of survival, gripping tales of ordinary heroes facing overwhelming odds? Like Theresa Pardo, who had to choose between buying Morgan, her nine-year-old daughter who suffers from asthma, an inhaler or a birthday present. Theresa is a government employee, but Harris County, for which she works, provides her with affordable insurance only for herself, not for her daughter. By the time she has paid for her rent, car, and day care, she is left with $200 for everything else.

Carol Johnston, also a single mother, living in Houston,

lost her job last spring and, after filling out over five hundred
job applications, still has not found another one. Carol has a
sixteen-year-old son with learning disabilities. She has cysts in
her breasts that she cannot afford to aspirate—not poor
enough for Medicaid, but too poor to buy her own insurance.
"Do I have to move to Iraq to get help?" she asks.

From roads and bridges to public schools and universities,
the nation faces a sobering challenge in preventing the
moldering infrastructure from becoming a drain on the
economy rather than an asset. According to the National
Center for Education Statistics, we need $127 billion to ren-
ovate our schools, and the American Society of Civil Engineers pegs the cost for upgrading our roads, bridges, and
tunnels at over a trillion dollars. Education and infrastructure
pay dividends, not just abstractly, but to every business in
America. Imagine if companies had to teach their employees
to count or read. To tell "on" from "off." Imagine if it took
a hundred hours to truck a product to market over potholed
roundabout roads rather than ten on a well-maintained, direct interstate.

This collapse of investment in our public infrastructure is a
breach of trust. It is not a question of money. It is, quite simply, a question of perverted priorities. In the midst of a $500
billion deficit, George Bush somehow found another $87
billion—on top of the initial expenditure of $79 billion—for
Iraq because he considers fighting that war to be our highest
national priority. The money is there. It's just being spent on
luxuries instead of necessities. On a fur coat of conquest and
grandiose schemes instead of a raincoat in the middle of a
storm.

The celebrations over the increase in our Gross Domestic
Product are also a breach of trust. As soon as news hit the

media that the GDP had gone up to 8.2 percent in the third quarter of 2003, many began to declare victory for Bush's economic policies. It was as premature as the "Mission Accomplished" banner on the USS *Abraham Lincoln*. First of all, by the fourth quarter the number had cooled down to 4 percent. But beyond that, I have a modest proposal: we need two GDP numbers. One would reflect corporate profits, which grew 40 percent during the third quarter. The other would reflect jobs and wages: during the same third quarter 165,000 jobs were lost, and even those who had jobs found that, despite great increases in worker productivity and profits, their wages barely kept up with inflation. That we are two nations is borne out as well by the Christmas shopping reports: fabulous at Neiman-Marcus and Saks, less cheery at Target and Wal-Mart.

In fact, what the Bush Republicans have done is not shrink government but shift its growth in the directions they prefer. Libertarian critics have noted with some perplexity that the footprint of government has actually expanded under the Bush administration. Spending rose by 16.9 percent in 2003 on top of a 13.1 percent increase in 2002, more than double the increases of the Reagan era. In all, defense spending has gone up 34 percent since the beginning of the Bush administration. The Cato Institute has even dubbed Bush the "Mother of All Big Spenders."

CRIME AND VERY LITTLE PUNISHMENT

When New York State Attorney General Eliot Spitzer concluded his settlement agreement with the corrupt titans of

Wall Street at the beginning of 2003, none of the wrongdo-ers involved had to admit any wrongdoing. This kid-glove treatment of Wall Street crooks—even in the hands of a real crusader for cleaning up the system—provides a profound example of how we continue to operate under two vastly different sets of rules in this country—one for a select group of elites and one for the rest of America. When I asked Spitzer if he was concerned about this disparity, he replied, "While I would prefer to have a statement of wrongdoing, the firms never admit wrongdoing because it would drive them to bankruptcy." So? Isn't the genius of capitalism to let the free market—not the attorney general of New York—pick winners and losers depending on how they play the game? Break the rules, and you lose. How dra-matically would the numbers change if we were as con-cerned about personal bankruptcies as we are about business ones?

Prof. Paul Lapides, director of the Corporate Governance Center at Kennesaw State University, ruefully describes the sleazegeist: "I used to tell my students that if you commit a white-collar crime, the time will come when you will serve your time. Now I tell my students, if you commit a crime, commit a big one." Lapides adds, "If you commit a big enough crime, you'll probably have to return only some of the money, and you won't have to do any jail time. Is America a great country or what?"

When common criminals are allowed to cop a plea, they plead guilty first as part of the bargain. Crooks in pinstripe suits, on the other hand, even those caught red-handed, don't have to come clean. It's the ultimate privilege—and the ultimate insult to our intelligence. What good is finding a smoking gun if the guys who fired it are allowed to pay a small fine, step over the bloody body, and reload?

Each day brings a fresh, stomach-turning revelation of the rampant corruption infecting corporate America. Last fall the 95 million people invested in the $7 trillion mutual fund industry had a rude awakening when an SEC investigation revealed that 25 percent of mutual fund dealers and 10 percent of mutual fund companies were using market timing and late trading—practices banned because they benefit the well-connected at the expense of average shareholders.

In Bush's second year in office, median compensation for CEOs rose by 14 percent, reaching $13.2 million, but this rising tide did not lift all boats. Indeed it occurred while the total return of the S&P 500 was down by 22 percent: one more example of the delinking of reward and performance. Incidentally, this trend is not restricted to the Bush years. Going back to 1980, we find CEO pay skyrocketing by 442 percent while worker pay has gone up by 1.6 percent. And yes, these figures are inflation-adjusted. In other words, while CEOs made 45 times what workers made in 1980, by 2002 they made 241 times as much.

And over a year and a half after the president declared "no more easy money for corporate criminals, just hard time" and the Sarbanes-Oxley Act was signed with much fanfare, the SEC is still allowing auditors to do tax consulting for the companies they audit; shareholders still have little say over executive compensation; stock options are still not treated as business expenses; and to prevent future crusading Eliot Spitzers, the financial services industry is pushing legislation through Congress that will limit the power of state regulators to oversee brokerage firms.

"Life is returning to normal," Bush proclaimed just two weeks after the fall of Baghdad. "Things have settled down inside the country." Just who is preparing his morning briefing papers? Polly-andy Card? Little Condoleezza Sunshine?

THE SECRET RESIGNATION FILES:
THE JOY OF QUITTING

The only thing better than getting a really great job is quitting one you're sick of. And what's the best part of quitting? Writing a scathing resignation letter to your boss gloating that you don't have to hate yourself anymore for stifling your conscience, your principles, and your self-respect. Only, you say it in a nice way. You never know, some day you may need a recommendation.

Government workers are no different. They really can't say anything bad to their boss either. After all, he's the president and the fourth most powerful man in government, after Rumsfeld, Cheney, and the guy who makes those "message" signs that appear behind the commander in chief whenever he gives a speech. So they tap-dance around the reason for their departure, applaud the administration's efforts, boast about the "accomplishments" they were proud to be a part of, and say they're looking forward to spending more time with their family. All of which, I can assure you, is total BS.

What follows are excerpts from actual resignation letters written by government officials who disagreed with the Bush administration's policies so violently that they preferred the uncertainty of the unemployment line to toeing the party line. Also included are excerpts from what I imagine were the first drafts of these letters—what the resigners knocked out before their significant others reminded them that every time you resign from one job, you need to go looking for another.

1. Mike Dombeck, Forest Service chief, resigned on March 27, 2001, after four years on the job.

What he wrote in his resignation letter: "It was made clear in no uncertain terms that the administration wants to take the Forest Service in another direction . . ."

What he might have written in the first draft: "It was made clear in no uncertain terms that the administration needs to kiss a little logging industry ass, having gotten nearly $300,000 in donations during the 2000 election (ten times more than Al Gore). Mr. President, after all that bark-bussing and timber-tonguing, it's a wonder you didn't get splinters in your lip or a very painful STD (Sequoia Transmitted Disease)."

Fact: Before the U.S. Forest Service approves a timber sale on federal land, loggers are currently required to study the impact on endangered animals and salmon runs. The Bush White House is pushing to overturn both of these requirements.

2. John Brown, PhD, was a Foreign Service officer for nearly twenty-five years, having served in London, Prague, Krakow, Kiev, and Belgrade. He resigned on March 10, 2003.

What he wrote in his resignation letter: "I cannot in good conscience support President Bush's war plans against Iraq. The president has failed to: explain clearly why our brave men and women in uniform should be ready to sacrifice their lives in a war on Iraq at this time; to lay out the full ramifications of this war, including the extent of innocent civilian casualties; to specify the economic costs of the war for ordinary Americans; to clarify how the war would help rid the world of terror; to take international public opinion against the war into serious consideration."

What he might have written in the first draft: Come to think of it, the above probably is his first draft. After twenty-five years as a diplomat, he had the good sense to edit out phrases like "monumentally stupid" and "worst White House decision since the Bay of Pigs."

Fact: By February 2004, since the start of the war in Iraq, well over 500 American soldiers had been killed and over 3,000 wounded.

3. Bruce Boler, an EPA state water quality specialist, resigned from his post on October 23, 2003, because his bosses at the EPA accepted the findings of a controversial study that concluded that Florida wetlands discharge more pollutants than they absorb.

What he wrote in his resignation letter: "Ultimately the politics of southwestern Florida have proven to be stronger than the science . . ."

What he might have written in the first draft: "This report, the people who wrote it, and my superiors at the EPA are all obviously off their collective rocker. Next thing you know, they'll be telling us that auto emissions are actually *reducing* global warming. Congratulations, Mr. President, you've just given greedy Florida developers lucrative tax credits for improving water quality by, get this: replacing pristine natural wetlands with golf courses, strip malls, and gas stations. I'm sure they'll reward your brother Jeb accordingly."

Fact: In January 2003 the White House recommended creating a new category of "isolated" waters that wouldn't be subject to the Clean Water Act. If the measure is adopted, hundreds of industries won't need permits to dump their potentially toxic sludge and waste into 20 percent of the nation's wetlands and 60 percent of streams that only flow intermittently.

4. Isam al-Khafaji, a member of the Iraqi Reconstruction and Development Council, resigned on July 9, 2003.

What he wrote in his resignation letter: "Having tried various avenues to convey my feelings of disappointment and frustration . . . it is with deep regret that I am submitting my resignation and appealing to you to intervene directly and personally to reverse the systematic attitude of sidestepping Iraqis, which makes our work within the Coalition Provisional Authority redundant."

What he might have written in the first draft: "Rather than working with allies in a democratic fashion, I'm collaborating with a fanatical administration that has lied about Iraq's 'weapons of mass destruction,' the Saddam–Al Qaeda connection, and Jessica Lynch's gun-toting 'heroics.' The Bush White House is more concerned with the free flow of cheap oil than with restoring power, water, or democracy in Iraq. I'd go on, but the candle in my bombed-out hut just went out . . ."

Fact: Over twice as many soldiers have died in Iraq since the president declared "mission accomplished" than before.

5. Eric Schaeffer, director of the EPA Office of Regulatory Enforcement, resigned on February 27, 2002.

What he wrote in his resignation letter: "I cannot leave without sharing my frustration about the fate of our enforcement actions against power companies that have violated the Clean Air Act. . . . We are fighting a White House that seems determined to weaken rules we are trying to enforce."

What he might have written in the first draft: "I can't leave without sharing my frustration, Mr. President. Your recent proposal to amend the new-source-review component of the Clean Air Act is—how can I say this?—stupendously moronic. It will, among other outrages, allow a coal plant in Monroe, Michigan, that already emits more than 100,000 tons of choking sulfur dioxide, nearly 46,000 tons of nitrous oxide, and 17.5 million tons of carbon dioxide into the air to emit about 40,000 more tons of sulfur dioxide a year. But the three hundred or so people who'll die prematurely from those pollutants are from Michigan. And Michigan was one of those uppity blue states that went for Gore. That's okay, I suppose."

Fact: In the 2000 presidential election, oil and gas companies, two of the leading sources for environmental pollutants, donated nearly $35 million to political candidates, 80 percent of which went to Republicans. In return for his 10 percent cut of that bounty, President Bush has been working hard to systematically weaken clean air standards.

6. John Brady Kiesling, a twenty-year veteran of the Foreign Service whose last job was that of political counselor, U.S. Embassy, Athens, resigned on February 27, 2003.

What he wrote in his resignation letter: "Until this Administration it had been possible to believe that by upholding the policies of my president, I was also upholding the interests of the American people. I believe it no longer. I am resigning because I have tried and failed to reconcile my conscience with my ability to represent the current administration. I have confidence that our democratic process is ultimately self-correcting."

What he might have written in the first draft: "I have confidence that our democratic process is ultimately self-correcting and that President Bush will be thrown out of office in 2004 when the American people discover that he stole the 2000 election, got us into a quagmire akin to Vietnam, turned the largest government surplus in history into the largest deficit in history, couldn't find Osama bin Laden, and ordered the assassination of beloved comic actor John Ritter. OK, I got carried away with that last one. I think."

Fact: The $87 billion President Bush has appropriated to fund the war in Iraq could instead have been used to pay the salaries of two million new teachers, or hire two million police officers, or provide nearly $8,000 of care for every child without health insurance.

7. Karen Kwiatkowski, Office of the Undersecretary of Defense, Near East Bureau, resigned on July 1, 2003.

What she wrote in her resignation letter: "While working from May 2002 through February 2003 in the office of the Undersecretary of Defense for Policy, Near East, South Asian, and Special Plans in the Pentagon, I observed the environment in which decisions about postwar Iraq were made. . . . What I saw was aberrant, pervasive, and contrary to good order and discipline. . . . If one is seeking the answers to why peculiar bits of "intelligence" found sanctuary in a presidential speech, or why the post-Hussein occupation has been distinguished by confusion and false steps, one need look no further than the process inside the office of the Secretary of Defense."

What she might have written in the first draft: "Don Rumsfeld is an idiot. Don Rumsfeld is a megalomaniac. If we lose this war, blame Don Rumsfeld. I hate Don Rumsfeld. Where was I? Oh, yeah, Don Rumsfeld is a duplicitous charlatan, Don Rumsfeld is . . ."

Fact: In 1986, when Don Rumsfeld was considering a run for the White House, an article about him in the *Chicago Tribune* listed helping "re-open U.S. relations with Iraq" when he served as Ronald Reagan's special envoy to the Middle East as one of his career achievements. According to the State Department, while Rumsfeld was opening relations with Iraq, Saddam Hussein was actively using chemical weapons to systematically murder thousands of Kurds.

8. Mary Ann Wright, deputy chief of mission, U.S. Embassy, Mongolia, resigned on March 19, 2003, after thirty years of diplomatic service.

What she wrote in her resignation letter: "I disagree with the administration's policies on Iraq . . . and curtailment of civil liberties in the U.S. itself. I believe the administration's policies are making the world a more dangerous, not a safer place. I feel obligated morally and professionally to set out my very deep and firm concerns on these policies and to resign from government as I cannot defend or implement them."

What she might have written in her first draft: "Dear Mr. President, you can take this job and shove it!"

Fact: According to a classified State Department report, "Anti-American sentiment is so pervasive that Iraqi elections in the short term could lead to the rise of Islamic-controlled governments hostile to the United States."

9. After two-and-a-half years as chief administrator at the EPA, former New Jersey governor **Christie Todd Whitman** resigned on May 20, 2003.

What she wrote in her resignation letter: "As rewarding as the past two-and-a-half years have been for me professionally, it's time for me to return to my home and husband in New Jersey. . . . I leave knowing that we have made a positive difference and that we have set the Agency on a course that will result in continued environmental improvement."

What she might have written in her first draft: "When you honored me by asking me to join your cabinet as administrator of the Environmental Protection Agency, I didn't know the title would be ironic. I naively assumed the post would have something to do with protecting the environment, as opposed to protecting the bottom line of your campaign contributors. I thought that was Don Evans's job over at Commerce. If I am ever to sleep at night again, I have no choice other than to send you this letter. I remember the lump I felt in my throat back in 1973 when Elliot Richardson resigned his cabinet post rather than acquiesce to Richard Nixon's demand that he fire Watergate prosecutor Archibald Cox. I had the same reaction seven years later when Cyrus Vance also took a principled stand and resigned as secretary of state in protest over President Carter's military action in Iran.

" 'You would not be well served in the coming weeks and months,' he wrote to Carter, 'by a secretary of state who could not offer you the public backing you need on an issue and decision of such extraordinary importance.' My feelings exactly. As Richardson told Nixon, 'Mr. President, it would appear that we have a different perception of the public interest.'

"And since I cannot face the prospect of looking my children in the eye and explaining why I stood by while the president I served was selling out their health, the health of their children, and the health of our planet, I respectfully submit my resignation and bid you good-bye."

What Gov. Whitman might have talked about with her husband:

Mr. Whitman: Honey, you can't scold the president for okaying the destruction of millions of acres of pristine Alaskan wilderness at the hands of greedy Texas oil companies. This is your resignation letter; you have to say something nice. What about something like "we've made incredible progress toward protecting the environment."

Gov. Whitman: But we haven't made "incredible progress." In fact, it's been the exact opposite.

Mr. Whitman: OK, then. What about "we've taken great steps"?

Gov. Whitman: Haven't done that either. Did you know that under my watch, inspections of polluting businesses dropped by 15 percent and the number of criminal cases we refer to the Justice Department dropped by 40 percent?

Mr. Whitman: What about "a giant stride towards . . ."

Gov. Whitman: Still not right.

Mr. Whitman: "Vast improvement"?

Gov. Whitman: No. Work with me here, OK?

Mr. Whitman: You made "big changes."

Gov. Whitman: Idiot! It's got to sound good, but be nebulous. That's the point I have to make!

Mr. Whitman: I got it. "Positive difference." Say you made a "positive difference."

Gov. Whitman: "Positive difference," it's perfect. It sounds like something, but it's totally meaningless. (*then sullen*) I'm so ashamed.

Fact: The Bush administration has initiated more than two hundred rollbacks of America's environmental laws, undermining the protection of our air, water, and public lands.

Do Your Part

If you or someone you know is a government worker who can no longer support the misguided, self-serving, asinine, and boneheaded policies of the Bush administration, yet can't muster the courage to write a scathing resignation letter, you're in luck. Clip out this helpful resignation form letter, fill in the blanks with your personal righteous indignation, and address it to

President George W. Bush
1600 Pennsylvania Avenue
Washington, D.C. 20500

Dear Mr. President,

I am submitting to you my resignation from _____ to take effect immediately, because I can no longer in good conscience support your _____ plan to _____.

I am proud that in my capacity as _____, I was able to _____. But we both know that your real intention is to _____, not _____.

I believe this _____ decision to _____ will be _____ for the American people and will _____ America's reputation and make us the target of hateful and recriminating acts like _____.

As I retire, my future plans include spending more time with _____, taking up _____, and becoming involved with my local _____.

Finally, I'd like to add a personal note. I think you are a total _____.

Sincerely,

(Your name here)

FANATICS IN ACTION, PART TWO: ICING THE YELLOWCAKE

Poor Karl Rove spent close to two years meticulously staging photo ops and carefully crafting sound bites to create the image of President Bush as a take-charge, man-the-controls, land-the-jet-on-the-deck-of-the-aircraft carrier, "Bring 'em on" kind of leader. And then, as you may have forgotten or blocked out, among the 5,413 words in Bush's 2003 State of the Union address were sixteen that proved to be, well, a little problematic: "The British government has learned that Saddam Hussein recently sought significant quantities of uranium from Africa." He hadn't. To avoid that unfortunate fact, the president's own people subsequently strove to portray him as a bumbling, detached figurehead in chief. Take George Tenet. While robotically impaling himself on his sword by taking responsibility for the president's confusion, the CIA director also took great pains to point out that he himself thought so little of the Niger/Saddam uranium connection that he and his deputies refused to bring it up in congressional briefings as far back as the fall of 2002. It just didn't meet his standards.

Same with Colin Powell. The secretary went on at great length about the intense vetting process—"four days and three nights" locked up with the leaders of the CIA, working "until midnight, one o'clock every morning," going over "every single thing we knew about all of the various issues with respect to weapons of mass destruction"—that went into deciding what information would be used in his United Nations presentation. A presentation that ultimately did not include the Niger allegation because it was not, in Powell's words, "standing the test of time."

Hmmm, just how hard is that test? Powell's UN speech came a mere eight days after Bush's State of the Union, leaving one to wonder what the expiration date is on patently phony data. About a week after a president uses it, it turns out.

So here's the picture we're left with: When faced with using explosive but highly questionable charges in vital presentations leading up to a possible preemptive war, both Powell and Tenet gave the information a thorough going-over before ultimately rejecting it. But not the commander in chief. Apparently he just took whatever he was handed and happily offered it up to the world. He was, therefore, little more than the guy in the presidential suit, mindlessly speaking the words that others had debated and polished and twisted and finally agreed he would say. Then when the yellowcake hit the fan, our stand-up-guy president decided that the buck actually stops with, er, George Tenet.

As the Niger controversy—Yellowcakegate—turned into a political firestorm, the question became, What didn't the president know, and why didn't he know it? And why does he seem to know less and less every day? After all, it became clearer by the day that just about everyone else involved in making the case for war knew that the president was using a bogus charge to alarm the nation about Saddam's nuclear threat. Whatever the opposite of "top secret" is, this was it.

The U.S. ambassador to Niger, Barbro Owens-Kirkpatrick, knew. She had sent reports to Washington debunking the allegations. Joe Wilson, the envoy sent to Niger by the CIA, knew. His fact-finding trip quickly confirmed the ambassador's findings. But the fanatics had such a firm hold on policy that they did the unthinkable: they leaked the name of a serving covert CIA operative, Wilson's wife, in order to send him a not-so-subtle message to shut the hell up.

The CIA knew. The agency tried unsuccessfully in September 2002 to convince the Brits to take the false charge out of an intelligence report. The State Department knew. Its Bureau of Intelligence and Research labeled the Niger connection "highly dubious." Tenet and Powell knew. They refused to use it. The president's speechwriters knew. They were told to remove a reference to the Niger uranium in a speech the president delivered in Cincinnati on October 7— three months before his State of the Union. And the National Security Council knew: NSC staff played a key role in the decision to fudge the truth by having the president source the uranium story to British intelligence.

And Marine General Carlton Fulford and his boss, Chairman of the Joint Chiefs of Staff General Richard Meyers, knew. Fulford was sent to Niger in 2002 to check on Niger yellowcake and found it well secured by the mining company that had extracted it. He also received personal assurances from Niger's president that it would remain so.

The bottom line: this canard had been thoroughly discredited many, many times over, but the administration fanatics so badly wanted it to be true, they just refused to let it die. The yellowcake lie was like one of those slasher movie psychos who refuses to stay buried no matter how many times you smash a hatchet into his skull. It had more sequels than *Friday the 13th* and *Halloween* combined.

Cherry-picking convenient lies about something as important as nuclear war is bad enough, but the administration's attempts to spin the aftershocks were even worse. They just didn't seem to grasp the concept that when you're sending American soldiers to die, the reasons you give—all of the reasons—should be true.

Condoleezza Rice was the worst offender in the frantic

cover-up of the Niger deception. Tenet had personally warned Rice's deputy, Steve Hadley, not to use the yellowcake claim back in October 2002. NSC staffers also played a key role in manipulating the State of the Union. Rice's widely publicized assertion that, at the time of the State of the Union, "maybe someone knew down in the bowels of the agency, but no one in our circles knew that there were doubts and suspicions that this might be a forgery" has since been revealed for what it is: a bald-faced lie.

Even when the truth came flooding out, Rice continued to play fast and loose with the facts—and to stand by her man. "The statement that he made," she said on the Sunday shows, "was indeed accurate. The British government did say that."

Joining the still-don't-get-it unit were Don "Haldeman" Rumsfeld, who termed the president's speech "technically correct," and Ari "Ehrlichman" Fleischer, who offered up this classic bit of spinsanity: "What we have said is it should not have risen to the level of a presidential speech. People cannot conclude that the information was necessarily false." Watergate gave us the nondenial denial. Yellowcakegate gave us the nonadmission admission.

And that wasn't the only parallel. In July 1973, at the height of the Watergate hearings, Richard Nixon announced, "What we were elected to do, we are going to do, and let others wallow in Watergate." George Bush took the same head-in-the-sand approach, letting it be known that, with Tenet taking responsibility for the Niger snafu, he considered the matter closed. "The president has moved on," Fleischer said. "And I think, frankly, much of the country has moved on as well." Let others wallow in Yellowcakegate, right? But wishing doesn't make it so, either for phantom uranium transfers or the evaporation of skepticism.

In the spirit of Tricky Dick, let me make myself perfectly

clear: I'm not saying that Yellowcakegate was the equivalent of Watergate. I'm saying it was much, much worse.

At its core, Watergate was all about trying to make sure that Nixon won an election. Yellowcakegate was much more than a dirty trick played on the American public. It betrays the Bush administration's pattern of deception as it pushed and shoved this country into a preemptive war—from the much-advertised but nonexistent links between Iraq and Al Qaeda to the sexing up of Saddam's WMD.

No one died as a result of Watergate, but more than 500 American soldiers have been killed and thousands more wounded to rid the world of an imminent threat that wasn't, to say nothing of the countless Iraqis who have lost their lives. And where will these numbers be at the end of the "long, hard slog?" With Yellowcakegate, George Bush came across as very presidential indeed: like his dad, he was out of the loop; like Clinton, he became a world-class word weasel; and like Nixon, he showed a massive propensity for secrecy and dissembling.

CORPORATE AMERICA DIVVIES UP
THE POST-SADDAM SPOILS

The collective insanity of the Bush administration is enabled by a posse of self-interested yes-men ready, when called upon, to swear on their mothers' graves that the moon is indeed made of green cheese. Whatever the delusion du jour is, be it a messianic sense of righteous purpose, an obsession with "tax relief," thirst for oil, daddy issues, or that old devil imperialism, one prime mover is always close to the heart of the fanatics' purpose: the corporate bottom line.

The dots leading from Wall Street to the West Wing situa-

With the Niger uranium scandal—Yellowcake-gate—George Bush came across as very presidential indeed. Like his dad, he was out of the loop; like Clinton, he became a world-class word weasel; and like Nixon, he showed a massive propensity for secrecy and dissembling.

tion room are easy to connect. There's money to be made in postwar Iraq. The nugget of truth that former Bush economic guru Lawrence Lindsey let slip in the fall of 2002 shortly before he was shoved out the Oval Office door says it all. Momentarily forgetting that he was talking to the press and not his buddies in the White House, he gushed, "The successful prosecution of the war would be good for the economy."

Even before the first smart bomb was dropped on Baghdad, we already had a winner in Iraq. The conquering heroes were not generals in fatigues but CEOs in suits, and the shock troops are not an advance guard of commandos but legions of lobbyists. The United Nations has traditionally overseen the reconstruction of war zones like Afghanistan or Kosovo. But in keeping with its unilateral, the-world-is-our-sandbox approach to the invasion, the White House decided to nail a "Made in the USA" sign on this Iraqi fixer-upper. Postwar Iraq is being rebuilt using red, white, and blueprints.

The Bush administration doled out over $1.7 billion in government contracts to American companies who lined up to cash in on the rebuilding of postwar Iraq before the destruction had even begun. Talk about advance planning: even while the people of Iraq were girding themselves for the thousands of bombs expected to rain down on them during the first twenty-four hours of the attack, the administration was already picking and choosing who would be given the lucrative job of cleaning up the rubble.

To further expedite matters, the war-powers-that-be invoked "urgent circumstances" clauses that allowed them to subvert the requisite competitive bidding process—the free market be damned—and invite only a select group of companies to bid on the rebuilding projects. No British companies were included, which left many of them seething. And you don't need to ask if any other foreign enterprises were cut in on the action. *Mais non!*

So just which companies were given first crack at the post-Saddam spoils? The common denominator among the chosen few is a proven willingness to make large campaign donations to the Grand Old Party. The top bidders—the Bechtel Group, the Fluor Corporation, and of course Vice President Cheney's old cronies at Halliburton—had donated a combined $2.8 million over the past two election cycles, 68 percent of which went to Republicans. A total of $8 billion in contracts, according to the Center for Public Integrity, has been doled out to seventy American companies that have made political contributions totaling nearly $50 million since 1990. More than half a million dollars went to Bush's presidential campaigns, surpassing the amount collected by any other politician in the past twelve years. A Nebraska contractor working in Afghanistan spelled it out: "It depends on who knows who in the administration, USAID, and the State Department."

THE LOVE TRIANGLE OF DICK, SADDAM, AND HALLIBURTON

The insider track given these fat-cat donors proves afresh that splurging on a politician is one of the soundest and safest investments you can make.

No one in the administration embodies this bottom-line mentality more than Dick Cheney. The vice president is one of those ideological purists who never let little things like logic, morality, or mass murder interfere with the single-minded pursuit of profitability. His on-again, off-again relationship with the Butcher of Baghdad is a textbook example of what modern moralists condemn as "situational ethics," a convenient code that allows you to do what you want when you want and still feel good about it in the morning. In the Cheney White House (let's call it what it is), anything that can be rationalized is right.

Cheney and Hussein were clearly on the outs back during the first Gulf War, when Cheney was Secretary of Defense and the first President Bush dubbed Saddam "Hitler revisited." Then Cheney waltzed over to the private sector, and suddenly things between him and Saddam warmed up considerably. With Cheney in the CEO's seat, Halliburton, through its foreign subsidiaries, helped Iraq reconstruct its war-torn oil industry with $73 million worth of equipment and services— becoming Baghdad's biggest such supplier. Kinda nice how that worked out for the vice president, really: oversee the destruction of an industry, then profit from rebuilding it.

When, during the 2000 campaign, Cheney was asked about his company's Iraqi escapades, he flat-out denied them. But the truth remains: when it came to making a buck, Cheney apparently had no qualms about doing business with "Hitler revisited." And make no mistake, this wasn't a case of hard-nosed realpolitik; it wasn't like the rationale for Don Rumsfeld's cuddle-up to Saddam back in '83 despite Hussein's almost daily habit of gassing Iranians. That, we were told, was all about "the enemy of my enemy is my friend." No, Cheney's company chose to do business with Saddam *after* the rape of Kuwait. After Scuds had been fired at Tel Aviv and Riyadh. After American soldiers had been sent home from Desert Storm in body bags. And as recently as 2000, before joining the GOP ticket and pocketing his $34 million

Halliburton retirement package, Cheney was pushing for an end to U.S. sanctions against Saddam.

But Dick Cheney's former cronies at Halliburton proved nothing if not flexible. They were at the head of the line of companies ready to reap the estimated $7 billion it will take to modernize Iraq's oil infrastructure. This of course comes on top of many other lucrative Pentagon contracts, including a ten-year deal to provide food services to the army that comes with no lid on potential costs.

In an act of good faith, the Army Corps of Engineers awarded Halliburton an open-ended contract to make emergency oil infrastructure repairs and fight oil fires as soon as the war started. This burn-and-build approach to business guarantees that there will be a market for Halliburton's services as long as it has a friend in high places to periodically carpet bomb a country or two.

Lenin once scoffed that "a capitalist would sell rope to his own hangman." And, while the man got more than a few things wrong, he's been proven right on this one time and time again. After all, Hewlett-Packard and Bechtel did help arm Saddam back in the '80s, and Loral Space, Lockheed Martin, and Boeing's Hughes Space and Communications did help China steal rocket and missile secrets—and point a few dozen long-range nukes our way.

Clearly, our national interest runs a distant second when pitted against the rapacious desires of special interests and the politicians they buy with massive campaign contributions. Oil and gas companies donated $26.7 million to Bush and his fellow Republicans during the 2000 election and almost $20 million in 2002. So does it really come as any surprise that Cheney's staff reportedly held secret meetings in October 2002, with executives from ExxonMobil, ChevronTexaco,

ConocoPhillips—and, yes, Halliburton—to discuss who would get what in a post-Saddam Iraq? As they say, to the victors—and the big-buck donors—go the sp-oil-s.

Thankfully, however, one aspect of Halliburton's Iraq rip-off came to glaring light last fall: oil price gouging. Under the terms of its sweetheart deal with the Department of Defense, in addition to repairing the country's tattered oil infrastructure, Halliburton, through its subsidiary Kellogg Brown & Root, is also obligated to provide U.S. forces with gasoline for their operations. This gasoline is procured in Kuwait, where it sells for roughly 70 cents per gallon. By the time it arrives in Iraq, a trip of approximately four hundred miles, the gas sells for more than twice that amount, at approximately $1.70 per gallon.

As of last fall, when Congressmen Henry Waxman and John Dingell finally received a response to their inquiry into Halliburton's profiteering, Halliburton had been paid over $300 million for importing gasoline worth roughly half that amount—a profit margin unconscionable in a time of war. The director of the Defense Energy Support Center, an office within the Pentagon, acknowledged that Halliburton appeared to be charging "excessively high" prices for the gasoline they were importing into Iraq and that fuel into Iraq can be transported for less than half that amount. The Pentagon's investigation concluded that Halliburton overcharged by as much as $61 million for oil from Kuwait, and along the way it found further evidence of overcharging—to the tune of an additional $67 million—in a now-rejected proposal for cafeteria services. The president's response to the wartime profiteering? "We expect that money to be repaid." And no dessert for a week! Further evidence that the good folk at Halliburton play by a different set of rules came when the Pentagon investigation exonerated them, and when they were awarded an additional $1.2 billion contract in January on the heels of revelations that Halliburton employees had received kickbacks from a Kuwaiti company.

But unethical behavior is old hat for Halliburton subsidiary Kellogg Brown & Root. It paid $2 million last year to settle charges that it had overbilled the government. According to a GAO study, the company boosted its bottom line by charging the army $85 for plywood that cost $14 and racked up profits by cleaning the same base offices as many as four times a day. More than likely, this bit of recent history was on the minds of Republican legislators in the House of Representatives when they stripped the Iraqi supplemental funding bill of a provision that would have held corporations accountable for war profiteering. How convenient! What other wonderful, costly surprises will be revealed over time? As cities and states scramble to patch glaring holes in their social-service budgets, corporate profiteering in Iraq represents a betrayal of every principle of patriotism and love of country that this administration claims to stand for.

As a first step toward Iraqi prosperity, the president's ambitious postwar plan earmarked $100 million to ensure that Iraq's 25,000 schools had all the supplies and support necessary—including books for 4.1 million Iraqi schoolchildren. I'm sure the schools in Oregon that were forced to shut down a month early due to inadequate funding or the low-income students in California who sued the state in a desperate effort to obtain adequate textbooks and qualified teachers of their own would have loved to see such "tangible evidence" of President Bush's support. The same goes for our flatlining public health-care system. As more than a mil-

lion poor Americans were about to lose their access to publicly funded medical care, the president was in the market for
a corporate contractor to oversee a $100 million upgrade of
Iraq's hospitals and clinics.

While most communities in the U.S. are facing deferred
school maintenance bills of tens of millions of dollars, the
Coalition Provisional Authority points with an obvious lack of
irony to the 1,600 Iraqi schools that have been refurbished
since the putative end of hostilities. Schools reopened for
business are clearly a symbol of some significance to an administration that is so rhetorically devoted to the cause of education. But as is the case on the home front, rhetoric and
reality quickly diverge as soon as the curious observer moves
past the pleasingly painted façade (which I suppose is even
more than most American schools can take for granted) of
these rebuilt Iraqi institutions of learning. One intrepid reporter from *Newsweek* found that in Baghdad's Camp Sara
neighborhood, five "rebuilt" schools were found to lack textbooks, desks, and blackboards. Most of these schools also experienced a problem that is unfortunately quite familiar to
students in many of America's inner-city schools—nonfunc-
tioning toilets. Great paint job, shame about the lack of books
and plumbing.

As with so many other aspects of the contracting process in
Iraq, the problem seems to be a lack of accountability. In this
instance, in a desperate desire to demonstrate success, Bechtel
set absurdly short deadlines for the reconstruction work. This
led to Iraqi subcontractors slashing corners already previously
cut. That explains how air conditioners ordered in writing for
classrooms are transformed into ceiling fans by the time of installation. Who profits from the air conditioner's transformation into an eleven-dollar ceiling fan? It isn't the sweaty kids.

During World War II, Franklin Roosevelt took the extra-ordinary step of levying heavy penalties against companies that sought to exploit the war for their own disproportion-ately large profit. "I don't want to see a single war millionaire created in the United States as a result of this world disaster," he declared. Clearly his spirit doesn't live on in the current White House.

SECRETS AND THE SECRET KEEPERS WHO KEEP THEM SECRET: A QUIZ

In the three years George W. Bush has been president, his administration has, in some ways, become like a Washington call girl. No matter what they say something will cost, be it rebuilding Iraq or "full service," it always winds up costing more. Plus, both have a laundry list of secrets they refuse to tell, the difference being that the White House's secrets aren't embarrassing pillow talk, they're vital facts the public has the right to know.

How much is the administration keeping from us? Take this secrecy quiz and find out what you know. And what you don't.

1. "Operation Iraqi Freedom: Strategic Lessons Learned" is an official Pentagon report that:

   A. "Concludes," in the words of Rep. Bob Wexler (D-FL), "that the postwar agenda for Iraq was flawed, rushed, and inadequately planned."

   B. Democrats in the House have tried to get a copy of, but have been blocked by the Department of Defense and the Bush Republicans.

C. Was called "brutally honest" one week and then weeks later referred to as "only a draft" by the Pentagon.
D. The Bush White House doesn't want Americans to see because it's hypercritical of the administration's flawed planning for postwar Iraq.
E. Attacks Defense Secretary Don Rumsfeld specifically for his hypocrisy: publicly supporting the war in Iraq, while privately expressing doubts.

(Answer: all of the above, except E. However, Rumsfeld did express his private doubts about the war—calling it "a long, hard slog"—in a memo to four aides dated October 6, 2003, which was leaked to *USA Today*.)

2. Which of the following was cut out of a 2003 Environmental Protection Agency Report on Global Warming by the White House Council on Environmental Quality and the OMB?

A. The fact that the 1990s are likely to have been the warmest decade in a thousand years in the Northern Hemisphere.
B. A section on the future risks posed by rising global temperatures.
C. A mention that humans are partly to blame for global warming.

(Answer: all of the above.)

3. Eleven months before President Bush declared that Iraq tried to buy yellowcake uranium from Niger in

the 2003 State of the Union address Vice President Dick Cheney's office was told:

A. "Niger" is a country in Africa, not a derogatory term for blacks. "Please advise the president to pronounce it correctly."
B. The claim is a hoax. The VP's office was told so by Ambassador Joe Wilson, sent by the CIA to investigate the allegations.

(Answer: B.)

4. When asked about his whereabouts, why do the vice president's staff members often keep Dick Cheney's location a secret?

A. National security concerns.
B. That's just the policy the doctors have in the cardiac care unit at the Bethesda Naval Hospital.
C. When a man's busy masterminding plans to conquer the world, he just needs his privacy.

(Answer: A.)

5. Before the war in Iraq, the Pentagon awarded a top-secret $7 billion no-bid contract to put out oil well fires to a company that:

A. Used to be headed by Vice President Dick Cheney.
B. Paid a $4 billion fine in 2002 to settle asbestos lawsuits.
C. Is being investigated by the SEC for inflating profits by $100 million in 1998 by the way it accounted for cost overruns on construction jobs.

    D. Paid a $2 million fine in 2002 to resolve allegations of fraud stemming from work done on a California military base.

(Answer: all of the above. The company, Kellogg Brown & Root, is a subsidiary of Halliburton, which was headed by Vice President Dick Cheney from 1995 to 2000.)

6. Thanks to Bush's military order, what is the legal burden of proof the administration must meet in order to classify a suspect "a terrorist" and remand him over to a secret military tribunal?

    A. "We just feel like it."
    B. "This guy totally gives us the creeps."
    C. "A preponderance of evidence."
    D. "C'mon. Just look at him."

(Answer: C.)

7. Despite pledging the White House's full cooperation in the Justice Department's investigation of who leaked the name of a top secret CIA operative, George Bush won't rule out which of the following?

    A. Lying to protect a senior administration official.
    B. Obfuscating until this whole ugly thing just goes away.
    C. Invoking "executive privilege" to thwart the investigation.
    D. Distracting the American people by running off to Iraq again to serve soldiers a plastic turkey.

(Answer: C. Bush isn't planning to run off to Iraq again until reporters start asking more questions again about David Kay and WMD.)

8. In an effort to convince Congress that Iraq could rebuild on its own following a U.S. invasion, Deputy Defense Secretary Paul Wolfowitz said Iraq would quickly produce $30 billion a year in oil revenue, despite:

   A. A top-secret Pentagon task force report that pegged the amount at 25 percent less.
   B. Saudi Arabian efforts to thwart such production.
   C. The fact that most of that money is earmarked for U.S. defense contractors with ties to the White House.

(Answer: A. By late summer 2003, Iraq was producing 1 million barrels a day but was forced to ditch up to 35 percent of that due to lack of storage and distribution infrastructure.)

9. The Bush administration's 2001 energy plan favors opening more public land to oil and gas drilling. Who were the members of Dick Cheney's task force that drafted the plan?

   A. Corporate oil and gas executives and lobbyists who stood to benefit from the proposed drilling.
   B. Scientists with no financial interest whatsoever.
   C. Toothless government yes-men.

(Answer: A. Bush has refused to release the names of Cheney's committee on the grounds it would interfere with his ability to get "confidential advice from his chosen advisors" and violate the principle of separation of powers. Plus, it'll look like he's getting environmental advice from companies that want to drill for oil.)

10. What reason did President Bush give for keeping classified a large section of a federal report on September 11 that allegedly implicates Saudi Arabia in the attacks?

    A. "It's none of your business."
    B. "National security."
    C. "It looks bad if our 'allies' are secretly trying to destroy our way of life."

(Answer: B. According to *Newsweek* magazine, the censored portions detail links between associates of the hijackers and Saudi Arabian princes and government officials.)

11. True or false? The Bush White House also classified details in the above-mentioned federal report indicating that high-level government officials were warned in 2001 that Al Qaeda was planning to hijack airplanes and launch a spectacular attack on the U.S.

(Answer: True.)

12. In 1995 President Clinton issued an executive order that most government documents will automatically be declassified after 25 years. In 2003 President Bush issued a new executive order that would declassify government documents after how many years?

A. 10 years
B. 28 years
C. 20 years
D. 5 years

(Answer: B.)

13. Three years into his presidency, how many formal news conferences has George W. Bush held?

    A. 33
    B. 61
    C. 9
    D. 18

(Answer: C. At this point in their presidencies, Bill Clinton had held 33 press conferences, George Herbert Walker Bush 61, and Ronald Reagan 18.)

14. President Bush issued an executive order giving ex-presidents the right to delay the release of records of their presidency to the public for how long?

    A. Indefinitely.
    B. Ten years.
    C. Until they damn well feel like it.
    D. Five years.

(Answer: A.)

15. In a little-publicized October 12, 2001, memo to federal agencies, Attorney General John Ashcroft directed them to do what?

    A. Answer all questions from the media honestly and truthfully, with no subterfuge whatsoever.

B. Fund any and all of his programs, regardless of cost.

C. Employ a much more stringent test before granting Freedom of Information requests.

(Answer: C. In his memo Ashcroft asked agencies to consider whether "institutional, commercial and personal privacy interests could be implicated by disclosure of the information.")

16. On the eve of the Iraq War, George W. Bush's administration banned the videotaping of:

   A. Ashton Kutcher's new MTV show *Punk'd: Tikrit.*
   B. Coffins of deceased soldiers at all military installations.
   C. Internet-ready homemade sex scenes in the Lincoln Bedroom.

(Answer: B. Some have accused Bush of hiding the casualties of the Iraq war in order to sustain its public support. Those people are right.)

17. True or false? The Bush White House has instituted a policy that severely restricts Democratic members of the House and Senate from questioning the administration.

(Answer: True. Timothy A. Campen, the director of the White House Office of Administration, sent an e-mail to members of the House and Senate Appropriations panels that said, "Given the increase in the number and types of requests we are beginning to receive from the

House and Senate . . . I am asking that all requests for information and materials be coordinated through the committee chairmen and be put in writing from the committee." In effect, Democrats won't get questions answered without the blessing of the GOP committee chairmen.)

So, how did you do? Remember, to the White House, anything worth saying is worth keeping secret.

PAY TO PLAY IN IRAQ

What's the most exclusive club in America? How about the Augusta National Golf Club, whose three hundred members withstood the slings and arrows of Martha Burk with nary a scratch? Or maybe it's the U.S. Senate, where a seat at one of the historic rolltop desks can go for as much as $60 million? Or what about ex-boyfriends of Jennifer Lopez?

No, in fact the most select body is the tiny group of contenders invited to bid for capitalism's crown jewel: the Iraq contract.

For full impact, we need a flowchart, like the ones the FBI uses to show the reporting structure of a mafia crime family. Instead of illustrating the interrelationships of the Soprano crew, this chart would lay out the connections that guaranteed that the big winners in the post-Saddam sweepstakes would be those two ultimate Washington insiders, Halliburton and the Bechtel Group. We've talked about Halliburton, so let's take a closer look at Bechtel.

The Bechtel chart is truly Byzantine—starting with George

Shultz, former Bechtel president, former Reagan Secretary of State, and currently both a Bechtel board member and chairman of the Committee for the Liberation of Iraq. Then there is Jack Sheehan, a senior vice president at Bechtel and a member of the Pentagon's influential Defense Policy Board. And then we have chairman and CEO Riley Bechtel, who in February 2003 was appointed by Bush to the highly influential President's Export Council.

Of course, using access, influence, and positions of ostensible public service to make a buck or two—or over a billion of them—off Iraq is nothing new to the fine folks at Bechtel. They offer their customers the most precious commodity of all: experience. Back in the 1980s, the company wanted to build a pipeline to carry oil from Iraq to the Jordanian port of Aqaba—a project ardently supported by the Reagan administration, which included Shultz and a fellow Bechtel alumnus, Secretary of Defense Casper Weinberger. Backers of the Bechtel pipeline lined up a veritable Who's Who of former Reagan-Bush power players to push for the scheme, including former Secretary of Defense and CIA Chief James Schlesinger, former National Security Advisor William Clark, former National Security Advisor Robert McFarlane, and former Attorney General Edwin Meese—I guess the thought being that all that political star power might help people forget Saddam's charmless behavior on the battlefield and in the torture chamber.

Even though he wasn't on the Bechtel payroll, one of those working hardest to convince the Iraqis to hop into bed with the company was the macho man himself, Don Rumsfeld. While working as Reagan's special envoy to the Middle East in 1983, Rumsfeld met with Saddam personally and tried to convince him to sign on to Bechtel's pipeline pipe dream. And Rummy isn't the only current administration official with a close encounter of the Bechtel kind on his CV. Andrew Natsios, administrator of the U.S. Agency for International Development, the agency responsible for handing the lucrative Iraqi rebuilding contract to Bechtel, used to be in charge of overseeing Boston's Big Dig, a massive highway project managed by Bechtel that overran its projected cost of $4.5 billion by nearly $10 billion. In a scathing letter sent to Natsios, the Massachusetts inspector general called Bechtel's contract for the Big Dig "an invitation to fraud, waste and abuse." Apparently, this amounted to a sterling recommendation in Natsios's eyes; three years later, when the time came to draw up the very short list of companies invited to bid on Iraqi contracts, he didn't hesitate to include the old gang at Bechtel. Hey, what's a little "fraud, waste and abuse" among chums?

It goes without saying that everyone involved in these cushy deals denies any impropriety. In fact, they are downright offended by the suggestion that these contracts—bid on by a very select group of well-connected companies and awarded based on secret criteria—were anything but on the up-and-up. "We won this work on our record, plain and simple," crowed Riley Bechtel in an e-mail to employees, making it sound as if their record of insider dealing were something to brag about. And a spokesman for the company assured reporters that Bechtel had not "attempted to bring any political pressure to bear." They didn't have to. When the fix is in, no one has to remind the referee to count to ten when the chump takes his dive. It's all done with a wink and a nod. So it's no wonder that in January 2004 Bechtel was awarded another government contract in Iraq worth nearly $2 billion over the next two years.

The perfect explanation for how this all works came from none other than Our Former Man in Baghdad, retired General Jay Garner. When asked about his uncanny success as a businessman following his long military career—especially how he helped Sy Technology boost its government contracts from $8.5 million in 1999 to $46.8 million in 2001, with much of that business coming from the army division he used to run—Garner replied, "I do not go to friends for business. I get business from my friends, but it's not solicited by me." Don Corleone couldn't have put it any better.

Here's another way of looking at the process: "The purpose behind the abuse," said Senator Charles Grassley (R-IA), "was so that cronies of the president could win the spoils of political gain for themselves." Although Grassley's description suits the Bechtel pact to a tee, he was actually talking about Bill and Hillary's Travelgate. Let's hope Senator Grassley—or anyone on his side of the aisle—can muster a similar fit of indignation over a recent epidemic of crony capitalism that makes Travelgate seem like a tempest in a Teapot Dome.

Here's my bottom line: in a time of war, at what point does subverting our national security in the name of profitability turn from ugly business into high treason? We have over 3,000 American casualties—lives lost and limbs sacrificed—young men and women who were sent to fight against a regime that did not pose a threat to us. Saddam Hussein was a monstrous dictator and getting rid of him is a humanitarian act. But how many Americans would have approved of spending over $150 billion and seeing 3,000 young men and women killed or wounded to get rid of an Iraqi dictator who had no weapons of mass destruction? Yet that is now the administration's position.

At what point does war profiteering turn from ugly business into high treason?

UNCLE SAM WANTS YOU . . . TO GIVE BACK A BILLION DOLLARS

In 1996 the Republican-controlled Congress enacted a law that permits U.S. citizens injured by terrorists to sue the foreign government that sponsored the attack. It's a surprisingly compassionate and pragmatic notion, especially when you consider it came out of a Congress controlled by Mr. Warmth and Personality, Newt Gingrich.

Cut to the summer of 2003, when seventeen U.S. servicemen who were tortured by Iraqi soldiers during the first Persian Gulf war—some for as many as forty-seven days—were awarded nearly $1 billion in damages by a U.S. federal judge. The soldiers had been beaten, burned, starved, threatened with dismemberment and castration, urinated on and forced to play Russian roulette, among other horrors. Clearly these were just the people this law was designed to compensate.

The money the soldiers were awarded was to have been paid from the ample Iraqi government assets frozen in the United States. Here's where the trouble starts: the Bush White House has moved—so far successfully, and with very little publicity—to have the decision overturned on the grounds that that money has been earmarked to rebuild Iraq, not for punitive and compensatory damages in a lawsuit. The president's spokesman Scott McClellan had this to say: "It was determined earlier this year by Congress and the administration that those assets were no longer assets of Iraq, but they were resources required for the urgent national security needs of rebuilding Iraq." What? It can't be.

And yet it is. The Bush White House wants tortured soldiers to give back money they were awarded in a fairly adjudicated lawsuit so the administration can spend it to rebuild the roads and bridges they just finished blowing up.

In the meantime, while injured soldiers are still recovering from physical and psychological wounds and wondering how they could have been betrayed by a government they swore to protect, lots of the president's cronies are cashing in. Which FOGs (Friends of George) and Washington insiders are getting rich off the war—other than Halliburton and Bechtel insiders, that is? Here's a sampling:

- Joe Allbaugh is George W. Bush's former campaign manager and close friend. He has set up a lobbying company to trade on his connections and, as he says, help steer corporate clients to government contracts and "business opportunities in the Middle East following the conclusion of the U.S.-led war in Iraq."
- Terry Sullivan of Sullivan/Haave was hired for four months' work in Iraq giving advice to emerging government ministries. Sullivan's wife, Carol Haave, is the deputy assistant secretary of defense for security and information operations at the Pentagon. When asked by the Center for Public Integrity if she knew anything about the government contract awarded to her husband's company, she said she had no knowledge of any work the company might be doing. That "company" has only one employee—her husband.

- Philip J. Carroll Jr. is the former chairman and CEO of Fluor, according to its website one of the world's largest engineering, construction, maintenance, and procurement companies. Although no longer in Fluor's employ, he collects a pension worth over a million dollars a year and has $34 million in company holdings. Carroll, who was also with Shell Oil for thirty-seven years, was appointed by the White House to be the chairman of the board advising Iraq's new oil minister, whose prime agenda will be hiring companies to excavate, construct, and maintain Iraq's oil wells. In an interview with the *Los Angeles Times*, Carroll said he would attempt to avoid a conflict of interest. "I will stay so far away from any consideration of the bidding process, evaluation process or even the administration and arbitration of things associated with any of those companies in which I have a financial interest." Sure he will. Not surprisingly, Fluor has contributed more than $3.5 million to political candidates in the last twelve years, and in the last two years, it has been on the receiving end of $500 million in contracts to rebuild Iraq and Afghanistan.

PORTRAITS IN FANATICISM: DICK CHENEY . . . THE MARGIN OF VICTORY FOR DEMOCRATS?

GOP inner circles continue to buzz with the rumor that President Bush is planning to drop Dick Cheney from his re-election ticket and replace him with someone less radioactive—Tom Ridge? Rudy Giuliani? Bill Frist? All I can say to this is: Please, Mr. President, say it ain't so!

Cheney is the Democrats' best—though sorely underutilized—weapon. A loose-lipped loose cannon who threatens to torpedo the Bushie ship of state every time he half-opens his mouth. If only we start paying attention. The Most Powerful Number Two in History just can't help telling it like he sees it, and the way he sees it is very, very telling. And frightening.

Take his dig-in-his-heels approach regarding Iraqi WMD and a Saddam/Al-Qaeda connection. While even Rummy, Condi, and Wolfowitz, the administration's true believers, were splitting verbal hairs trying to back away from their apocalyptic prewar claims—"Did I say 500 tons of sarin and 25,000 liters of anthrax? I meant 'weapons of mass destruction-related program activities.'"—Cheney merely reloaded and kept on firing with both barrels.

To his hawkish eyes, a lone pair of souped-up flatbed trucks are "conclusive evidence" of Saddam's WMD, and a memo the Pentagon has labeled "inaccurate" provides, according to Cheney, "overwhelming evidence" that the former Butcher of Baghdad and Osama bin Laden had "an established relationship."

Like a Flat-Earther who has sailed around the world ten times but keeps waiting to topple off the edge, Cheney has got his story and he's sticking to it.

He even persists in serving up that thoroughly moldy chestnut about head-hijacker Mohammed Atta hooking up with an Iraqi spy in Prague, despite the fact that the FBI has long since concluded that Atta was actually tooling around Florida in a rental car at the time of the alleged meeting.

In a recent biography of Tony Blair, an aide to the British

prime minister accuses Cheney of having "waged a guerilla war against" Blair's attempts to seek U.N. approval of the invasion of Iraq, and calls the Vice President "a visceral unilateralist."

He's also a visceral corporate apologist. Remember when the idea of having a CEO vice president was a campaign selling point? Now we see that the only thing being sold is the public good. Exhibit A is the way Cheney's corporate cronies at Halliburton have benefited from having a friend in the very highest of places.

In the blink of an eye and the toppling of a statue, the company has gone from facing looming losses to scoring billions in no-bid and no-ceiling contracts tied to the invasion and occupation of Iraq. As for the rest of us, we've been rewarded with a company that squanders our tax dollars at every turn.

In February 2004 we learned that Halliburton had consistently overbilled the Pentagon for meals at Camp Arifjan, a U.S. military base in Kuwait. According to auditors, the Pentagon paid the company $16 million for nearly four million meals that were never served. And Camp Arifjan is just one of over 50 dining facilities in Kuwait and Iraq the company serves. Maybe Halliburton can steal a page from McDonald's playbook and put up a giant golden H outside their mess halls, with a sign keeping tabs on the number of meals they billed taxpayers for but didn't actually provide: "Over 4 Million Never Served!"

This phantom-food fiasco came right after the gasoline overcharging scandal, which came right after the Kuwait kickback debacle. Pardon me for bringing this up, but shouldn't there be three strikes and you're out? Instead, we get yet another example of how there are two sets of rules in our country—one for the elites (and the former companies of the elites) and one for everybody else. When caught with its hand in the taxpayer-funded cookie jar, Halliburton doesn't get tossed in the brig for life; it merely apologizes, pays back the money it's pilfered, and goes on to win another hefty cost-plus contract.

Despite this avalanche of sleazy profiteering and corporate misconduct, Cheney stubbornly insists on defending his erstwhile company—from which he still receives a hefty deferred salary ($162,392 in 2002), and in which he still holds 433,333 stock options. "They get unfairly maligned," he said in the midst of these damning revelations, "simply because of their past association with me."

No, they get maligned because they can't seem to keep themselves from gouging American taxpayers. It makes one wonder what the company would have to do for Cheney to feel criticism of Halliburton was justified—cater John Kerry's victory party?

If Cheney's relationship with Halliburton represents the evils of crony capitalism, then his relationship with Supreme Court Justice Antonin Scalia epitomizes the evils of crony democracy.

It's not just that Cheney and Scalia had dinner together and went on a duck-hunting trip—with the Vice President picking up the travel tab—while the Supreme Court was being asked to overturn a lower court's decision requiring Cheney to reveal the names of his energy task force members. It's that these guys can't, for the life of them, see why anybody would have a problem with this overly cozy state of affairs.

Why bother with "justice for all" when you've got hunting buddies who don't give a flying duck about fairness, impartiality, or the public's right to know?

On the upside, this behavior turns a blazing spotlight on the defining traits of the Bush White House: secrecy and arrogance.

"I do not think my impartiality could reasonably be questioned," said Scalia, responding to questions about the propriety of a sitting judge rubbing elbows—and blowing small game birds out of the air—with a named party and material witness in a case he's about to hear. That ranks up there with Justin Timberlake's infamous post-Super Bowl claim that the boob shot seen 'round the world was due to a "wardrobe malfunction."

I can already hear those committed to seeing Bush back home in Crawford come January 2005 warming up the chant: "Ho, ho . . . hey, hey . . . Dick Cheney's got to stay!"

THE REFORMER WITH RESULTS PRODUCES NEITHER

A hallmark of the Bush years has been watching the president being let off the hook for his actions while being given credit for his words. In the spring of 2002, a week before an international development conference in Mexico, the president's rhetoric reached new levels of unreality. "The growing divide between wealth and poverty, between opportunity and misery, is both a challenge to our compassion and a source of instability. We must confront it."

Could any statement be more disconnected from the president's actual domestic priorities?

"We cannot," said the president, "leave behind half of humanity as we seek a better future for ourselves. We cannot accept permanent poverty in a world of progress. There are no second-class citizens in the human race." This pie-in-the-sky speechifying was prompted, according to Jim Wolfensohn, the warm-and-fuzzy president of that supposedly sinister instrument of U.S. global hegemony, the World Bank, by 9/11. "On September 11 the imaginary wall that divided the rich world from the poor world came crashing down. . . . There is no wall. There are not two worlds. There is only one," Wolfensohn explained. Speaking to the heads of state of some fifty countries at a UN conference in Monterrey, President Bush emphasized the destabilizing impact of having 1.2 billion people living in extreme deprivation. "We fight against poverty because hope is an answer to terror," he said. But the president has yet to acknowledge the destabilizing impact of poverty here at home, where the gulf between rich and poor continues to widen and where there are 12 million of our kids living below the poverty line.

While Bush accurately articulated the immense challenge of poverty, there was no commensurate, meaningful shift in policy abroad or at home. The president made it clear that overcoming global poverty is not only a moral but also a national security imperative. But once again Bush's rich language was followed by a poverty of action.

So was his rich language of reform. In 2000 he ran as "a reformer with results," but the Bush administration has, at every turn, championed the status quo and subverted reform, including campaign finance reform. A fine illustration of this is a promise the president made to John McCain—and then broke as soon as he had what he wanted.

Back in July 2002, the White House cut a deal with McCain: the president would appoint ethics lawyer and reform advocate Ellen Weintraub to one of the three Democratic positions on the six-member Federal Election Commission, and in exchange, McCain would stop holding up a slew of Bush judicial and administrative nominations. The Weintraub appointment was seen as crucial by reformers, since the FEC was in the process of deciding the specifics of how McCain-Feingold—reluctantly signed into law by the president in the spring of 2002—would be implemented.

But in a move McCain called "calculated, orchestrated, and cynical," the White House held off appointing Weintraub until the day after the FEC had finished carving up the new rules, leaving gaping loopholes through which millions in soft money continue to be funneled to the political parties—exactly the kind of thing the new law was designed to prevent. Considering McCain's propensity to stray off the ranch, he'd been a pretty loyal soldier, but he had finally had enough and opened fire on the White House. "They flat-out broke their word," he told me. "We usually do business in Washington with a handshake. From now on, that will be very hard to do with them. I'll have to question the sincerity of any promises they make."

The senator also decried the shameless way the White House tried to collect PR points by hopping on the reform bandwagon and then doing everything in its power to ensure that the bandwagon wasn't going anywhere. "While the administration wanted to share in the widespread public approval of campaign finance reform by having the president sign the legislation into law," McCain said, "he's cooperating behind the scenes with opponents of the law in Congress and on the commission to weaken it as much as possible." If there is a standard operating procedure in this White House, this is it.

As a result, McCain predicted, the next few years will bring a persistent rash of new scandals stemming from the ongoing flood of money into the political process. "It's inevitable," he told me. "More money mixed with more loopholes will lead to more paybacks like the one Eli Lilly was given in the Homeland Security Bill. But politicians have become completely addicted to money, so trying to change the system is like trying to take heroin from a heroin addict."

With Republicans controlling the White House and both branches of Congress for the first time in forty-six years, we have seen corporate America go on a D.C. shopping spree in an all-out effort to purchase a wide range of legislation. Actually it's more of an investment spree: a few hundred thousand in cash now will generate a few hundred million in the next legislative cycle. It worked like a charm for Bechtel and for Halliburton. Hell, if you've got $10 million to invest in bad government, it might even work for you! Factor in the Democrats' growing reliance on corporate donations, and all the conditions seem set for an unprecedented special interest onslaught.

As Nick Nyhart, the executive director of Public Campaign, put it, "If the National Weather Service had a political forecasting unit, it would have to issue the following advisory for Washington, D.C.: A 'perfect storm' of special interest demands and policy paybacks has hit the nation's capital, as a Congress and White House more beholden to corporate contributors than any in memory come under pressure to deliver on a host of anti-consumer and anti-environment measures." This is indeed a perfect storm. Except in this version, it's the public that gets dragged overboard.

Among the things being swept away by the tsunami of money are the foundations of our democracy and the values of our elected officials. Before he announced that he would not be seeking reelection, Senator Zell Miller (D-GA) confessed that the never-ending need to cozy up to donors had left him "feeling like a cheap prostitute who'd had a busy day."

"I know firsthand, and from working with colleagues, just how beholden elected officials and their parties can become to those who contribute to their campaigns and their parties' coffers," says former senator Warren Rudman, winning a "Duh" award by reminding us that a quid pro quo always goes along with that kind of dough.

PORTRAITS IN FANATACISM: THE KARL ROVE DIARIES

When Senator Bob Graham dropped out of the presidential race in October 2003 and announced he would not be running for reelection, we were left with his diaries. (Since 1977 he's filled some four thousand 2-by-3-inch notebooks with the daily details of his life, including where he slept, what he ate, whom he met, and what he wore.) Some labeled Graham's practice a disturbing fetish; others have praised it as a sign of extreme self-discipline. Still others wonder whether it was necessary for so many trees to make the ultimate sacrifice just so that we might know that Senator Graham wore khakis and had the grilled salmon at his 12:47 lunch yesterday.

Apparently, this quirky habit is catching on, and by an amazing stroke of good luck, I came across (in my fevered imagination) what appears to be an obsessively detailed running log of the daily activities of Karl Rove—the man his biographer dubbed "the most powerful unelected person in America."

LOG 2.09.04 (MONDAY)

5:05 Awake. Castigate self for sleeping in. Remove snooze bar from clock radio with pliers.

5:05–5:15 Bathroom. Brush teeth, massage gums, trim nose hairs. Practice affable grin (in mirror).

5:15 Exchange customary morning greeting with Darby: "Good morning, Mr. Co-President," "Good Morning, Mrs. Co–First Lady."

5:17 Kiss Darby (cheek).

5:18 Start to get dressed. Hesitate over underwear drawer. Boxers or briefs?

5:19 Call Frank Luntz to ask him to run quick Insta-poll. Luntz asleep. Not fully on board?

5:25 Crunch numbers (they come back inconclusive).

5:26 Decide to go commando. It's more on message: all about liberation.

5:35–6:35 Kitchen, b'fast: Waffles (syrup), Lucky Charms w/milk (2 percent), coffee (black), Metamucil (orange). Skim sampling of fair and balanced news coverage: *Washington Times,* FreeRepublic.com, *Wall Street Journal* editorial page, *Weekly Standard,* Newsmax.com, Fox News. (Remember to send Ailes another gift basket for coverage of Democrats' lack of patriotism.)

6:50–6:55 Walk to car, enter car, close car door, fasten seat belt, adjust rearview mirror. Realize I've forgotten keys. Use family-friendly exclamation "Darn!" Undo seat belt, exit car, walk back to house, locate keys. Repeat initial car entry. Then repeat again (just to be sure).

6:55–7:12 Drive to work. Listen to Dobson's *Focus on the Family*. Notice that he hits talking points word for word. Smile w/ satisfaction. Switch to lesbian strippers on Stern (guilty pleasure).

7:13 (LATE!!!)–8:00 Staff meeting in WWO (West Wing Office). Answer e-mails and excoriate low-level aide for no good reason while meeting w/ Dan Bartlett and Margaret Spellings to discuss best way to counter negative fallout from latest job growth numbers. Orange alert? Red alert? Invade Syria?

8:03–8:05 Exchange pleasantries in hallway w/ A. Card. Utilize distant but disarmingly affable smile. Note Card has switched aftershave. (Sign that he's looking for private sector job?)

8:06–8:07 Walk to Oval Office (feel the awe and fear of those I pass).

8:08–8:48 Oval Office. Meet w/ W, discuss next phase in Operation Landslide: W will scuba dive to submerged submarine to meet with Navy SEALS and serve them Fourth of July hotdogs. Secret Service opposed (still fail to grasp political realities).

Undermine A. Card (too easy!) by mentioning aftershave change to Bob Novak.

8:48–8:53 Stay behind to talk to W about nickname problem: stress overwhelming preference for "Boy Genius" over "Turd Blossom."

8:54–8:55 Walk back to West Wing (feel chafing; regret earlier decision re: underwear).

8:56 Call Darby, ask her to bring over boxers (the ones with American flags).

9:14–9:16 Call Scott McClellan. Tell him to blackball next reporter who asks when I am going to attend a military funeral.

9:17–9:47 Meet w/lobbyist for tobacco industry. Swap war stories from my Philip Morris days. Smoke two Marlboro Reds (old times' sake).

9:51 Suddenly not sure which to be today: fox or hedgehog.

9:52 Realize I can be both (hell, I'm Karl Rove). Feel the power.

9:55–10:55 Leave screaming, over-the-top phone message for author James Moore. (Show him how "Bush's brain" really works!)

10:56 Take high-blood-pressure medicine and lozenge for sore throat (cherry).

12:10–1:00 Working lunch (salmon, garlic mashed potatoes, iced tea). Map out entire day-to-day strategy for 2006 midterm races (early prediction: barring blowback from '04 invasion of Syria/Iran/Pakistan, we gain five seats in Senate and twelve in House with demonization of unpatriotic Democrats).

2:15 Show John McCain what war is really like by spreading vicious rumor about him. Black lovechild arrested for Al Qaeda ties.

2:17 Watch McCain rumor being disseminated on Fox.

3:05 Have fleeting, unprovoked sympathetic thought about old benefactor Ken Lay.

3:06 Banish thought forever.

5:01–7:30 Attend RNC fund-raiser. Mingle. Accept praise and adulation. Also checks. (Overuse affable smile?) Wonder if I am officially a rock star now. (Yes!)

7:35–8:00 Drive home. Listen to books on tape recording of *Treason*. (Make joke to self regarding Coulter being our hottest WMD.)

8:01 Walk from driveway to house. Open front door. Karl Rove's front door.

9:28–10:15 Watch TIVOed replay of the Grammy Awards. Smile to self for engineering Beyoncé's five wins.

11:07 Shower and dress for sleep (blue striped PJs). Draft tomorrow's to-do list: Give grief. Make threats. Impugn patriotism. Intimidate media. Pursue bait-and-switch policies. Strong-arm donors. Manipulate. Plot. Connive. Pick up dry cleaning.

12:05 Kiss Darby good night (lips, but no tongue).

12:06 Asleep. Dream that I'm the most powerful un-elected person in American history. (Oh wait, I am!)

THE LATE, GREAT ESTATE TAX

A fair and just society would not engage in the tax policies that Bush and the Republican Congress pushed forward in the last three years. Take the Republican attempt to repeal the estate tax, one of the principal drivers in the creation of philanthropic foundations in America. This move comes just as increasingly pinched federal and state agencies are looking to food banks and homeless shelters administered by nonprofit organizations to feed and house the poor. But who pays the bills for them? Often it's foundations that might never have been established if the estate tax hadn't been created. As much as we would like to believe that American citizens are simply more charitable than their counterparts in Europe, Japan, and other developed countries, the truth is that we depend increasingly on the philanthropic sector (and individual tax deductible donations) to pick up the cost for social services that in other countries are paid for with taxes.

Now, with the planned phase-out of the estate tax, private philanthropy will almost certainly be reduced just when the need for it is growing exponentially. In fact, some of the nation's wealthiest individuals, who also happen to be ardent philanthropists, are strenuously opposed to the repeal of the estate tax. They don't feel that they are in need of relief. Foremost among them is Bill Gates Sr., who coauthored *Wealth and Our Commonwealth,* in which he excoriates the estate tax repeal on both economic and moral grounds. In the book's introduction, Paul Volcker, the former Federal Reserve Chairman, ties his opposition to the repeal to our country's founding principles: "From the days of our founding fathers . . . the concept of equality of opportunity and dispersion of wealth and economic power has been part of the American psyche. The inheritance of huge fortunes, far beyond any reasonable need for education, for medical care, and for a comfortable—even luxurious—standard of living, has never rested easily with that political philosophy."

Gates's economic case against the repeal rests on the fact that "the government is the biggest venture capitalist there is . . . there would be no Internet without federal government research money." Gates draws the unavoidable conclusion that "there's no such thing as a self-made millionaire." But thanks to the many fans of neofeudalism in the Republican Party's right wing, the estate tax is gradually being reduced. It is slated to be completely repealed by 2010.

The estate tax reduction and eventual repeal will also have a large impact on cash-strapped states, depriving them of $3.5 billion in revenue this year, increasing to $8 billion in 2005. The result, of course, will inevitably be either cuts in services or hikes in taxes or both. But once again the Democratic opponents of the estate tax repeal have done a miserable job making the case to the American electorate.

THE FANATICS SPEAK

"Stuff happens. But in terms of what's going on in that country, it is a fundamental misunderstanding to see those images over and over and over again of some boy walking out with a vase and say, 'Oh, my goodness, you didn't have a plan.' That's nonsense." (Don Rumsfeld on the looting of the National Museum in Baghdad. Pentagon News Conference, April 11, 2003.)

"I think in this case international law stood in the way of doing the right thing . . . international law . . . would have required us to leave Saddam Hussein alone, and this would have been morally unacceptable." (Richard Perle, London, November 11, 2003.)

"Honestly, it's a little tougher than I thought it was going to be. If we have to, we just mow the whole place down, see what happens. You're dealing with insane suicide bombers who are killing our people, and we need to be very aggressive in taking them out." (Trent Lott, *The Hill,* October 29, 2003.)

"There are different kinds of truths for different kinds of people. There are truths appropriate for children; truths that are appropriate for students; truths that are appropriate for educated adults; and truths that are appropriate for highly educated adults, and the notion that there should be one set of truths available to everyone is a modern democratic fallacy. It doesn't work." (Irving Kristol, *Reason,* July 1997.)

"You know, I've been around this business a long time. I know how some feel about alternative energy, and I respect their opinions. But I have to tell you, alternative energy is something long into the future. There's nothing we can do with it that helps us much now. People have got to understand that energy independence means more oil. And that means we've got to drill." (George W. Bush during a meeting in Tom Daschle's office in January 2001.)

"My ideal citizen is the self-employed, homeschooling, IRA-owning guy with a concealed-carry permit because

There are no gates or walls high enough, there are no bank accounts large enough to isolate you from the fear and suffering of those left behind. We're all in this boat together. And the fact that there isn't a hole at your end of the boat doesn't mean you are safe.

that person doesn't need the goddamn government for anything." (Grover Norquist, *Washington Times*, December 23, 2003.)

"Nothing is more important in the face of a war than cutting taxes." (Tom DeLay, Washington, D.C., March 3, 2003.)

HEALTHY MARRIAGES ARE FROM VENUS, GEORGE BUSH IS FROM MARS

Who needs bread and circuses when you've got manned missions to Mars and "Healthy Marriage" initiatives?

Signaling that the Pander Countdown to Election Day 2004 had begun in earnest, in mid-January President Bush rolled out a pair of Caesar-worthy proposals that are literally out of this world (and by that I don't mean to imply that they are wonderful, but rather that the person who thought them up must be living on a different planet than the rest of us).

Let's start with healthy marriages. Tossing a bone, if not a garter belt and a bible, to his conservative base (which is up in arms over the thought that gay people may soon have the right to legally tie and untie the knot—and thus make a mockery of the sacred institution that Britney and Jason are such big fans of), the president spiced up his 2004 State of the Union speech by tiptoeing up to the edge of saying "I do" to a constitutional amendment defining marriage as the exclusive province of heterosexual couples.

"Our nation must defend the sanctity of marriage," he declared to ringing applause from Tom DeLay and the "Amen" chorus on the right.

The president's connubial rhetoric came on the heels of the announcement of his "Healthy Marriage" initiative—aka "The Leave No Bride Behind Act." The president plans to spend $1.5 billion protecting and promoting marriage, especially among poor, minority couples.

The money will be used to teach couples how to manage their conflicts in healthy ways, and, yes, to fund ad campaigns publicizing the value of getting hitched. I can just picture the PSAs starring Trista and Ryan: "Hey, kids, we were paid millions of dollars to tie the knot on national TV. So don't believe anyone who tells you that marriage isn't worth the trouble!" Federal dollars will also be earmarked for mentoring programs that use married couples as role models. Here's a suggestion: why not start with conservative icons such as Bob Dole, Newt Gingrich, and Phil Gramm. They can all tearfully testify how much those ads might have meant in their own unsuccessful attempts to keep a marriage together.

Now I'm not saying that helping married couples stay together is a bad thing. I'm just saying that it's not a job for the federal government. Especially not for a government faced with far more pressing problems than what to do when he wants to watch football and she wants to cuddle. We have 9% unemployment, 12 million children without medical insurance, record-breaking deficits, unfinished business in Afghanistan and Iraq, porous ports, vulnerable airports, and every state in the union cutting back on vital social programs, and the president wants to spend precious resources convincing young people that marriage is better than shacking up? Just whom is he protecting here? Aside from his own electoral backside.

"Marriage programs do work," insisted Dr. Wade Horn, assistant secretary for children and families of the Department of Health and Human Services. "On average, children raised by their own parents in healthy, stable married families enjoy better physical and mental health and are less likely to be poor." Yeah, well so are children who can read. And those raised by parents who have a job. Or health insurance.

What makes the president's proposal particularly galling is that it's being offered up by a politician who came into office attacking federal programs like the one he is proposing for being too intrusive. "I trust people," said candidate Bush during one of his debates with Al Gore. "I don't trust the federal government."

Indeed, the very people who have been complaining for decades that government programs are not the way to fight the war on poverty are now determined to use federal tax dollars to fight the war for matrimonial bliss. And they're using the same line of argument they excoriate liberals for using to explain why we need to invest in education, health care, and poverty fighting: "For every $1,000 we spend on public programs addressing family breakdown," said Tony Perkins, president of the conservative Family Research Council, "we only spend one dollar trying to prevent that breakdown in the first place. The President's initiative puts the emphasis in the right place—prevention."

Of course, the $1.5 billion the president has earmarked for his Healthy Marriage proposal is a drop in the bucket next to the $12 billion he plans to spend trying to imitate JFK's inspiring look toward the heavens.

The president obviously believes that offering a big and bold idea such as sending an American to the Red Planet by 2020 will capture the imagination of voters here on the third rock from the sun (and keep their minds off the steadily mounting body count in Iraq and steadily mounting domestic problems here). If I didn't worry he'd take me seriously, I'd suggest he just combine it all—announce that the mission to Mars will be manned by unmarried poor people with no access to health care or education, along with those who keep asking where the WMD are. All problems solved.

But if it's really big, bold ideas Bush wants, how about forgetting Mars and concentrating on another planet that's in need of some attention: Earth. Starting with the steadily deteriorating condition of our environment. It's not like Mother Earth is exactly the picture of health.

I don't mean to play psychologist, but I do think it's worth noting that Bush's Mars initiative is yet another step toward completing his father's unfinished business. Papa Bush also proposed a manned mission to Mars—a program that was shot down due to its projected $400 billion to $500 billion price tag. And those are 1989 dollars. I'm not sure how Junior is planning to pull it off for a mere $12 billion. Maybe he went shopping for his Martian chronicle at Target.

Speaking of Bush family dynamics, let's not forget that George the First was voted out of office due in no small part to the perception that he was thoroughly disconnected from the reality of most Americans' everyday lives: he didn't know how much a quart of milk cost or how a grocery store price scanner worked. Well, George the Next's policy priorities show that he is even more remote from the struggles of the average voter than his dad was. Far worse than not knowing how much milk costs, W is working to ensure that our children and grandchildren won't be able to afford it anyway.

These two pandering proposals prove once again: average Americans are from Earth, George Bush's policies are from an entirely different solar system.

PORTRAITS IN FANATICISM: TOM DELAY, FUND-RAISER AND FUN-RAISER

Hey, lucky Bush Republicans! Guess what? You may already be a winner! That's right, look outside your front door. It's Ed McMahon, Dick Clark, and right next to them, House Majority Leader Tom DeLay!

Unless you were recently dug out of a 20,000-year-old glacier, you may find it hard to muster much beyond a weary shrug at the fund-raising antics of our public officials. Yes, they expend more time and imagination on gathering money than they do on governing. *Sigh.* Sure, they sell whatever influence they have to anyone and everyone who will pay. *Ho-hum.* Perhaps the only living soul who professes surprise at our pay-to-play politics is DeLay himself. He once looked the camera in the eye at a press conference and soberly announced, "It never ceases to amaze me that people are so cynical, they want to tie money to issues, money to bills, money to amendments."

But the fund-raising machinations of Tom DeLay are so elaborate and sneaky that they clearly exceed the usual high level of graft in Washington, D.C. Tom DeLay is a fund-raising fanatic whose schemes go far beyond the greedy and into the realm of the pathological. In order to slake his unquenchable thirst for cash, DeLay has constructed an elaborate network of PACs, charities, donor groups, and shell organizations. The Texas Republican seems to have modeled his efforts on those of another great Texas institution now defunct. It's the Enron-ization of fund-raising.

If you're wondering what the hell Tom DeLay needs all that money for, considering that he raises it year in and year out, regardless of whether or not he is up for reelection, the answer is that he has become a sort of super-fund-raiser who spreads the money around to fellow Bush Republicans willing to kiss his ultra-fanatical ass. Along with his pioneering efforts on the ethical fringes of our toothless campaign finance laws, DeLay seems to take unbridled glee in bending moderate Republicans to his will. Besides his scintillating personality, DeLay's most potent tool is his firm hand on the campaign cash faucet. He can irrigate the parched campaign of a potential ally and impose a drought on a moderate who provokes his wrath, all at the flick of a wrist. His squashed opponents are never allowed to forget that DeLay began his professional life in the field of pest control.

DeLay's preferred mechanism for hunting and gathering donations is something called, innocuously, the DeLay Foundation for Kids. Lest I be accused of the sort of cynicism that Tom seems so distraught about, let me say that, as far as I can tell, the DeLay Foundation does, indeed, try to assist children, especially in the area of foster care, and that DeLay and his wife have themselves cared for three foster children. And that's admirable.

OK, now that you've read the disclaimer, here's what you need to know about "Tommy's Kids." At a 2003 foundation fund-raiser, a celebrity golf tournament held at the Ocean Reef Club in Florida, corporate sponsors were afforded an unusual form of access, the opportunity to play golf with key Republican lawmakers like Majority Whip Roy Blunt and De-Lay himself, all nominally in the name of a good cause. Further, corporations could, for an additional donation, get their name in the tournament program or on special signage.

The event, not surprisingly, was a sellout—in more ways than one. While the lobbyists and corporate mendicants got to hit the links and bend the ear of a congressman or senator, their cost was entirely tax deductible as a charitable donation.

So basically for the needy CEO class it was a free golf vacation with the chance to push its agenda. And because the DeLay Foundation for Kids is a charity, not a political fund-raising entity (wink-wink), donations to it are unfettered by campaign finance restrictions. Unfortunately, there was a small impediment to a good time being had by all: a pesky antijunketing restriction barred companies from paying for travel and meals for members of Congress. So DeLay, as majority leader, expressed his displeasure, and lo, the rule disappeared. Now corporate kid-lovers could rest assured that there would be no shortage of legislators.

The personal charity dodge is so effective that, as a *Roll Call* editorial put it, "Frankly, we're amazed that more Members have not identified favorite charities as opportunities for special interests to buy influence. They would seem to be a natural. They can serve a worthy purpose, be it children, disease research, the arts or environmental betterment. They can add luster to a Member's political persona. And they can offer special interests a place to show their appreciation for the Member's performance. With soft money banned, we would expect more corporate money to find its way to politically connected charities."

Tsk, Tsk. Roll Call sounds a little cynical there. Maybe that's because they got wind of Tom's newest enterprise, a completely, totally, utterly different charity by the name of Celebrations for Children, Inc., which was set up in September 2003 as a sort of travel agent for visitors to next summer's Republican Convention in New York City.

According to the *New York Times*, Celebrations for Children offers conventioneers a smorgasbord of package deals in all price ranges, from economy to first class. High rollers willing to spend a tax-deductible $500,000 get the "Upper East Side" package, which includes a seasickening yacht cruise with Mr. DeLay and his wife. (The *Times* doesn't say whether DeLay intends to actually pilot the craft himself, but with that sticker price, it's a sure bet that a few people on board will know their way around a yacht.) Other perks include a golf tournament, a late-night rock concert (now, even I'd pay good money to see a bunch of Tom DeLay fans at a late-night rock concert), and tickets to Broadway shows. At the bottom end is the "Greenwich Village" package, which offers a yacht cruise with an unnamed VIP and tickets to President Bush's speech at the convention. Although the Texan can be excused for his poor understanding of Manhattan real estate prices, the hierarchy offended many New Yorkers, since Greenwich Village property is actually some of Manhattan's most expensive. Maybe they thought it wouldn't be politically correct to put a "Harlem" or "South Bronx" package at the bottom.

Some hands-on attention from a member of Congress is promised to all donors at all levels and, given Mr. DeLay's ability to single-handedly fund their campaigns and pass their bills, you can bet that many will attend—if they know what's good for them.

At the risk of drifting into cynicism again, despite my best efforts, I should point out that one child who will certainly be there celebrating courtesy of the charity is Mr. DeLay's own: his daughter, Dani DeLay Ferro. Ms. Ferro is one of three managers of Celebrations for Children, and she has made something of a career, entirely on her own merits I am sure, of the interest she shares with her dad in a better world. She earned almost $60,000 in 2000 as a consultant to DeLay's innumerable political action committees and is the manager of his reelection campaign. Still, she does sound well qualified to ensure that donors, be they high up on the Upper East Side or down low in humble

Greenwich Village, have a great time at the Republican Convention. At a kickoff party at her suite in the Rio Hotel in Las Vegas, that kid-loving town, Dani told friends that a lobbyist poured champagne on her while she was relaxing in the hot tub.

Ah, champagne well spent!

CLEAN AIR: MORE MOTHERING, LESS SMOTHERING

If we're going to get off our asses and change our world, not tomorrow but today, it's critical to understand just how much of a mess we're in now, as the presidential election of 2004 unfolds before our eyes. For starters, while there was a titanic struggle in Congress over its provisions, Bush and his scheme team have realized how an incumbent president seeking reelection can turn the McCain-Feingold campaign finance reforms to his advantage. The key is the biggest concession reformers made to get the law passed: they allowed the limit on individual contributions to candidates ("hard money") to be doubled from $1,000 to $2,000 per election. Advocates for this change noted that it had been nearly thirty years since Congress had set the $1,000 limit; they argued that thanks to inflation, a $1,000 limit today was equivalent to having a limit thirty years ago of only $300. Doubling the limit wouldn't even compensate for the rise in the cost of living, they said.

All very reasonable, but the new higher limits left literally 99.9 percent of Americans out of the picture. Only one-tenth of 1 percent of all Americans made a contribution of $1,000 or more in the presidential election of 2000, according to the Center for Responsive Politics. Surveys of donors of $200 or more in the 1996 elections (we're talking about one-quarter of 1 percent of all Americans) revealed that four-fifths had an annual family income of more than $100,000 a year. By comparison, just 8.5 percent of U.S. taxpayers had a family income of over $100,000 in 2001. Handing to a rarified group of wealthy white Americans the ability to give even more money to candidates for office—while doing nothing to relieve the pressure on those candidates to amass huge war chests—can mean only one thing: more access and influence for wealthy interests and less for ordinary Americans.

Let's speak plainly, shall we? Access and influence—the two things that big donors admit they are seeking when they "max out" on their contributions to politicians—are just apt euphemisms for power. Former Senator Paul Simon used to tell an illustrative story of what such a check buys you. At the end of a long day on the road, Simon arrives at his hotel and sees a stack of phone messages. Flipping through them, he comes to one from a big donor. Whose phone call do you think he's going to return first?

Big money contributions get your phone calls returned, and they buy you a seat at the table when policy is made. Energy industry executives gave $20.5 million to Bush-Cheney and the Republican National Committee in 2000, and in exchange they and their lobbyists were invited to secret meetings with Dick Cheney to draft our energy policies, including such brilliant ideas as billions in fresh subsidies for the failing and dangerous nuclear power industry and more oil and gas drilling in our pristine wilderness areas. Coal-using electric utilities gave Bush and Co. $4.8 million in 2000, and in response the administration trashed a key Clean Air Act rule that companies like Southern and FirstEnergy had been accused of violating. Dozens of government investigations against polluters have been dropped too.

The result? Listen to what the American Lung Association's president, John Kirkwood, had to say about the Bush administration's air pollution legislation.

The administration plan would hurt public health and help big polluters by delaying and diluting cuts in power plant emissions of sulfur, nitrogen and mercury . . . in fact, the U.S. Environmental Protection Agency's own analysis shows that timely enforcement of the current Clean Air Act will provide greater pollution reductions sooner than those proposed by the administration.

Unfortunately, the administration remains focused on attempts to avoid and delay implementation of existing clean air regulations, thus weakening one of the most effective environmental laws Congress ever passed.

Meanwhile, millions of Americans—including children with lung diseases like asthma and seniors with chronic lung and heart problems—continue to breathe dirty air, especially on the high pollution days we see during the summer months. Nearly half the American population— more than 137 million people—still breathe unhealthy amounts of ozone, a toxic air pollutant. The EPA estimates that over 65 million people live in counties that will violate the health standard for fine particulate (soot) pollution, linked to tens of thousands of premature deaths each year and a host of other health effects including asthma attacks. The current still-polluted state of the air in this country is indefensible.

If that seems a bit abstract to you, take just one state, Ohio. There are twenty-seven power plants in Ohio. These plants will be allowed to pollute more under Bush's new policy. There are another forty-six pollution-spewing power plants within thirty miles of the state borders. Nearly 2.5 million children in Ohio live within thirty miles of those plants. Just over 175,000 children in Ohio have asthma. These kids and their schools don't have a political action committee fighting for their interest in Washington. The American Lung Association does fine work, but it doesn't have a PAC either. And while parents of children with asthma can certainly make campaign contributions, very few of them are in an income bracket where they are able to buy access and influence in Washington.

LEAVE NO DONOR BEHIND

In May 2003, when the president launched his reelection fund-raising drive, his campaign aides said that he was aiming to raise $170 million, all for a primary in which he had no Republican opponent. To get to this astonishing number—more money than was raised by all the previous Republican presidential candidates from 1980 to 1996 combined—his campaign came up with a new level of enhanced access and influence. "Pioneers," people who raised at least $100,000 for him, have been superseded by "Rangers," people who manage to bundle $200,000 or more. Of course, all those dollars come from donors whose wallets have been fattened with tax cuts, regulatory cutbacks, no-bid contracts, and the like.

It's like an Amway scheme, only instead of selling brushes and cleansers, they're selling power and prestige. Anyone seeking to be a Bush Ranger or Pioneer is given a tracking number to tell potential donors to write on their checks. And this number isn't just for accounting purposes. In 2000

Newsweek obtained a memo from Tom Kuhn, a top energy industry lobbyist, where he explained to other energy executives the importance of using the tracking system. "It does insure that our industry is credited, and that your progress is listed among the other business/industry sectors." Nothing gets the juices flowing for the phony free marketers like a little friendly competition. In 2000, 68 of the 538 known Pioneers came from the energy industry. (No wonder Cheney handed over energy policy to them.)

In a system where money flows to power (and vice versa), one party now has a monopoly on power in Washington, and the deep-pocketed donors who helped put it there have pent-up demands they expect to see satisfied. Not only do the Bush Republicans have the means to reward their friends, they have the motive: their margins in Congress are still narrow. To expand their majority in 2004 and secure their power, they need to widen their already substantial lead over Democrats in the money chase.

The result is a special new program that perhaps we should call "Leave No Donor Behind." As the president and his campaign team do for fund-raising what Henry Ford did for manufacturing, the astonishing thing is how little shame they display. In June 2003, at a gala event in Washington that brought in an astonishing $3.5 million for the president's re-election in one evening, one of his aides told a reporter, "We should raise that much because we can, because we can always use the money, and because there's no political downside for him in doing it." Wayne Berman, a former Commerce Department appointee under Bush's father who is now a well-connected lobbyist, was interviewed by CNN's Jonathan Karl during the fund-raiser; Berman crowed about how easy it was to rake the money in:

Berman: I think it's possible the president will raise more money in his first month of fund-raising than the Democrats have been able to raise combined. All nine of them.

Karl: That's a staggering fact considering the days of unlimited million-dollar contributions are over. Under new campaign finance laws, no donor can give more than $2,000. Even so, the president expects to raise at least $170 million for his campaign. That's a lot of $2,000 checks. How hard a sell is it for you?

Berman: It's not a hard sell at all. The most difficult thing is finding somebody who hasn't been called by someone else who's raising money.

Karl: So what do you do when you're making calls, you're asking people to contribute? What's your pitch?

Berman: Well, my pitch is, you know, pretty straightforward. The president has done a fantastic job of leading the country. He needs your support, and I would appreciate it if you would write a check and send it into the campaign. I hope you'll come to the event and listen to what the president has to say.

Karl: People like you raised $100,000 last time. . . . What do you get in return?

Berman: Last time, you got a chance to buy some good cuff links. I should have worn them today to show them to you. You had to pay for them, but they were very attractive. I don't know what the goody is this time. I'm sure it will be cuff links or maybe, this time, we'll get—

maybe get a necktie or something. But you don't get anything. You get to participate in the process. And you get to feel as if you contributed to supporting somebody you believe in.

Wow, cuff links and ties and "participating in the process." And that little matter—not worth mentioning on CNN—of buying public policy.

WAYNE BERMAN: PORTRAIT OF A LOBBYIST EXTRAORDINAIRE

Wayne Berman was just one of at least forty-seven Bush 2000 Pioneers who were lobbyists, including such luminaries as Randy DeLay, brother of Tom, and Haley Barbour, the former GOP chair and current Mississippi governor. What was interesting about Berman's emergence as a cheerleader for Bush in 2004 is that, just a few years earlier, he was considered too hot to handle by the Bush team. In 1999 he had proudly signed up as a Pioneer and predicted he'd raise "$250,000++" on the personal information form he filled out for the Bush finance committee. But he was reportedly asked to stop raising money that October, after his name surfaced in connection with a scandal in Republican-controlled Connecticut, where the state treasurer, Paul Silvester, was convicted of taking kickbacks from money managers. Silvester testified that he invested $50 million of state funds with the Carlyle Group, a deal that generated a $900,000 finder's fee for Berman, because he was seeking a job with him. (And indeed he got that job, in a firm Berman ran with former Senator Al D'Amato.) Although Berman denied any wrongdoing, the events left a cloud over his head. But that was in 2000, when Bush had to deal with McCain's primary challenge. There obviously was no longer any worry over at Team Bush about letting Berman loose at the June 2003 fund-raiser.

A few weeks before that event as the president was appearing at a dinner to raise money for the national Republican Congressional and Senatorial committees, Berman went on TV with an even more brazen message, that thanks to McCain-Feingold, fund-raising was now all "about the little people."

Asked about Bush's unrivaled dash for cash, then–White House spokesman Ari Fleischer denied that the president was doing anything extraordinary. "I think the amount of money that candidates raise in our democracy is a reflection of the amount of support they have around the country," he said. "The president is proud to have the support of the American people, and the American people will ultimately be the ones who decide how much funding goes to any Democrat or any Republican." Does anyone else remember when the number of votes a candidate received was the ultimate measure of his support, rather than the number of dollars?

A BRIEF SURVEY OF REPUBLICAN HISTORY

I wonder if today's Republicans understand their own political history. After all, it was Lincoln who rescued the nation from the disgrace of slavery, and it was Teddy Roosevelt who dragged the Republican Party kicking and screaming into a modern world in which government has the right and obligation to regulate industry. Both would be ashamed of today's Bush Republicans.

Perhaps a quick survey of American history would be helpful here. It was under Teddy Roosevelt's stewardship that pivotal laws were passed to regulate the railroads and the food and drug industries. By the 1920s, however, the momentum for social reform had sputtered to a halt. The Republicans' focus turned, instead, toward limiting immigration, and minimizing government regulations. The result, as Lewis Gould writes in *Grand Old Party: A History of the Republicans,* was that the United States stood alone among other industrialized countries in that it had no "system of old-age insurance, no provision for unemployment during an economic downturn, no effective regulation of financial markets, no measures for insuring safety of bank deposits, and no real limits on child labor." These issues were brought home with great force by the crash of 1929, but it took another Roosevelt to mobilize the nation to confront these structural inequities in American society.

FDR was astoundingly productive in a time of crisis. It helped that dismay and disgust over the rule of his Republican predecessor gave him a convincing national mandate. Capitol Hill was so cowed by public support for Roosevelt that many of the early New Deal measures were passed unanimously. But early Republican support for the New Deal soon transmuted into hostility that persists to this day. Conservative Republicans were particularly galled at the creation of Social Security. They also bridled at Roosevelt's support of organized labor and his willingness to impose new taxes on inheritances and the incomes of the superwealthy.

Nevertheless, Republican presidents from Eisenhower to Reagan conceded that Social Security and other entitlement programs were, in fact, too popular to eliminate outright. As Gould notes, Reagan, in particular, "put forth a conservatism with a smiling face that asked little of his fellow citizens. Reduce taxes, spend more on defense, oppose Communism, and all would come out right in the end. . . ."

Indeed in the 1980s and 1990s the Republican Party didn't scale back government, despite all the rhetoric and all the pledges. Instead it reallocated the financial resources of the government to those sectors of society that it favored. Which is exactly what has been happening under the current regime. Per-household spending by the federal government has soared to $20,000, the highest level since World War II.

The Bushies, though, are determined to take another whack at the New Deal and the institutions that emerged in its wake. This time, to avoid antagonizing seniors and swing voters, there is no direct confrontation. Yet the recently passed Medicare bill prohibits the government from negotiating a better price for prescription drugs, gives windfall profits to drug companies, and subsidizes HMOs to take over Medicare. Bush Republicans are determined to privatize as much of the social welfare infrastructure as possible. And where they can't eliminate or privatize a program, they will simply starve it for capital in the years ahead. Thus, the tax cuts of today are sticks of dynamite being planted around the foundation of Social Security, Medicare, and unemployment insurance. Each of these sticks is linked to a timer that ensures that when the explosion goes off and the smoke clears to reveal the resulting carnage, the guilty parties will be long gone. You have to hand it to these guys. They know they would be beaten in a fair fight in the present, so they adopt stealth tactics that leave it to a future Congress or president to bury popular social programs that they have doomed by their present actions.

Lincoln is another great Republican who likely wouldn't recognize his own party. Here's a man who was elected as the first Republican president and gave his life to the causes of defending the Union and eliminating slavery. Today his party enjoys almost no support within the African American community.

For conservatives like Barry Goldwater, the argument wasn't so much against civil rights for minorities as it was a defense of states' rights against expanding federal authority. That argument created convenient political cover under which Goldwater and those who derided entitlement programs for coddling people could make common cause with southern Democrats threatened by an ascendant African American population.

It was during Richard Nixon's successful presidential candidacy that these two strands of conservatism—fiscal and cultural—explicitly came together. Nixon wooed many conservative voters by talking a strong game about how overtaxed Americans were. He complemented this appeal by successfully using race as a wedge issue with which to lure disaffected Democrats. Many blue-collar Democrats in the Midwest believed that efforts to aid African Americans would impinge on their own economic prospects. Others wanted to be shielded from the desegregation of exclusively white neighborhoods and schools. Nixon was particularly successful in attracting former Democrats from the South by promising to oppose busing, limit the activism of the courts in matters of race, and appoint a southerner to the Supreme Court. He was explicit in this strategy: "I am not going to campaign for the black vote," he said, "at the risk of alienating the suburban vote."

Once in office, however, Nixon defied most predictions by creating the Environmental Protection Agency, supporting affirmative action, expanding rights for Native Americans on tribal lands, enacting wage and price controls, and creating the National Endowment for the Arts. He also pursued détente with the Soviet Union, and normalization of relations with the People's Republic of China. All the while, however, Nixon railed against the size of government and the pernicious growth of agency bureaucracies.

Nevertheless, conservative Republicans felt they had been duped. But it was too late to undo many of the social reforms that Nixon had either enacted or expanded. The fallback strategy became to ensure that government would have to shrink by restricting its financial wherewithal, i.e., tax-cutting. Which brings us to today, when Bush doesn't need to turn up for NRA conventions to maintain his bona fides, as long as he keeps the faith on cutting taxes. And Arnold Schwarzenegger can be a social moderate on issues like guns and abortion so long as he makes his first act as governor the repeal of a tax increase.

STILL YOUR FATHER'S REPUBLICAN PARTY

Since George W. Bush ran as a compassionate conservative, Bush Republicans have become the transvestites of the political world. They can put a dress and makeup on, make themselves all pretty, and promise to care about the poor, schoolteachers, and quality health care, but behind the mascara, cheap perfume, and come-hither looks, they're still the same guys who march us into war, plunge us into huge deficits, and rail against gay marriage and taxes. And through it all, they raise money day and night.

Here are excerpts from an actual frequently-asked-questions memo sent to New York State fund-raisers from the "Bush-Cheney '04" reelection committee in the fall of 2003. It's a pocket guide to solving problems only very rich people have.

Question: Can I use my personal aircraft for campaign business?
Answer: No, you may not use your personal aircraft for campaign business. Corporate aircraft may be used, but only if each person boarding the plane pays the equivalent of a first-class airplane ticket.

Q: Can I have a fund-raising cocktail party for my friends at a private club or hotel and pay for the party?
A: No. You may have them come to your house and treat them up to $1,000 in expenses per adult in the household without it counting against your $2,000 contribution limit.

Q: Can I use my executive assistant to help with my fund-raising activities?
A: Any person can volunteer to help. Employees may volunteer a maximum of 1 (one) hour per week during working hours and an unlimited amount outside of the office.

As a bonus, I've included a few FAQs of my own that I suspect "Bush-Cheney '04" might find useful.

Q: How much money do I need to donate in order to be considered a George Bush "Pioneer" and get something specific from the president?
A:

- For $250,000 we can arrange to have your daily newspaper thrown directly onto your porch, not in the bushes or near the sprinklers. For three months.
- For $100,000 you can get the ambassadorship of your choice.
- For $75,000 you can get an ambassador post of *our* choosing (probably someplace like Kosovo, the West Bank, or Somalia).
- For $50,000 you can get a lucrative no-bid government contract, assuming you are, in fact, a military contractor. And even if you're not, we'll work something out.
- For $25,000 you'll be invited to join the president at his table for a fund-raising dinner. For $10,000 more, the president will be instructed to *not* eat off your plate.
- For $10,000 you can have your photo taken with the president. Or have three parking tickets fixed.
- For $5,000 the president will record one of those hilarious answering machine messages for you. *"Hi, you've reached (INSERT YOUR NAME HERE). Just kidding, it's President Bush . . ."*

- For $2,500 the president will send you an auto-graphed photo. For $100 more, he'll even spell his name correctly.
- For $1,000 the president will send you an Instant Message greeting, suitable for framing.
- For $500 . . . you know what? Don't even bother.

Q: I know individuals can only donate $2,000, but since my wife is four months pregnant, can I donate $6,000 on behalf of the "three" of us?

A: This is a dilemma facing many Republican Party faithful. Like so many before you, I hope you'll consider delivering your child prematurely, since the party can't legally accept donations from the unborn (at least not yet). However, the president sure could use the money. And despite what you've heard from so-called scientists, babies are surprisingly well developed at four months. In fact, many have working lungs. And even some of their toes.

Q: If I send a delicious plate of sugar cookies or a wreath with garland and bows with my donation, will the president use his influence to have obstruction of justice charges against me dropped?

A: Unfortunately, no, Ms. Stewart.

Q: Can you assure me that the money I give will be used to run negative ads that smear the president's Democratic opponents?

A: Not 100 percent. But, how's a 99.7 percent assurance? After all, we do need a few bucks to buy off state voting regulators and the people who count the punch card ballots in Michigan.

Q: Is there any way around the $2,000 dollar individual donation limit?
A: No! And if you don't want to find out more, absolutely do not call the Republican Party headquarters weeknights between 11 PM and 2 AM. Operators won't be there to help you.

Q: Will the president take a donation even if it is in Confederate money?
A: Yes, he will. (Note, this only applies to Senator Lott.)

Q: If I have obtained the money for my donation by illegal means, will that present a problem for the president?
A: No, assuming you haven't been caught and are not currently the subject of a federal investigation. Otherwise, give the money to a distant relative or friend and ask him/her to donate the money on your behalf.

Q: How can I be assured the president knows I sent the money?
A: Thanks to the PATRIOT Act, the president knew you were going to donate even before you did. He also knows you're out of checks; it's time to reorder. The ones with the animal prints are nice. Your wife likes those.

SECTION II

A BUSH REPUBLICAN TAKES CALIFORNIA

THE BUSH GAME PLAN HEADS WEST

The writing of this book presented me with a quandary. Had I not been a participant in the California recall race, there is no question that I would have used the recall election and the improbable rise of Arnold Schwarzenegger as important illustrations of the rise of the fanatics. Arnold's method, a velvet glove of charm and sham compassion concealing an iron fist squeezing the poor and the vulnerable, displays the latest refinement in George Bush's game plan. By looking at the recall, we can see what to expect in 2004 and figure out how to beat it.

These are powerful reasons for writing about Arnold. But there is also a powerful argument for avoiding the subject of Schwarzenegger altogether. As someone who, well, *didn't* win the gubernatorial election, I could be perceived as having a personal beef. Any negative comment might seem like sour grapes, Parthian shots in a lost cause.

Still, at the risk of seeming like a poor sport, I feel compelled to dissect—only lightly, I promise—the Arnold Experience, not to refight the recall but because of its high level of relevance to what is at stake in 2004.

But before I bury him, allow me to praise Arnold Schwarzenegger.

Watching CNN two days before last Christmas, I saw Arnold visiting the Paso Robles area in California, which had just been hit by a devastating earthquake. Looking great, as he always does, and speaking with warmth and authority, he said, "We will rebuild this town square. We will restore the energy that made it a place that people want it to be. These buildings may have crumbled under the pressure of the quake, but I know for sure that the people will not buckle that easily." The governor was genuinely reassuring and comforting. You could see it on the faces of the people in Paso Robles, and you could feel it even over the television.

And then it hit me.

Arnold would have made a great king. If California were a constitutional monarchy (and, who knows, maybe someone will get a referendum for that on the next ballot), Arnold would make the perfect figurehead. He could console victims of natural disasters. He could cut ribbons, hand out T-shirts, and sign autographs. He could preside with dignity over ceremonial events, wear fancy sashes and robes and swords, ride around in a gold-plated, open-air Hummer, and give distinguished visitors a genuine movie star welcome. And, in the bargain, the people of California would not just get the perfect king, they would get a wonderful royal family with a beautiful and talented queen and four adorable princes and princesses.

Unfortunately, Arnold wasn't crowned king. He was elected governor in a recall process that, at first, seemed too ridiculous to take seriously. For once, the late-night monologue jokes seemed superfluous. But once the impact of Arnold's budget cuts began to hit home, the laughter quickly faded, until the only ones still giggling were the governor himself and his big-money backers.

GOVERNOR SCHWARZENEGGER: A VERY FAMILIAR KIND OF REPUBLICAN

Like Bush, Schwarzenegger ran as a compassionate, bipartisan Republican, and like Bush, he gave a compassionate, bipartisan inaugural speech. But unlike Bush, he didn't even wait a few weeks before targeting programs benefiting the poor and disadvantaged.

The first round of cuts he proposed, just eight days after taking office, included canceling a cost-of-living increase for 500,000 families on welfare and repealing a law that would allow 66,000 poor families to get food stamps even if they own a car worth more than $4,650.

His first full budget, introduced in the beginning of January 2004, was headlined in the *Los Angeles Times* as "Budget Ax Would Fall Heavily on the Poor, Ill." Here are some highlights (or lowlights):

- Taking $1.3 billion in property taxes from cities and counties, putting at risk many of the local police and fire services that depend on these funds.
- Cutting $1.9 billion from the state's legally guaranteed funding for K-12 schools and community colleges.
- Cutting $729 million from higher education, which would force tuition increases at CSU and UC campuses of 10 percent for undergraduates and 40 percent for graduate students.
- Trimming California's public universities' incoming classes by 10 percent, which would turn away 20,000 students next fall.
- Making financial aid harder to get by lowering the maximum qualifying income for Cal Grant re-

cipients by 10 percent, hitting many middle-income families.

- Slashing Medi-Cal by nearly $900 million, including cutting payment by 10 percent to doctors serving 6.8 million low-income patients, which would lead to increases in many co-pay charges.

- Capping a program that treats 37,600 children and teenagers whose families earn too much to be eligible for Medi-Cal but who have severe medical needs. (Some children with cancer, for example, will no longer get state help to pay for chemotherapy.)

- Capping enrollment in the Healthy Families program that provides health care for children of the working poor.

- Cutting 2 percent from AIDS and HIV treatment and prevention programs.

- Cutting cash payments for 1.2 million families that rely on government support to survive.

- Slicing $55.6 million from Public Health funding, including a cap on enrollments in a program aiding people with genetic handicaps.

- Freezing certification of new Adult Day Care Centers, and denying the centers reimbursement for therapy or transportation costs.

- Slashing the CalWORKs temporary cash assistance program by $800 million, reducing benefits for 481,000 poor families on public assistance.

- Cutting by $373.5 million the support services that help the elderly and disabled remain in their homes. Family members would no longer get paid to care for relatives.

- Taking $59 million from the state's trial courts, including innovative programs like drug courts.

The supreme irony is that we are willing to invest tens of thousands of dollars a year on a child who goes wrong and winds up in the criminal justice system, but we begrudge the far smaller amount it would cost to help keep these kids out of jail in the first place.

The sense of foreboding I felt about the kind of governor Arnold would be has become a tragic reality. California Treasurer Phil Angelides called the Schwarzenegger budget "morally and economically bankrupt." How did we get to the point where eliminating the car tax is more important than all of these things—health care for kids, college scholarships, aid for the elderly and disabled? How many dreams have been eliminated as a result? What kind of people have we become when the measure of our humanity—how we treat the weak, the infirm, and the less fortunate—has been sacrificed for a cheap political stunt that will save most of us about a hundred and fifty bucks a year? Why is it that the car tax had to go, while corporate tax loopholes continue to drain the revenues we need for a small modicum of social justice?

Why, for example, is it OK for Disney to pay only a nickel per square foot in property taxes for much of its land while the average new homeowner in the area pays over 3000% more? As Assemblywoman Loni Hancock put it, "This is like the rhinoceros in the living room. It is one of the major loopholes in our tax structure." Ending the commercial property tax injustice or a modest increase in taxes for the wealthiest one percent of Californians would preserve so many of these essential programs. How is it that just proposing a tax increase, saying the t-word, has become a declaration of war?

Not only are these cuts punitive and unfairly aimed at the most vulnerable Californians, they are not even fiscally sound. In fact, they are the kind of cuts that have unintended—and very pricey—consequences. They make California weaker, in every way. Take the cuts to programs designed to help the blind, elderly, and disabled be self-sufficient. Without these services, many of them will be forced to move into much costlier nursing homes—at taxpayers' expense. The same is true of the rate cuts for doctors, a move that will force many poor patients to use hospital emergency rooms as their primary (and more expensive) means of medical treatment—again with California's taxpayers footing the bill.

As for cuts to the state's food stamp program, these will deprive the state of tens of millions of dollars in federal funds. In fact, nearly $1 billion more in federal money would be coming to California if the state didn't have some of the most stringent food stamp eligibility requirements in the country. Meanness, it turns out, doesn't come cheap.

Meanwhile, back at Fanatics' HQ in Washington, the brutal realities of three years of declining federal revenues are reflected in the president's 2005 budget. The administration is planning to place a drop in the revenue bucket by cutting $1.6 billion from the housing budget, which will keep local agencies from issuing housing vouchers to over 250,000 low-income families. Another drop is to be added by forcing veterans to pay more than twice as much for their prescription drugs. Indeed, the 2005 budget cuts funding for veterans by $13.5 billion over five years. And just as SARS, Mad Cow, and a deadly Asian bird flu are topping the news, the administration is scaling back funding for the National Institutes of Health. All to help finance the president's tax cuts. These measures barely make a difference to the budget deficit, but each one makes a world of difference in the lives of hundreds of thousands of people.

And in states, cities, and towns across the country, the consequences of Bush's reckless tax cutting have been disastrous as local governments are finding out the true meaning of trickle-down economics. Faced with a cumulative shortfall of $200 billion, states have resorted to desperate measures like deferring employee salary payments, cutting health care coverage and child care assistance to low-income working families, cutting back K-12 education, instituting double-digit increases in college tuition, borrowing against future revenues from the tobacco settlement, and raising fees for divorce filings—assuming, no doubt correctly, that a $50 increase won't reduce the number of divorces.

Alabama provides a startling case in point. Seeing no other option, the conservative Republican governor, Bob Riley, proposed a $1.2 billion tax increase to begin to bridge a deficit canyon and guarantee some protection for the state's millions of poor citizens. The antitax fanatics waged a relentless and well-funded campaign against it, the voters defeated it, and now Alabama's schools are unable to afford textbooks or computers, state troopers work a four-day work week, and five thousand inmates have been set free from the state's prisons.

In George Bush's home state of Texas, meanwhile, the nationwide collapse in public health insurance programs, especially those protecting children, has meant that 160,000 Texas children lost their health care coverage. The state has also been forced to cut back on Medicaid for pregnant women. Punishing the weak and vulnerable simply because they lack the resources to fight back is not the American way. But, thus far, responsibility for the pain these very real cuts are inflicting on millions of Americans has not been laid where it belongs: on the welcome mat at 1600 Pennsylvania Avenue.

ARNOLD SCHWARZENEGGER: WHAT HE SAID AND WHAT HE DID

What he said: "We have to make sure that every child in California is insured. That is the most important thing. I'm very passionate about children's issues. It is very important because they cannot fend for themselves. The children, we have a Healthy Families program here in California, and it is a very, very good program." (Gubernatorial debate, CSU Sacramento, September 24, 2003)

What he did: Proposed freezing enrollment in the "very, very good" Healthy Families program, a move that will force as many as 100,000 children to go without health insurance—in a state where one in seven children is already uninsured.

What he said: "I am only going to make cuts to a certain point. I'm not going to cut dog food for blind people." (KFBK Radio in Sacramento, November 20, 2003)

What he did: Five days later he proposed cuts that would deny transportation and vital at-home services to blind people.

What he said: "I teach my kids: don't spend more than you have. We have to teach that to Sacramento. . . . They borrow, borrow, borrow." (Interview with ABC's Peter Jennings, October 5, 2003)

What he did: Proposed $4 billion in borrowing in his first budget.

What he said: "As soon as the campaign is over, I will— I can get into all of those kind of specifics [of the groping charges] and find out what is really going on." (Interview with NBC's Tom Brokaw, October 5, 2003)

What he did: First, according to spokesman Rob Stutzman, Schwarzenegger "decided to engage a well-respected investigative firm to look into the allegations."

Later he reversed himself and announced he didn't need to investigate himself after all.

What he said: "I want to have an outside audit so I know exactly where the waste is. I want to see the waste; I want to open up the books to the people of California so they can see where the waste is." (Press conference, Los Angeles, October 8, 2003)
What he did: Hired Donna Arduin to conduct an audit, which resulted in dozens of spreadsheets being dumped in the laps of dumbfounded reporters but no reported waste.

What he said: On how he would balance the budget: 1) "I already told you that I will find it in medical; I will find it in worker's compensation; we'll find it with the Indian money. We'll find it by going to the federal government for the money. I will find it by finding the waste that is in the government. I will find it because there are so many programs that are overlapping that we can cut, all of those kind of things. You know, agencies, regulatory agencies that are overlapping." (Interview with ABC's Peter Jennings, October 5, 2003)
2) "I hate making cuts. Because it hurts me. . . ." Press conference, Sacramento, December 1, 2003
What he did: He proposed $1.9 billion in cuts for 2003–2004, then another $4.6 billion in cuts in the 2004–2005 budget in education and health and human services.

What he said: "We also know there's so much trickery in this year's budget . . ." (Interview with Sacramento radio host Eric Hogue, August 26, 2003.)

What he did: After denouncing the trickery of Gray Davis's budget, he produced a budget that relied on tricks of its own to close a $14.4 billion budget hole. It calls for nearly $10 billion in borrowing, funding shifts, and other budget gimmicks, including diverting to the state's treasury $1 billion in gas tax revenue reserves for funding roads and extending light-rail lines.

THE DEAL-IN-NATOR

As he did during the campaign, Governor Schwarzenegger continues to define "special interests" as those interests that are at odds with his policy goals. Everyone else is fair game to be hit up for a contribution.

Roughly a month after taking office, Schwarzenegger held a fund-raiser, sponsored by the California Manufacturers and Technology Association and megadeveloper Alex Spanos, among others. About six hundred deep-pocketed contributors, lobbyists, and their corporate clients paid up to $21,200 for the privilege of rubbing elbows with the governor.

And how's this for audacious? During the dinner, the Governor delivered a speech in which he noted that he had spent much of his campaign attacking the same "special interests" that he was now partying with—and thanked them for being such effective straw men. If there is one thing Arnold has learned over the course of his moviemaking career, it's how important it is to have a good villain for your hero to lock horns with.

Special interests were the villain. During the recall campaign, Schwarzenegger claimed that he didn't "need to take money from anybody," then plunged into fund-raising like a man possessed, eventually taking in $12 million in campaign cash and a $4.5 million bank loan—$4.4 million more than California election law allows. In January, a Superior Court judge declared the loan illegal and ordered the governor to stop raising money to repay it.

As governor, Schwarzenegger has exhibited a very familiar Republican proclivity for cozying up to special interests, appearances be damned. Just three days after taking office, he paid a special visit to a large Los Angeles area auto dealership, Galpin Ford, to celebrate his repeal of the state's unpopular car tax. "Go out there," he exhorted a crowd of four hundred at a midday rally. "Buy cars. Buy new cars. Buy used cars." Buy, buy, buy! It must have been music to the ears of Galpin Ford's owner, Bert Boeckmann: imagine having a world-renowned cinematic superstar hawking your product on the nightly news. The event was worth millions in free advertising. And it only cost the dealer a little over $50,000 to make it happen. Boeckmann, along with his wife, contributed $42,400 to Arnold's gubernatorial campaign and doled out another $10,000 for his inauguration.

Sometimes payback isn't a bitch, it's a heartfelt pitch.

Displaying his usual deft touch for irony, Governor Schwarzenegger used the Galpin Ford appearance to rail against politics as usual—all while putting on a display of pay-to-play politics that would have made Gray Davis feel right at home.

Auto dealers, who donated over $800,000 to Schwarzenegger's campaign, weren't done cashing in on the governor's priced-to-move specials. They also rolled off the lot with a sweetheart deal: the firing of Steve Gourley, the head of California's Department of Motor Vehicles, an official with an admirable history of investigating and punishing shady auto industry financing practices. One of Gourley's investigations led to the 2001 indictment of a group of employees at a dealership accused of selling used cars as new, resetting odometers, and peddling fraudulent car loans. That dealership is owned by AutoNation, a company that donated $21,200 to Arnold's campaign. Do you think the gang at AutoNation felt that was money well spent when Governor Schwarzenegger canned Gourley just hours after taking the oath of office? One thing you can say for car dealers: they know a sweet deal when it comes their way. Buy, buy, buy!

Car dealers weren't the only ones hopping aboard Arnold's post-election gravy train. In the three months following his recall victory, Schwarzenegger raked in nearly $3 million in political funds. More than a few of the firms and individuals contributing to the governor have business before the state, including AT&T and developers Donald Bren and Alex Spanos. The new governor also took in $100,000 from a company that is the leading underwriter of workers' compensation insurance—even as he announced plans to put a workers' compensation reform initiative on the ballot in 2004.

But that's not all: Schwarzenegger accepted a $53,000 donation from Wackenhut Corrections Corporation, a company that operates private prisons in the state. The contribution came a little over a month before California was set to close down a 224-bed facility run by the company. "We have a large investment in California," explained Wackenhut president Wayne Calabrese. "We want to do everything we can to preserve our business base in California," including buttering up the new guy in charge. Helpfully, the firm's Florida lobbyist, David Ericks, is a good buddy of Donna Arduin, the governor's budget-slashing finance director. Team Schwarzenegger, of course, has denied any connection between contributions and state affairs, saying that a decision on the Wackenhut facility wouldn't "rise to the level of the governor's consideration." Funny how that distinction was never made during the campaign, when Schwarzenegger regularly hammered Gray Davis for accepting money from the state's prison guards' union—a group that, it just so happens, frequently clashed with Wackenhut over the push to privatize California's prisons.

Of course, we could have seen this coming from the moment he insisted that he was not taking any money from special interests, only from "powerful interests"—a distinction that seemed to have been lost in translation. Call them what you like, "special interests," "powerful interests," or "extremely self-interested interests," Arnold's donations include $100,000 from Yellowstone Development, a company accused by the EPA of illegally polluting rivers and wetlands, $21,200 from the giant HMO Health Net, which contracts with the state for programs like Healthy Families, $50,000 from Affiliated Computer Services, a Texas computer consulting company that specializes in government contracts, and $363,700 from real estate developer Alex Spanos and his family, along with large donations from other major real estate developers, car dealers, and agribusiness kingpins. So when you look at Arnold's contributors, they aren't, in fact, very "special" interests, just run-of-the-mill big-business interests Republicans have been in thrall to for decades.

While Arnold might be understandably shy about discussing George Bush's policies and the part they irrefutably played in what's happened to California, he's not so coy when it comes to tapping Bush's donors. The president's big boosters, the Rangers and the Pioneers, courageous multimillionaires who have tamed the wild frontiers of influence peddling, also turned out their pockets for Arnold. And among his campaign donors was President Bush's father.

Arnold's backers included some who hedged their bets by supporting both the actor and Gray Davis. Big developers, who knew that, no matter who was in office, there would always be a few rules that needed bending and one or two loopholes that needed stretching, donated $400,000 to Schwarzenegger and $300,000 to the then-governor.

The body politic is no different from the human body: you are what you eat. Arnold's claim of independence from the backroom boys evaporated when he endorsed his $100,000 check from Yellowstone Development. By their donors, ye shall know them. He may claim to be a public servant, but he's only on loan from his corporate donors.

His failure to conduct his long-promised independent audit of the state's accounts underlines the contradictions between his campaign rhetoric and his actions. In speech after speech on the campaign trail, he vowed that his first act as governor would be an exhaustive audit that would uncover billions in waste. "There is more special tricks and special effects than *Terminator 3*," he said about California's budget. "I'll send accounting firms to really look at that, and do auditing for sixty days, then we can find out exactly where we can cut." In other interviews, he predicted there would be "billions of dollars to be played around with when you open those books." Schwarzenegger spokesman Sean Walsh pledged that the audit would be "real" and "forensic." And the day after his election, Schwarzenegger reiterated his plan to have a "line-by-line" examination of the state's books.

Soon after taking office, however, the new governor began singing a different tune. The promised thorough, wide-ranging audit was replaced by a cursory assessment of earlier budget reports already produced by state agencies, and vows to "open the books" to the public were quickly scuttled. "I would not view this as an audit," said former state controller Kathleen Connell, one member of the three-person team Schwarzenegger had chosen to review the "audit" findings. Talk about an anticlimax.

In one of the campaign TV ads Arnold blanketed the airwaves with, he made solving the budget crisis sound like a no-brainer. "Here is my plan: audit everything, open the books, and then we end the crazy deficit spending."

Easier said than done. Those "billions of dollars to be played around with" have proven as elusive as Iraqi WMD.

As galling as Schwarzenegger's audit flip-flop was, it can't hold a candle to the jaw-dropping about-face he executed on his pledge to protect local governments from the loss of revenue caused by his rollback of the state's car tax. Local governments have become the front lines—the "leading indicators," if you will—of the damage that is being wrought all across the country by the fanatical obsession with cutting taxes and "shrinking government." Not satisfied with plunging itself into a sea of red ink, the federal government continues cutting aid to cities, causing budget deficits and underfunded safety net programs. Before taking office, the governor-elect had personally guaranteed that California's cities and counties would be compensated for the close to $4 billion the rollback would cost them—three-quarters of which is earmarked for police, fire, and other public safety services. "I can guarantee you that we will not take money away from them," he said. "They need the money." During the campaign he had even promised that he would provide an alternative source of funding on the same day that he cut the car tax.

Well, true to his vow to the tax-cut crowd, he repealed the car tax on his very first day in office, but he clearly had no plan for how to keep his word on the second half of the bargain.

All across the state, local officials cried bloody murder. Even the notoriously mild-mannered mayor of Los Angeles, James Hahn, a Democrat who had been a part of Schwarzenegger's transition team, went ballistic: "We now have a governor who made a personal pledge to me, made a personal pledge to the people of California . . . I think it's immoral for people to break their word, to go back on pledges."

The outcry caused Schwarzenegger to change course and direct that local governments be reimbursed for the loss, but he did not identify a funding source. Then, three weeks later, he reversed course yet again, taking back $1.3 billion in property taxes from local governments. It was downright dizzying.

These two Schwarzenegger promises—one immediately kept and one so casually broken—speak volumes about the mind-set of the tax-cut fanatics. It's particularly striking how blithely the pain and suffering resulting from scaled-back services is dismissed: Hey, it's not my fault.

THE LEAVE-US-ALONE COALITION
OR
THE GROVER-JEB-DONNA-ARNOLD NEXUS

Welcome to the America long dreamt of by the "Less Government Is Best Government" crowd.

The spiritual guru of this bunch is conservative activist Grover Norquist, head of the Leave-Us-Alone Coalition. Norquist is the central theorist behind a brutal, un-American plan that adds up to the Third Worldization of our society. "I hope a state goes bankrupt," he told the *New York Times*. "I hope a state has real troubles getting its act together, so that the other 49 states can say, 'Let's not do that.' We need a state to be a bad example, so that the others will start to make serious decisions they need to get out of this mess."

That Norquist is willing to advocate the bankruptcy of an entire state shows how disconnected these fanatics have become from the pain that such a disaster would cause. Imagine all the social programs that would have to be abandoned by a bankrupt state. Picture real people, many of them defenseless children, going without health care, without shelter, and without the possibility of improving their lives through education or job training.

And it isn't just Grover Norquist. It's now the mainstream of the Republican Party. Here is what Gov. Jeb Bush had to say on the subject during his 2003 inaugural speech while standing in front of Florida's Old Capitol: "There would be no greater tribute to our maturity as a society than if we can make these buildings around us empty of workers; silent monuments to the time when government played a larger role than it deserved or could adequately fill." So Norquist wants the states to go bankrupt and the president's brother wants government to wither away. Is anybody paying attention?

It doesn't appear so. The woman responsible for bringing Jeb Bush's chilling vision to life was none other than Donna Arduin, who, immediately after Schwarzenegger was elected, was summoned to California. Arduin, whom Schwarzenegger called "my genius," was responsible for cleaving $8.1 billion out of Florida's budget, resulting in, among other things, the elimination of 21,000 government jobs and the denial of social services to 55,000 children. And in the fanatics' world, that kind of achievement deserves a promotion.

Schwarzenegger tasked her with ferreting out all the billions of dollars of fraud and waste that he had promised he was going to terminate. Instead she offered to the governor, and the governor offered to the state, more than $6 billion in cuts mercilessly targeting the most vulnerable people in California.

My response to Grover, Jeb, Donna, Arnold, and the rank and file of the Leave-Us-Alone Coalition is simple: Sorry, no can do. We have created a democracy that links us all, and with it come not only opportunities but obligations. There are no gates or walls high enough. There are no bank accounts large enough to buy you and your family and your friends protection from the fear and hunger of those left behind or to isolate you from the consequences of growing social inequities. We are all in this boat together. And the fact that there isn't a hole at your end of the boat doesn't mean you are safe.

A VERY SCHWARZENEGGER THANKSGIVING

I joined the board of the Points of Light Foundation, founded by the first President Bush, when I was a Republican, and I stayed on it through my political transformation—in fact, until last February—because I still believe in the power of being a point of light, although I no longer believe that points of light alone, even thousands upon thousands of them, will be enough to solve the social crisis in our midst.

So it was really good to see Maria Shriver and her twelve-year-old daughter doling out food at a Sacramento food bank over this past Thanksgiving holiday. There was no doubt about her genuine warmth and concern. But it was a disconcerting blast from my Republican past to hear her at the same time and in the same venue defend her husband's first round of budget cuts—cuts that targeted health care and food programs serving some of the same people lining up at the food bank that day.

"Nobody likes the cuts," was Shriver's defense. "Arnold doesn't like the cuts. There is nobody who takes joy in that. . . . It's painful for everybody in California. But I think it is a time when people need to come together." That kind of rationalization lies at the heart of the problem. The truth is it's not painful for everybody in California. It's not painful for me, and it's not painful for her, and it's not painful for any of the people who donated to her husband's campaign. It's painful for the poor. And inflicting pain on the poor is not the way for people "to come together."

There are $2 billion in revenues just waiting to be collected, if only Schwarzenegger would be willing to ask his corporate cronies to share the pain by having their property tax loopholes closed. And another $1.3 billion if Schwarzenegger would be willing to put an end to offshore and California-based tax shelters. That might cause some pain in 90210 and a few other choice zip codes but, overall, I think rich and poor would be much closer together in a fairer California.

Incoming California Assembly Republican leader Kevin McCarthy also saw the Schwarzenegger cuts as "painful," saying, "We have had a cancer growing on our budget, and to cure this we are having to go through the chemo. It is painful, but we do have to shrink this tumor." GOP Assemblyman Ken Maddox was equally compassionate: "I can't think of one group that is not going to squeal when the cuts are made." Of course, we'll never know whether the wealthy corporations and special interest groups that helped fund Schwarzenegger's campaign would squeal or not; the governor has not prescribed any budgetary chemo for them. The prognosis for their financial health is just fine.

THE CHARM WARS

Arnold's election shows what can happen when a charming, affable celebrity, abetted by a starstruck media, runs a content-free campaign complete with special effects and taps into the public's deep anger and dissatisfaction with politics as usual. Of course, it wasn't the first time.

In 2000 another charming, affable cardboard cutout with high name recognition ran a manipulative, shameless, button-pushing campaign that tapped into the public's longing for an outsider who could unite Republicans and Democrats to shake things up in Washington. He cracked the notoriously tough exterior of the Washington press corps with his unassuming good-old-boy manner and his oh-so-charming penchant for giving people nicknames. Over the course of his three debates with Al Gore, George W. Bush mentioned the need for a different kind of leader to go to Washington to bring Republicans and Democrats together a whopping total of sixteen times, and he compared his "outsider" status to the business-as-usual mess in Washington nineteen times.

Here is a sampling of quotes from the mainstream media about just how charming George W. Bush was:

- "Call it the charm offensive. Texas Governor George W. Bush worked on winning hearts and votes in New Hampshire and Massachusetts yesterday with a roll of the eyes, the lift of an eyebrow, and plenty of irreverent asides. (June 16, 1999, Jill Zuckman, the *Boston Globe*)

- "Regardless of one's political persuasion, it's hard not to like Texas Gov. George W. Bush. The Republican front-runner for president in 2000 may not be the brightest bulb on the subject of foreign affairs, having flubbed a reporter's mini-quiz on world leaders last week. But at least he has the good sense now to make light of it. . . . Much like the man in the White House he is seeking to replace, Bush exudes the impression that he sincerely enjoys the company of people and genuinely would rather spend all his time mingling with those who adore him, brushing off aides who attempt to rush him to the next campaign event." (November 11, 1999, James F. McCarty, the *Cleveland Plain Dealer*)

- "As the lead partner of a Major League Baseball team and governor of a state with a weak chief executive post, Bush has used his powers of persuasion to get his way. His charm is bipartisan, which is important in Texas, where the state House is controlled by Democrats." (April 5, 2000, Owen Ullmann, *USA Today*)

By 2003, the media were ready to fall in love all over again.

- "We now know the value of charisma in California politics. It's the distance between Peter Ueberroth and Arnold Schwarzenegger in the race for governor. . . .

Arnold Schwarzenegger might have the charm to win over leadership-hungry voters while glossing over these sorts of details. Peter Ueberroth clearly does not." (August 28, 2003, Daniel Weintraub, the *Sacramento Bee*)

- "Schwarzenegger captivates. There is the plain language. There are those zingers from old films. Remember, in the movies, he's a protagonist of few words. And what a relief to hear reassuring action-hero talk on the campaign stage." (September 7, 2003, Joseph Honig, *Los Angeles Daily News*)

- "Schwarzenegger gave me absolutely nothing—and yet he made me feel like I was the only person on his planet. . . . It wasn't cold celebrity that overwhelmed us, but the inclusiveness of the Arnie charm. He had us in his big, outstretched palm. Seven years later, I am not surprised that this astonishingly warm and slippery diplomat managed to seduce an entire state." (November 29, 2003, Kerry Gold, *Vancouver Sun*)

Bush and Schwarzenegger share a capacity for intimacy that is rarer than one would think among the political class—and conspicuously absent in Gray Davis and Al Gore. Should that be our standard for political office now? Elections essentially becoming just another reality dating show? Perhaps C-SPAN could change the name of *Road to the White House* to *Joe President*.

George Bush told us that he was "a uniter, not a divider," a "compassionate conservative," and a "reformer with results." And the press, pierced by Cupid's arrow, let him slide. Arnold Schwarzenegger followed the same strategy. In care-

fully staged public appearances and no-holds-barred interviews with Jay Leno, Oprah Winfrey, and Howard Stern, he
paraphrased his pal George Bush's assertion that he was "a
uniter, not a divider," by repeating again and again that he
wanted "to be the governor for everybody, not just for Republicans or not just for Democrats, but for everybody." But
the key to Arnold Schwarzenegger's appeal to the right-
wingers behind the recall was that he was the perfect front
man, just like that other figurehead at the fanatics' feast,
George W. Bush.

The parallels between the two men's campaigns are nu-
merous and sometimes downright eerie. Proving an adept
student of Bush's unlikely rise to power, Schwarzenegger
produced the sequel, with himself starring in the role origi-
nated by the president. The bamboozled press played its part
perfectly by focusing on the few differences: Arnold was pro-
choice, pro–gun control, and pro–gay rights. But these social
issues are not the issues that are front and center in the governing of California and, indeed, the nation. Nor are they the
issues that the corporate interests dominating the Republican
Party give a damn about.

Token opposition to them is the red meat that George Bush
tosses to his party's ravenous radical base to keep them coop-
erative on Election Day. In California the party faithful were
willing to overlook these chinks in Arnold's conservative ar-
mor in order to get an antitax, anti-regulation Bush Republican seated behind the governor's desk. When the road forks
between social issues and making a few hundred million dollars for corporate interests, the GOP bosses will always choose
the latter. Every time. Tom McClintock, Arnold's rock-
ribbed, socially conservative intraparty foe, always saw himself
as "the real Republican" in the recall race. But by the time the

recall rolled around, we'd seen enough of how the Republican Party operates to know that—sorry, Tom—Arnold would become the GOP darling. He's got the ties to the business cronies. You don't. Ergo: He's the real Republican.

During the election, the Bush-Schwarzenegger symbiosis was kept carefully under wraps. The theory was simple: you say what you have to say to get elected. If a few "liberal" platitudes help soften your image in a strongly Democratic state, fine, say them; just get elected. Bush wisely kept his distance during the race. But no sooner was Schwarzenegger elected than the president and the governor-elect appeared together for an orgy of mutual backslapping at, inevitably, a Bush fund-raiser—the most holy sacrament of an elite order devoted to the worship of money.

The president told the crowd that Schwarzenegger will "be a fine and strong leader." Schwarzenegger gushed in return, "There is no greater ally that this Golden State has in Washington than our president, my dear friend." Then the new governor sat and applauded as the president reasserted in the strongest possible terms his doctrine of preemption. "America is following a new strategy," Bush told the crowd. "We are striking our enemies before they can strike us again." At this appearance, Arnold's Kennedy relations were noticeably absent. Understandable. We all have relatives we don't like being seen with when we are basking in the glow of the testosterone-giddy commander in chief. But did Arnold agree? You bet he did. As he told Sean Hannity, "I think that he is doing a great job. I supported the war in Iraq. . . . I believe in all that, yes."

Throughout the campaign, Schwarzenegger's seasoned handlers were very careful to position him as a different kind of Republican. Hmmm, does that sound familiar? In 2000, Karl Rove sold us a Texas governor and big-business stooge with an undistinguished résumé as a different kind of Republican who bonded readily with minorities, spoke *un poco* Spanish, cared about education, and spent his vacations at an environmentally sensitive ranch in Crawford, Texas. In one of the debates Bush even brought up "valuable rain forest lands." Funny—we haven't heard a lot about those valuable rain forests since the election. Three years later we had Arnold Schwarzenegger pledging to retrofit one of his six Hummers to run on clean hydrogen gas. But it will take more than this stirring promise to compensate for his having introduced to America the single most fuel-inefficient vehicle on the road.

The words "George Bush" never crossed Arnold's lips during the campaign except to tell me during the debate that if I wanted to campaign against Bush, I should go to New Hampshire. And somehow the media and the public did not see an irony in Schwarzenegger's railing against Gray Davis for taking a $12.8 billion surplus and turning it into a $38 billion deficit while putting his fingers in his ears and humming whenever someone pointed out that Bush took a $281 billion surplus and turned it into a $521 billion deficit. But consistency has never been the Bush Republicans' strong suit.

Bush and Schwarzenegger also share that most powerful invisible bond: a pathological fear of taxes. Bush gave expression to his taxophobia by cutting $2 trillion in taxes—mainly for the superrich, but also, to be fair, for the merely rich—in the middle of a war and a recession. For his part, Schwarzenegger repeated his juvenile antitax ravings almost as often as he told his audiences that he would "terminate" everything they didn't like while Gray Davis had "terminated" everything they loved including, yes, "our hopes." Arnold was firmly opposed

We've gotten to the point in this country where you couldn't raise taxes to repel an invasion from Mars unless you were able to disguise them as an economic stimulus package.

to bad things and, courageously, didn't care who knew it. I guess when you drive a Humvee you don't actually need frivolous little tax-funded things like roads.

Early in the campaign, he said about taxes, "I feel that the people of California have been punished enough. From the time they get up in the morning and flush the toilet, they're taxed. Then they go and get a coffee, they're taxed. They get into their car, they're taxed. They go to the gas station, they're taxed. They go for lunch, they're taxed. And this goes on all day long: tax, tax, tax, tax, tax."

Clearly, Arnold and W both ardently believe in the first edict of the fanatical right-wing religion: taxes are the root of all evil. Arnold went so far as to say in one of his ads: "I am in principle against taxing." Really? Then how could he also promise to cut nothing from our education budget? Where does he think schools get their funding? Where does he think the roads that kids get to school on come from? Or the police officers that make sure they get there safely? Or, yes, the water that they flush the toilets with? From box office grosses? From General Motors or Halliburton?

During his trip to Washington, Schwarzenegger got a lot of laughs by calling himself "the Collectinator," but where does he think the money he wants to collect from the Feds for California is coming from? He promised to come to the nation's capital "as many times as possible to make sure that we get more federal money to California." That's taxpayer money he wants to bring back, right?

But the public was too deeply invested in a rescue fantasy, a magical solution to all our problems in the form of an action hero with a can-do attitude. To get out his core message—anti–bad things, especially taxes, pro–good things, especially himself—to the desperate-to-be-saved voters, Arnold spent

$22 million on his campaign. Never has so much been spent to say so little.

BREAD AND CIRCUSES:
THEN AND NOW

In October 2003 at a Costa Mesa campaign stop, Arnold Schwarzenegger had a 3,600-pound wrecking ball dropped onto a white Oldsmobile Cutlass marked "DAVIS CAR TAX." On cue Arnold shouted, "It's *hasta la vista*, baby, to the car tax." The crowd ate it up, shouting in response, "Arnold! Arnold!" The media were thrilled; they had a fantastic video clip to promote their evening newscasts, and political consultants everywhere were considering adding "wrecking a car" to their criteria for what gets a candidate on the evening news.

Voters are used to seeing politicians using stunts and props, usually ham-fisted ones, to get attention on the campaign trail. Tasting the pies at the county fair, waving some document in the face of an opponent—this is the daily bread candidates offer the hungry beast of the twenty-four-hour news cycle, hoping for a moment's notice from the public's short attention span. But by using his Hollywood savvy, Arnold was able, just by crushing a Cutlass, to raise the standard for political stunts to a whole new level.

Elaborate special effects have always been a hallmark of Arnold's movies, so maybe it's not surprising that they played a role in his campaign, along with cinematic applause lines like:

"In the movies, if I didn't like a character, you know what I did, I destroyed it." Or, "This endless litany of taxing schemes by Messrs. Davis and Bustamante reminds me of the androids that I fight in the Terminator movies, which I keep shooting dead, but keep coming back to life."

Arnold's formulaic movies provided a magic formula for election success. And, like everything else about his campaign, they may offer a window on things to come, as the Schwarzenegger Effect spreads outward from California. Will other politicians now be forced to match his Industrial Light and Magic level of campaign production value?

But Arnold's "Hey, look at me!" campaign stunts, designed to answer the voters' concerns about policies with pyrotechnics, is not the ultimate in distracting extravaganzas. No, to see where we may be headed, as is so often the case, we have to look back at where we've been, back to the reign of the Roman Caesars.

During the tenure of Julius Caesar, officially-sponsored public spectacles marked celebrations of military victories, thanksgivings, the emperor's personal accomplishments, and the emperor's birthday. The Roman satirist Juvenal coined a phrase when he said, "The public has long since cast off its cares; the people that once bestowed commands, consulships, legions, and all else, now meddle no more and long eagerly for just two things—bread and circuses."

The circuses included wild animal shows, where deer, boar, bears, bulls, lions, panthers, leopards, ostriches, crocodiles, hippopotamuses, rhinoceroses, apes, lynx, and giraffes were forced to fight each other and sometimes humans. Augustus alone held twenty-six "bait-ings," killing 3,500 animals. Trajan's games in AD 107 saw 11,000 slaughtered beasts. Commodus, in one bloody afternoon, single-handedly killed five crocodiles and, on another, did away with two elephants, several rhi-noceroses, and a giraffe.

The more PETA–acceptable gladiatorial combat, be-tween men rather than men and animals, produced dis-tracting spectacles that must have been overpoweringly effective in taking the minds of average Romans off their problems. It's hard to worry about your dire job prospects when someone is getting his head chopped off right in front of you.

When watching gladiators hack each other to pieces got boring, Julius Caesar and Augustus turned to naval battles. The Colosseum would be flooded, and thou-sands of gladiators would dress up in historically accu-rate gear and duke it out on the "high seas." Claudius in AD 52, staged a battle that pitted fleets with 19,000 men (each!) against each other.

Judged purely by his ability to distract the public, President Bush must have been a Caesar in a previous life. He's a public spectacle machine—part P. T. Barnum, part juggling, sword-swallowing, fire-eating sideshow monkey. For his first great trick, he managed to con-vince the Supreme Court to award him the presidential election, despite his losing the popular vote by some-thing like a half million votes. Sometime later he dressed up like a Navy fighter pilot and landed in an S-3B Viking on the deck of the USS *Abraham Lincoln* to announce the end of "major combat operations" in Iraq—an event that had the singular distinction of be-

ing both distracting and disturbing. Then, in the grand-
daddy of all distractions, in the fall of 2003 President
Bush mounted a supersecret operation in which he
snuck out of the country to serve turkey and stuffing to
soldiers in Iraq on Thanksgiving (for exactly two hours
and thirty-two minutes). The news of Bush's trip—and
the sight of the commander in chief holding a turkey
(an inedible prop, as it turned out) as if he had just finished basting it—effectively distracted the voters from
the fact that more U.S. soldiers have died since the end
of major combat operations than during the war itself.
Bush reversed a slide in his approval rating, which shot
up by five points.

At least no one has been torn apart by lions, eaten by
alligators, or trampled by chariots at Arnold Schwarzenegger's campaign events or during W's publicity
stunts. Not yet.

TOTAL LACK OF RECALL

Among the many bonds between doppelgängers W and
Arnold is the employment of a key campaign tool, selective amnesia. Bush developed it and Schwarzenegger pumped it up.

Take the controversy that first sprang up just a few weeks
before the 2000 election over the discrepancy between
Bush's claims that he had flown with his Texas Air National
Guard unit until he was released from service in September
1973 and records indicating he hadn't been allowed to fly after August 1972. After talking things over with his candidate,
Bush's communications director, Dan Bartlett, told the press
that Bush could not recall ever being grounded.

Bartlett also claimed that the Governor (Bush, not Arnold) could not recall specifically how many times he reported for duty during his months in Alabama. This explanation came after Bush's campaign had been unable to provide any documents proving that he had reported for duty at all during his service with the Texas Air National Guard in Alabama. And when Bush was asked during the campaign why he checked the "do not volunteer" box (which meant at the time "do not volunteer for service in Vietnam") when he took his air force officer's qualification test, he responded that he did not recall checking the box.

He also could not recall any antiwar protests when he was a student at Yale. No one bothered to ask whether he actually recalled that there was a war at all in Vietnam, or whether he recalled the dustup that we had with the Germans and the Japanese sometime in the midcentury. Now, it's possible that his lack of recall is due to what he does recall about his college years: drinking. Lots of it. The president describes his drinking during those days as normal youthful carousing. Arnold would later echo this sentiment when attributing his behavior toward women to the atmosphere on rowdy movie sets. What a couple of fun-loving fellas!

Like Arnold, the president also has a history of apologizing for transgressions he cannot recall—like the time during the 2000 campaign when Bush declared that he could not remember what he had said to Al Hunt when he ran into the journalist at a Dallas restaurant, but that he nevertheless regretted offending him. Hunt, who is not suffering from the same memory problems, remembered that Bush had approached him and said, "You fucking son of a bitch, I saw what you wrote. We're not going to forget this." This was a reference to Hunt's prediction in *Washingtonian* magazine that Jack Kemp, rather than Bush's father, would lead the 1988 GOP ticket—proof that, when it comes to holding a grudge, W has a very fine memory indeed. Nevertheless, even certain softball questions during the 2000 presidential primary proved difficult for the mnemonically challenged Bush, who once claimed he could not "remember any specific books" he read as a child.

In February 2003, Senator Peter Fitzgerald, a Republican from Illinois, caused an uproar when he divulged that Bush told him he would repeal the 1976 ban on assassinations with an executive order, setting up the possibility that he could order Saddam's assassination "if we had a clear shot at him." Later Ari Fleischer said Bush could not "recall if he said it or didn't say it."

In July 2002, Dan Bartlett, now serving as White House communications director, was once more called upon to cover for the president's oh-so-conveniently spotty memory. Back in 1990, Bush sold 212,140 shares of Harken Energy for $848,560 while sitting on its board. A week prior, Bush had received a memo from Harken's outside counsel, Haynes and Boone, warning the board of directors against selling shares if they had insider knowledge that would affect the share price. According to Bartlett, Bush did not recall receiving the warning from Haynes and Boone.

Why is the president so willing to play the doddering dolt? Simple: it's better than the alternative. In 1998 a reporter asked if Bush had been arrested since 1968. That time around, he responded with an emphatic "No." (He was in fact arrested for drunken driving in 1976.) Which makes you understand why he's so vague. When he answers directly, he tells a lie. Of course, when he was asked about his "no" answer two years later, Karen Hughes responded that "he does not recall saying that."

Considering how well it seems to have worked for Bush, you can't blame Arnold for relying on a fuzzy memory when addressing uncomfortable facts from his past. On May 17, 2001, in the middle of California's energy crisis, Schwarzenegger joined a group of prominent Bush Republicans, including Mike Milken and Dick Riordan, at the Peninsula Hotel in Beverly Hills for a private audience with Enron energy huckster Ken Lay. After I held a press conference early in the campaign, asking Arnold to explain why he attended the meeting and what transpired during it, he suddenly morphed from the Terminator into the Absent-Minded Professor, telling a reporter, "I don't remember the meeting. Do I remember all the meetings I had in the last decade?"

Now, this was no ordinary meeting, coming as it did just days after Californians had suffered a second round of rolling blackouts—blackouts tied inextricably to the actions of crooked energy firms like Enron. But Arnold was given a pass by the press. The lesson was clear: when in doubt, don't recall.

On October 2, 2003, five days before the recall election, Arnold's capacity for convenient forgetfulness would be pushed to the limit. On that day the *Los Angeles Times* ran a front-page story headlined "Women Say Schwarzenegger Groped, Humiliated Them." It detailed Arnold's alleged sexual harassment of six women. Over the next few days, ten more women would come forward with similar claims.

When confronted with the charges, Arnold fell back on his favorite fudge: "I don't remember so many of the things I was accused of having done," he told CNN's Candy Crowley. Arnold's amnesia is not reserved just for sex and

Lay. On October 3, the *New York Times* reported that Schwarzenegger had told *Pumping Iron* director George Butler in 1975 that he admired Hitler "because he came from being a little man with almost no formal education, up to power," and because he was "such a good public speaker" and had a "way of getting to the people." Asked by *ABC News* to respond to these statements, Schwarzenegger said, "I cannot remember any of these."

This was the same kind of response he gave Judy Woodruff when she asked him two months after his election about the lawsuit Rhonda Miller, a Hollywood stuntwoman, has filed against him and his campaign for smearing her reputation. "This is all news to me," he replied. "I really don't know anything about that case."

It's enough to make you wonder whether these men should be allowed to get behind the wheels of their cars—let alone govern the state of California or the country.

ADVENTURES ON THE CAMPAIGN TRAIL

DIARY OF A SEVEN-WEEK-CANDIDATE

In case you haven't heard, I ran for governor of California in 2003. In case you haven't heard, I didn't win. But during the seven weeks I was a candidate, I did learn a hell of a lot—both about myself and about what it's going to take to fix our broken political system. My experience as a candidate was inspiring and frustrating, exciting and exhausting, fun and funny, maddening and surreal. When people ask me if it was worth it, I answer unequivocally "Yes." When people ask me if I would ever do it again, I answer unequivocally "maybe."

To give you some small sense of the recall as I experienced it—frantic, fractured, and, at times, bizarre—I have chosen a few resonant vignettes from the campaign trail.

THE RUBICON

In the weeks leading up to my crossing the Rubicon and entering the recall race, my friends were all drawing up lists of "pros" and "cons." The momentum seemed to shift on an hourly basis. There were days when at 10 AM I was absolutely, 1,000 percent sure I would never, ever do anything as crazy as run for governor; and by 11:15 I was absolutely convinced that nothing short of a runaway Hummer would stop me.

Hoping to avoid a serious case of mental whiplash, I decided to seek a very wise man's advice and gave Bill Moyers a call. "Whatever you do," Moyers told me, "don't do a cost/benefit analysis of the situation. Follow your heart, not your fears."

American progressives have traditionally been pushed to the fringe of the political spectrum, forced to "run to the middle" or hold their noses and half-heartedly support the lesser of two evils. All of a sudden, here was an opportunity for an all-out progressive run at the statehouse of the world's sixth-largest economy.

At the same time, a group of social activists in Northern California, led by Van Jones, who runs the Ella Baker Center for Human Rights, was trying to convince me to—in the words of the website they created—RunAriannaRun. Dot-com.

By the time I had decided to run, everyone—including former L.A. mayor and Schwarzenegger confidant Dick Riordan—was convinced that Arnold wouldn't. Indeed, in the middle of the campaign, I was sitting next to Riordan at a dinner party and he told me that he had received a "courtesy" call from Schwarzenegger at 11 AM on the day he announced, during which Arnold told his longtime pal he wouldn't be running. All the better to eat you with, my dear.

Then came the *Tonight Show* and Arnold's announcement, and I suddenly found myself in the middle of the Perfect Media Storm: The Battle of the Accents. The Hybrid vs. the Hummer.

But I also knew that even with all the free press, it wouldn't be enough. In a state the size of California, 770 miles long with 35 million people, it would take money—lots and lots of money for lots and lots of ads—to get my message out to the public. Those in the know told me it would cost a minimum of $10 million to do it right.

A daunting prospect to say the least. Little did I know just how daunting. Especially once, the day after I announced, a Democrat—Lieutenant Governor Cruz Bustamante—broke ranks and entered the race. Ninety-nine percent—99.9% really—of traditional Democratic money immediately dried up.

So I was left with the generosity of a few good friends and a great Internet-based fund-raising effort that led to my campaign having more individual donors than the other four main candidates combined.

I have been writing about the corrupting influence of money in politics for a long time. But now that I've seen it up close, I can tell you—it's much, much worse than I thought. I absolutely hated having to raise money. The begging, the cajoling, the schmoozing—and that was just my fund-raising team trying to get me to "work the phones." The need to dial for dollars is one of the most dehumanizing aspects of being a candidate. But it becomes an obsession. The Moby Dick of running for office. Even though you know it's wrong, you find yourself habitually checking your daily take. Your running total becomes the perverted bellwether of your success as a candidate.

It's fund-raise or perish. Or, at least, fund-raise or forget about buying TV time—and then perish. The biggest problem with this money chase, however, is how it takes you away from dealing with the people you want to connect with—average voters. Instead of going where the need is, our leaders spend most of their time going where the money is.

Consider: less than one-tenth of one percent of the U.S. population donated 83 percent of all campaign contributions over $200 in the 2002 elections. And there is a stark and telling disparity between those who bankroll political campaigns and the general population. While a third of Americans are people of color, nearly ninety percent of the over $2 billion donated by individuals in the last two elections came from predominantly white neighborhoods.

Talk about not getting the full picture.

That's why I announced my decision to run at A Place Called Home, a center for at-risk children—whose board I've been on for nine years—located in a gang-ridden part of South Los Angeles. And it's why, whenever possible, I held campaign events at places where the media don't normally go.

So I made speeches at an under-funded public school in Oakland, at a fund-raising dinner to buy textbooks for elementary school kids, and in an African-American neighborhood in San Francisco polluted by the noxious fumes of a nearby power plant. I believed I was calling attention to important issues, but the time spent raising consciousness was time away from raising money. I couldn't very well have asked those parents to pay for television advertising when their kids needed schoolbooks.

The recall campaign can serve as a cautionary tale of many things—but above all of the soul-destroying nature of modern, money-driven campaigns. Between Gray, Cruz, and Arnold, it was the Rise of the Fund-raising Machines.

And at the national level, where Bush is breaking every money-raising record in sight, we are facing the prospect of having only two kinds of candidates in the future: those completely beholden to special interests or mega-rich millionaires willing to buy their way into office.

Of course, with Arnold Schwarzenegger, we got both.

"ARNOLD ON LINE FOUR"

The day after Arnold and I each announced our candidacy, I was sitting in the office of my campaign strategist, Bill Zimmerman. Bill is a laconic, hardened veteran of progressive campaigns including Gary Hart's 1984 run for president and the battle to pass California's Proposition 36, a major victory in the war against the drug war.

In the midst of a brainstorming session with my team, Bill's assistant interrupted us with the unexpected news that Arnold Schwarzenegger was on the phone for me. Arnold and I had known each other socially ever since he had campaigned for my ex-husband Michael in his unsuccessful run for the Senate in 1994. I met Maria at the same time, when I was the political wife and she spent a few days following me on the campaign trail for a piece she was doing for *Dateline.*

I had always liked Arnold and Maria and had particularly admired what a great mother Maria is. She had given me some very effective parenting advice when, one Christmas over lunch in Sun Valley, she said, "Turn off the phone between the time the kids are back from school and the time dinner is over. Just be with them, undistracted." This echoed the advice of my late mother; she had once gotten really angry with me when she saw me opening my mail while talking to my daughters. My mother, like Maria, knew that multitasking is inimical to mothering.

Over the phone line, Arnold was his usual affable self. "I watched your announcement on CNN," he told me. "It was really good. I liked what you said." I wasn't too surprised by this, since a few hours after I had announced, he had made his surprise announcement on Jay Leno's show and said very similar things. I had railed against special interests; Arnold had too. I had said I would clean house in Sacramento; so had Arnold. I asserted my outsider status and promised to take on politics as usual; so did Arnold. I said it all with a thick accent. So did Arnold. If you had just heard the sound-bites, you would've thought we were running mates rather than ideological opposites.

Populist rhetoric can be a tricky thing: it's often used to disguise more than it reveals. It's all in how you fill in the blanks. Astonishingly, Arnold would be allowed to campaign for the next eight weeks without ever filling in those blanks. And only rarely being asked to.

During the course of our friendly conversation it was easy to see why so many people like Arnold.

At one point he mentioned my ex-husband, who, after toying with the idea of entering the recall race, had released a statement that morning backing Arnold. "So," I joked, "should I be expecting Maria's endorsement anytime soon?"

He laughed. "Don't count on it."

It was all very charming—a charm that over the course of the campaign made it so much easier for Arnold to construct and perpetuate his populist masquerade. Like a squid that squirts ink to evade pursuers, Arnold oozes charm to evade scrutiny. And it works.

THE WORST DAY OF MY CAMPAIGN

Just five days after officially filing my candidacy papers, I woke up to a front-page story in the *Los Angeles Times* headlined "Huffington Paid Little Income Tax." Anyone who tells you that there is no such thing as bad publicity has never run for office.

Given the adversarial tone of my conversations the day before with the reporters who wrote the story, I was not surprised at the slam. After spending a day examining my tax returns (which I voluntarily made public), the reporters had called me on my cell phone as I was walking through the airport in San Francisco to board a flight back to L.A.

Again and again I had repeated the simple facts:

- As a writer, my income is cyclical. There are years where I spend money on writing and research, and years when the income comes in, when the investment made in a lean year pays off in a fatter one. In the years in question I had not made a profit as a writer and thus my expenses exceeded my income.
- The majority of my business expenses went to salaries—salaries on which both my employees and I paid payroll taxes.
- My deductions were so conservative I didn't even deduct the cost of my home office although that is where I do all of my work.
- I had, in fact, paid $98,042 in property taxes and $44,216 in employer payroll taxes in the two years in question.
- I had given almost a quarter of my income to charity.

Contrary to public speculation, I hadn't received an enormous divorce settlement. I got a beautiful home and receive a large monthly child-support payment on which my ex-husband has already paid the taxes, so they don't appear on my tax returns.

But that morning there was little time to go into these details or fume about the injustice of it all. As is almost always the story on campaigns (and especially one as compressed as the recall race), another deadline was looming just ahead. In this case it was a press conference my campaign had scheduled for that morning to call attention to a meeting that had taken place in the midst of California's energy crisis between Arnold Schwarzenegger and "Kenny Boy" Lay. I planned to lay out a point-by-point argument making the connection between Arnold, his good friends in the White House, and the way the Bush administration's policies had negatively impacted the people of California.

Things didn't exactly go according to plan.

Instead of talking about Lay, Bush, and the energy crisis, I found myself facing a barrage of questions about my taxes. It was a wild scene, as dozens of reporters and camera crews closed in around me.

The truth is, I was never able to fully put the trumped-up tax story behind me. The narrative had been set. I had railed against corporations using tax shelters not to pay their fair share of taxes, and mine was seen as another case of hypocrisy. The fact that I actually had no profits to pay income taxes on during those two years, and that I had paid almost a hundred and fifty thousand dollars in other taxes, did not fit the narrative. So it was mostly excluded from the news stories. Political reality obeys its own rules, I discovered. And truth is subservient to it. This was the hardest lesson I learned, but in many ways the most significant. It was an "Aha!" moment when I started thinking about November 2004. I knew without any reservation that it would not be enough to keep pointing out the truth, however effectively, about Bush's statements and Bush's policies. We had to change the narrative.

If I were an average voter who read the original tax story I'd have been ticked off at me, too. But I'd have been even more ticked off when I found out that, in fact, there had been no loopholes and no taxable income. But when it comes to a juicy story that fits the story line, a little thing like the truth cannot be allowed to get in the way.

THE BEST DAY OF MY CAMPAIGN

Fortunately, bad days on the campaign trail were few and far between. My greatest source of inspiration and the foundation for the optimism of this book came during the week I spent touring college campuses up and down the state of California in my environmentally friendly, biodiesel bus, nicknamed the Independent Streak.

The very best of these best days was, somewhat ironically, September 11, 2003. First stop: the auditorium at Sacramento City College. The 1,200-seat hall was filled to standing room only. Campaign volunteers mingled with the buzzing crowd, handing out bumper stickers, buttons, and campaign materials and—most importantly—registering dozens of new voters. The atmosphere was electric—not all that surprising when you consider that California's community colleges have the most politically active student bodies in the country.

I started my presentation with a moment of silence in recognition of the second anniversary of the 9/11 attacks, and then called on the crowd to renew the values and spirit— the incredible sense of unity and community—that had come to the fore that day and which our leaders subsequently squandered. I then took the opportunity to lambaste the Bush administration, which a few days before had requested an additional $87 billion to fight the war in Iraq: "That $87 billion is more than it would take to balance the budget of all fifty states. And it's more than the money the president is earmarking next year for Homeland Security and the State Department combined. I don't know about you, but I certainly don't feel more safe and secure knowing that we are spending more in Iraq than on protecting us here at home."

After my speech, I spent time talking with the students. I remember a sophomore passionately telling me about his friend who was not able to stay in college because of the fee increases. He railed against the injustice of community college fees increasing over 60 percent while prison guards were getting pay raises. "If we had given Gray Davis $3 million the way the prison guards did, you know that wouldn't have happened," he said. "That's what's wrong with politics. And that's what we've got to fix." I knew that he and his fellow students were the key to doing just that. Mingling with them and experiencing their energy and enthusiasm, it was easy to believe that as long as they stayed involved, we would fix what's wrong with our democracy.

Then it was back on the bus, headed for Berkeley. We arrived forty-five minutes ahead of schedule. My campaign staff urged me to use the downtime to make fund-raising calls, but I wasn't in a masochistic mood, so off we went around town. At one point we came upon a store that had the feeling of a farmer's market, where we shopped, talked, and sampled the wares. Picking out figs, purple grapes, and blueberries—all beautifully laid out like a still life—I felt as if I were back in Greece. As we came out, laden with all our fruit, an elderly woman shouted from across the street: "Give 'em hell, and go in peace!"

We eventually made our way to the Berkeley campus for a rally held in the blazing sun at Sproul Plaza—epicenter of the '60s Free Speech Movement—followed by a Q&A session with graduate students at the school's Institute for Government Studies.

As they had been at every stop on my college tour, the students were bursting with insights and enthusiasm. It was heartening to see how committed, engaged, and passionate about the issues they were, and how involved in a whole host of social causes—from the war in Iraq to international sweatshops to living wage initiatives to homelessness to the environment.

Over the course of the tour, one thing became abundantly clear: America's young people haven't stopped caring about the world they live in, but many of them have stopped believing that politics is the way to make a difference on the issues they care about. If our democracy is to last for another 228 years, we're going to have to change that perception.

Back on the bus that evening we ate, drank, and sang our way across the Bay Bridge as the sun dipped below the San Francisco skyline, bathing the bay in warm autumn light.

At that moment, as far as I was concerned, the campaign could go on forever.

"I'M A WOMAN, PLEASE HEAR ME ROAR"

The one thing I had not anticipated when I decided to run for Governor was that being a woman would have any significance in the campaign. The reason may be that I have been very lucky in my life and career personally not to have encountered any discrimination. I've never had any problem speaking out, and therefore I'd reached the conclusion that, in this day and age, speaking out was not an issue for women. Although I make my living observing the world as it really is, I can be as guilty of wishful thinking as anyone.

For better and for worse, I was definitely disabused of these notions during my short career as a gubernatorial candidate. Let's start with the better. At the end of each of our four debates, I would be inundated with e-mails, mostly from young women, thanking me for "speaking out." The main theme was: "Watching you take on the men in the debates was empowering . . . It helped me be less afraid to use my voice . . ." At about the same time, there was formal validation of this feeling in a survey of Ivy League colleges where women expressed their concerns about standing out intellectually, and how this would affect the way men saw them. Views that one might suppose had vanished at some point during the second term of Dwight Eisenhower.

At the end of the one debate with Arnold Schwarzenegger, the reaction was particularly intense. As soon as I came off the stage, I was surrounded by dozens of young female students who thanked me for taking a stand and not backing down. I was moved by the gratitude—but also stunned by it. I certainly didn't think I deserved any special thanks for speaking my mind. Nor did I think that young women in 2003 still needed role models in order to have the courage to find their own voices. And it wasn't just young women. There were older women, even very successful women, who got in touch with me. There was one e-mail that especially sticks in my mind: "That debate brought back to me all the memories of being the only woman around the boardroom table, being endlessly condescended to by the men."

Oh, yes, I forgot about the condescension. "Yes, Arianna. Yes, Arianna," was Cruz Bustamante's refrain, sounding weary and bored, barely tolerating a typical nagging female.

It was the equivalent of "take two Midol and you'll feel better in the morning." Arnold's version was to suggest that I drink more decaf, a comment that is hard to imagine being addressed to a man. As Marlo Thomas once said, "A man has to be Joe McCarthy to be called ruthless. All a woman has to do is put you on hold."

I remember an exhibition at the Folger Shakespeare Library in 1997 on Shakespeare's "Unruly Women." There were many. Portia in *The Merchant of Venice* took on the legal world in Venice. Beatrice in *Much Ado About Nothing*, and Rosalind in *As You Like It* would have definitely been invited today to make the switch to decaf. After all, unruly women ruffled feathers and rattled cages just by having the guts to take on the big boys.

It's hard to challenge prevailing orthodoxies and be sweet and adorable at the same time, but while a man who doesn't toe the line can be seen as an appealing rogue, a woman is far more likely to be seen as a ball-busting bitch.

IN 2004, IT'S REALLY NOT EASY
BEING GREEN

I love the Greens. And it's impossible not to love Peter Camejo, the Green Party candidate for governor in the California recall election: he's bright, sensitive, passionate, and unwavering in his commitment to economic and social justice.

Back in 2000, the Greens and I agreed that stopping Bush was less important than changing the system. We also shared the belief that the Democrats had effectively become the Republican-lite Party as they veered ever further away from Democratic principles in search of money and votes. Indeed, I was as disgusted by this lemming-like approach to politics as Peter and Ralph Nader were. But by 2003, I had become convinced that Bush's reelection posed an imminent threat that had to take precedence over all other considerations.

The fundamental difference is that, both in 2000 and during the recall, Peter and the Green Party were thinking in the long term, which is, generally speaking, a smart idea. Reform always takes longer than reformers want it to and, as Peter kept reminding me during the campaign, the Greens are still in the process of building a party.

But in 2004 I have to ask Greens everywhere to ask themselves if modest gains in building party infrastructure can really offset major losses in areas of core concern to most Green Party members: the environment, social equality, criminal justice, and civil rights. The fact is that having someone in the White House who sees the value of instituting electoral reforms like instant run-off voting will open up the system and dramatically improve the prospect of smaller political parties. And that someone ain't going to be George Bush. The urgent must now take precedence over the important—as well as over making mountains out of molehills.

Let me explain what I am talking about. Backstage before the first debate of the campaign, in Walnut Creek, just outside of San Francisco, moving between talk-show style dressing rooms, it was hugs and kisses all around—even with the Republicans in the race. At one point, I got caught in a Peter sandwich, wedged between Peter Camejo and the other Peter in the race, Peter Ueberroth. I had gotten to know both Ueberroth and Tom McClintock in my Republican incarnation and I like them both, even if the list of things we agree on could fit on the head of a pin, with room left over for

It's all well and good to dream about how wonderful it would be to remodel your home, but when your house is going up in flames, your first priority must be putting the fire out. Our collective priority for the near term must be to evict the Crawford squatter from the White House. Only then can we set about remodeling our democratic home. We simply can't do it in reverse.

"The Lord's Prayer." As for Cruz Bustamante, he was down-right cuddly.

Out front it was a different story. In particular, Cruz and I crossed swords early and often.

At one point, one of the journalists on the debate panel asked me if I was worried that I might become a spoiler in the race. As an answer, I turned to the lieutenant governor and asked him if he stayed awake at night worrying that he might "spoil" California's chance to have a truly progressive governor.

"Cruz, please," I mock-pleaded. "Do not be the Ralph Nader of 2003!"

It was a throwaway line that got a laugh.

So imagine my surprise when, five days later, I received a letter signed by a quartet of high-ranking Green Party officials asking me to apologize for having "referred to the Green Party presidential candidate from 2000, Ralph Nader, in a disparaging manner."

I immediately called Peter to ask if the Frowning Foursome were joking. They weren't. Peter was upset, too. I could not believe it. Here we were, a pair of progressive allies struggling to compete with a slew of exponentially better-funded opponents, and the Greens were getting huffy about a Nader joke—one that wasn't even a slam on their guy?

I wrote back to the Greens, explaining that "my jibe to Cruz Bustamante, cautioning him 'not to be the Nader of 2003' was clearly a satiric comment designed to publicly castigate Democrats using the specter of 'spoilerism' as a cudgel with which to undercut those who challenge the two-party system and fight for the right of alternative political voices to be heard."

But the damage had been done. Believe it or not, my relationship with Peter Camejo never fully recovered from my having implied—even satirically—that Ralph Nader could ever be considered (gasp!) a spoiler.

CRUZ BUSTAMANTE, MATCHMAKER

I had just finished giving a speech in front of a group of business people committed to social responsibility (calling themselves, appropriately enough, Business for Social Responsibility) when my cell phone rang. It was my office calling to let me know that Cruz Bustamante had called twice and was very anxious to speak to me.

It was three weeks after the recall election. The last time I had spoken to the lieutenant governor was backstage after one of the final debates—a perfunctory "good luck" exchanged as we passed each other on our way out the door. My curiosity was piqued. I told my office to have him call me on my cell. A minute later the phone rang.

"Hello, Arianna," said the dulcet baritone voice I had come to know so well over the course of the campaign. "This is Cruz."

"Hi, Cruz," I chirped, wondering what the hell this could be about.

"Arianna, I'm calling about something completely unconnected."

Unconnected to what? I thought to myself, but held my tongue.

He continued, "There is a good friend of mine who watched you on television a lot during the campaign and, well, he would really like to take you out on a date."

"And Cruz, you haven't been able to dissuade him?" I replied.

"Why would I? You're a charming woman."

Really? My mind quickly flashed back to the first debate of the campaign, the one at which I had accused him of engaging in "legalized bribery" and told the audience that he would never keep his promise to impose a tax on cigarettes because of the large contributions he had taken from Big Tobacco. Oh, well, maybe all men are masochists at heart.

Cruz continued his pitch. "My friend is six-four, looks just like Tom Selleck, and is a labor leader."

"Have him give me a call," I said. The next thing I knew (OK, it was actually the next day), a huge bouquet of white tulips arrived at my office—an offering from my prospective date.

Hmm, tall, handsome and chivalrous . . . Then the phone rang. It was him. With visions of *Magnum PI* reruns jogging through my head, I quickly thanked him for the tulips. He then told me that his pal Cruz had surveyed the women in his office to decide which kind of flowers I should be sent. Tulips had beaten out orchids two to one. Damn, I thought, these guys even use focus groups for dating!

Anyway, Cruz, if your day job in politics doesn't pan out, you may have one hell of a future as a matchmaker. Now about my sister . . .

SECTION III

THE FOOLS

SHEEP IN SHEEP'S CLOTHING

"I a little bit disagree with Chairman Roberts on that." That was Senator Jay Rockefeller, the senior Democrat on the Senate Intelligence Committee, on May 25, 2003, kinda, sorta, uh, not really taking exception to Committee Chairman Pat Roberts's assertion that we had turned the corner when it comes to keeping the peace in postwar Iraq. But it could just as easily serve as the motto for the whole Democratic Party: "Vote for us—we kinda, sorta disagree." The party leaders have been so timid, spineless, and lacking in confidence that to compare them to jellyfish would be an insult to invertebrates.

Call them the pusillanimous opposition.

These dithering poltroons have been so paralyzed by the fear of doing or saying something that could be turned against them in GOP attack ads that they've rendered themselves impotent when it comes to mounting any kind of challenge to President Bush on the two most important issues of the day: tax cuts and Iraq.

Exhibit A comes from Senate Minority Leader Tom Daschle, who, when asked on *Meet the Press* why the Democrats didn't offer a bold, full-throated alternative to the Bush tax cut plan, including the repeal of the 2001 cuts, timorously explained, "Well, we—you got to take it one step at a time." You do? Why? Is this an AA meeting? Bush doesn't take it one step at a time. He's comfortable leading by leaps and bounds. And he's dragging us along with him—straight over a cliff. We're facing a trillion dollars of new debt, incurred by a president with the worst economic record since Herbert Hoover, and the best the leader of the opposition party can muster is a meaningless cliché? Quick, get that man a dose of political Viagra! At least get the blood flowing *somewhere*.

Flash forward to late last year and the battles over Medicare and the energy bill. Senator Daschle was on *Fox News Sunday* being interviewed by Tony Snow. (Why he even bothered I have no idea.)

Snow: If the [Medicare] bill is as you understand it, would you filibuster it?

Daschle: Too early to say. We want to have a chance, first, to look at it, talk with our caucus, and come up with some plan for our own strategy.

Snow: Energy bill—filibuster or vote?

Daschle: Same way. We haven't seen the language . . . again, we want to take a look at the details. It's a thousand . . . maybe even a sixteen-hundred page bill.

With Daschle trumpeting such an uncertain call of "Charge! Retreat!" it's no wonder that the Democrats lost the battle over Medicare. They won the battle over the energy bill, but hard though it is to believe, Daschle was on the Republican side. Why? Because he added an amendment to increase ethanol requirements, and there are a lot of donations from the corn lobby to be had in his home state of South Dakota. It was the same reason he prevented a vote on expensing stock options in July 2002, shortly after meeting with venture capitalist and big Democratic Party supporter John Doerr.

Daschle was equally confusing—and confused—when it came to the war on Iraq. First he helped draft the Senate's resolution on the use of force. Then, after sticking his finger in the political wind and catching a zephyr of antiwar sentiment, he blasted the president for failing "so miserably at diplomacy that we're now forced to war." When that comment, made the day before the war started, unleashed a torrent of criticism from ever-vigilant Republican attack dogs, Daschle, instead of simply attacking back, hemmed, hawed, and executed another political pirouette, claiming that he "probably would have avoided making the statement" if he'd known we were on the brink of war. But a quick check of the record reveals this to be an utterly disingenuous dodge: word of the impending invasion was all over the media when Daschle opened fire on Bush. Maybe the senator's TV—and his staff—were on the fritz that day.

It is precisely this kind of craven vacillation that has made possible the triumph of the fanatics in the White House. Democrats are wringing their hands over the "tactical genius" of Karl Rove and the "brilliant political stagecraft" of his TV experts, who always present the president in the most flattering way. Such is the Democrats' fragility that the mere smoke and mirrors of posing the president in profile at Mount Rushmore or asking the people standing behind him during a speech on the economy to take off their ties so they look more like average Joes have Daschle *et al.* quaking in their boots. Anyone can look like a political genius in a room full of political nincompoops.

As we've seen with Bush's "Mission Accomplished" land-

The leaders of the Democratic Party have been so timid, spineless, and lacking in confidence that to compare them to jellyfish would be an insult to invertebrates. Call them the pusillanimous opposition.

ing on the *Abraham Lincoln,* the GOP is actually capable of overreaching and self-destructing. But will the Democrats be ready to fill the vacuum? Instead of worrying about the Bushies using the *Top Gun* landing in campaign ads, they should worry about Democratic leaders too afraid to offer an alternative moral vision to the White House fanatics' chilling worldview. If they can't compete on style, they should at least give it a shot on substance. After all, the problem isn't that Democrats are on the wrong side of the issues. It's that they are afraid to make an issue of being on the right side— not to mention smack dab in the middle of the American mainstream.

For example, only one out of four Americans believed the last round of tax cuts would significantly reduce their taxes, and just 29 percent thought the cuts were the best way to help stimulate the economy. Yet Democrats have been congenitally incapable of challenging a president whose domestic agenda centers on more and more tax cuts for the wealthy.

On the foreign policy front, the Democrats sat idly by, their thumbs otherwise engaged, while the administration's Iraqi tar baby has grown stickier by the day. And on and on it goes. On the environment, Social Security, greater access to affordable health care, gun control, and abortion, the majority of the American people are with the Democrats. Which makes the Democrats' inability to offer an alternative to the White House juggernaut all the more nauseating. And disgraceful. And tragic.

If this sorry state of affairs is going to change, the Democrats have to jettison their reliance on the consultants who botched the 2002 midterm elections by advising party leaders to avoid taking on the president on tax cuts and Iraq. They must instead offer an unambiguous alternative to Bush's well-crafted image as a straight-shooting man of conviction. It's time for the Democrats to give up their broken play-it-safe politics and risk offending a few vocal members of a radical minority. They seem to have forgotten the old sports adage that sometimes the best defense is a good offense. And it can be achieved without Howard Dean's Iowa animal hooting. So, here's a scoreboard update for Mr. McAuliffe, Mr. Daschle, and all of the Congressional party leadership: you're down by three touchdowns and the electoral clock is running. It's long past time to stop taking things "one step at a time" and start throwing deep.

The Democratic leadership has been in complete denial about this political reality. Remember November 2002? Understanding what happened then, may prevent history from repeating itself in November 2004.

THE 2002 TRAIN WRECK

Election Day 2002 offers a textbook example of what not to do in 2004. If only the Democrats can admit their mistakes. Heading into Election Day 2002, the party leadership had been positively giddy. Democratic National Committee Chair Terry McAuliffe even went so far as to guarantee a win in the Florida governor's race, crowing, "Jeb Bush is gone." In fact, the Republicans got it all in November 2002. They got the House. They got the Senate. And they got a massive boost of political momentum—just as those increasingly unreliable polls were hinting at a leak in the president's high-flying popularity balloon.

McAuliffe had gladly accepted Tim Russert's skeptical challenge to put his money where his mouth was by agreeing to donate $2,000 to charity if his prediction of surefire Senate wins for Walter Mondale and Jean Carnahan didn't pan out. Even as the disastrous results rolled in, McAuliffe refused to admit the obvious. "I think it's going to be a very good night for the Democrats," he told Larry King, moments after CNN had called yet another Senate win for the GOP. A good night perhaps for those Democrats with no television. But no matter. "I think it's going to show that we can win north, south, east and west," McAuliffe McSpun.

In the end, all the Democrats got on election night was a kick in the butt and some good experience at giving concession speeches. The morning after, the parade of ashen-faced Democrats appearing on the morning shows resembled the cast of *Night of the Living Dead*. As they tried to piece together the causes of the previous night's train wreck, they looked everywhere for clues except the one place that held all the answers—the mirror. McAuliffe attributed the shellacking to "the president out there actively campaigning," as if no president had ever thought of hitting the campaign trail before. House Minority Leader Dick Gephardt, who in his twenty-six years in the House came to personify the get-along-by-going-along approach of the political lifer, pointed his tentative finger at an enduring post–9/11 bounce, declaring 9/11 "the big factor in this election." Tom Daschle, the South Dakota Spitfire, agreed: "You had a president who talked a lot about 9/11." I hate to break it to you, boys, but there's going to be a September 11 before the first Tuesday in November for a long time to come. That excuse has a shelf life.

Memo to Tom, Dick, and Terry: The problem wasn't that the president was out there delivering his message. The problem was that you failed to have anyone out there delivering any kind of galvanizing opposing message. And it's not as if there weren't plenty of urgent issues to choose from: the limping economy, the soaring deficit, corporate corruption, an energy plan crafted by the oil industry, the undermining of virtually every regulatory agency, the insanity of Bush's tax cuts. Well, I guess that last one would have been a bit tricky, since twelve Democratic senators sided with Bush to vote for them, including former senators Jean Carnahan and Max Cleland, both of whom also voted yes on the Iraq resolution. Pandering to the president didn't seem to help them much.

To update Clausewitz, politics is war by other means— civil war. The Bush Republicans understand that. And they understand the value of denying weapons of mass distraction to your enemy. A case in point is the administration's masterful handling of the 250 or so pounds of political baggage known as Harvey Pitt. Dark wizard Karl Rove staved off the embattled Securities and Exchange Commission chairman's inevitable stroll to the guillotine until the embarrassing drop of the blade could no longer be used against Bush Republicans—right about cocktail hour on Election Day. It was crude, cold-blooded, and brilliant. Once Pitt became a threat to their security, they simply exchanged him— when the time was right.

The Democrats' historic defeat demanded a bloodletting as ruthless as Pitt's meticulously timed ouster. On Black Wednesday, Gephardt announced that he would not be seeking reelection to his so-called leadership post. He was seeking instead—in vain as it turned out—a promotion to 1600 Pennsylvania Avenue. Twelve-step programs teach us that recovery can only begin after you've bottomed out. If the Democrats are going to bounce back in 2004, they need to stop living in denial and start accepting responsibility for their crash and burn.

OUR FANATICAL AND FOOLISH SOCIETY: THE SYMPTOMS

1. Fewer people voted on Election Day 2002 than watched the World Series (even though it was one of the lowest-rated Series in history).
2. Osama bin Laden is still on the loose.
3. The president still believes an $8 billion a year missile defense shield will protect us from terrorists with box cutters, suitcase nukes, and vials of smallpox.
4. Dick Cheney was able to find a judge—albeit one appointed by the president—to side with him in the General Accounting Office suit that sought information about which energy industry executives met with Cheney's energy task force.
5. The NRA maintained its bullheaded resistance to creating a national database of ballistic "fingerprints," even as the D.C. snipers were randomly gunning down thirteen people.
6. Trent Lott, toastmaster.
7. The Bush administration sued the state of California for requiring that carmakers put more energy-efficient models on the road.
8. The governor of California introduced the country to the Hummer, a metal monstrosity that struggles to cover ten miles for every gallon of gas it burns.
9. How little we have been asked to sacrifice to help win the war on terror.
10. The appalling way the Bush administration played the national security trump card to promote every-

thing from tax cuts to drilling in ANWR to the drug war to subsidies for corporate fat cats.

11. Ken Lay has not even been indicted—let alone spent a day in jail.

12. We have our first MBA president and a CEO cabinet.

13. Tom Ridge's laughably lame color-coded terror warning initiative. It was enough to make us all see red.

14. Before he became the treasury secretary, John Snow was the CEO of a company that, despite close to a billion dollars in profits, paid not a penny in federal taxes for three of the last four years.

15. John Ashcroft felt it necessary to spend $8,000 of tax-payer money on curtains to cover a bare-breasted statue.

16. John Ashcroft's Holy-Roller war against medical marijuana clubs.

17. Prince Bandar of Saudi Arabia, a country that has been holding telethons for suicide bombers, is treated as an honored guest at the president's Crawford ranch.

18. The feds still haven't arrested anyone for the anthrax attacks.

19. In a time of war, sales of gas-guzzling SUVs were up 7 percent in 2003.

20. If an SUV is massive enough, it is entirely exempt from federal fuel economy standards.

21. Before 9/11, more than twice as many FBI agents were assigned to fighting drugs as to fighting terrorism. Even post–9/11, over 2,000 agents are still spending their valuable time fighting a fruitless drug war.

22. The tragic way the FBI failed to see all the red flags leading up to 9/11.

23. Companies avoid paying $70 billion in U.S. taxes a year simply by opening post office boxes in Bermuda.

24 Dick Cheney's serial use of offshore tax shelters while running Halliburton.

25. The White House's desperate and ongoing attempt to link Saddam Hussein and Al Qaeda.

26. The uproar that ensued in conservative circles after Colin Powell endorsed condom use as an anti-AIDS measure.

27. The number of personal bankruptcies in the United States continues to rise each year. It soared to a record 1.6 million in 2003 from 1.47 million in 2001.

INVASION OF THE POST-ELECTION BODY SNATCHERS

There was one change following the Democratic debacle. Dick Gephardt was succeeded by Nancy Pelosi as House minority leader. Pelosi's first Sunday morning TV appearance following her election was not reassuring. She was appearing on *Meet the Press,* but it might as well have been the Sci-Fi Channel. The woman answering Tim Russert's questions might have looked like Pelosi, but she sounded like a character from *Invasion of the Body Snatchers.* What had happened to the congresswoman from California? Gone was the bold, combative, impassioned politician we'd come to know over her fifteen years in the House. In her place was a soulless pod person—mouthing the kind of inoffensive, focus-group-tested, and cringe-inducing platitudes that have driven two-thirds of the American electorate away from politics and more than half of the remaining voters away from the Democratic Party. I couldn't help but wonder: had Head Pod Terry McAuliffe given her a whiff of some life-sucking spores?

How else to explain, for example, Pelosi's mealy-mouthed response to the all-important question of war with Iraq? The only member of the Democratic leadership courageous enough to vote against the president's use-of-force resolution, she had been unequivocal in her opposition to the war. "I have not seen," she said in September 2002 following a White House meeting with President Bush, "intelligence to justify the action that the president is suggesting." Turns out, she was right. But there she was, just seventy-two hours after her historic ascendance to her new post, vowing to back the president—even if he decided to attack Iraq unilaterally and without UN approval. "If our young people are called to duty," she said, "certainly we'll support the action of the president."

I had to turn up the volume on my TV set to make sure I was hearing her right. Sure enough, Pelosi was coming out foursquare in favor of backing our fighting men and women, having conveniently skipped right over the question of whether they should be put on the front lines in the first place. When Russert asked her to reconcile this stance with her previous opposition, she dismissed him with a curt, "That's neither here nor there now. Let's put that aside." And so they did. Even when the specter of Pelosi's former self appeared and suggested, "I do think that we can raise some questions before sending [our troops] into harm's way," she still refused actually to raise even a single one. Who, if not one of the heads of the opposition party, is going to raise these questions? Paul Wolfowitz perhaps? Isn't asking hard questions about why they're being called to lay down their lives the ultimate way of "supporting our troops"?

Pelosi was similarly compliant when it came to the president's handling of the war on terrorism. She gave the president two thumbs up in November 2002, contending that when it comes to combating terror, Americans "are in better shape now than we were last year."

Pelosi even tried to put a positive spin on the fact that Osama bin Laden is still on the loose, making the startling claim that the Al Qaeda mastermind isn't really "such an essential piece" of the war on terrorism. And John Muhammad was only tangentially involved with the sniper attacks, I suppose. So we had reason enough to bomb Iraq into the Stone Age, but Osama isn't worth losing sleep over?

To hear Pelosi tell it, leadership is all about finding the political middle—the elusive m-spot. "We must seek our common ground with the administration," she told Russert. And I lost count of the number of times she used the word "consensus" during her appearance. In truth, the last thing the Democrats need right now is a call to compromise. Do they think Dick Gephardt, who finally sank below the Iowa cornstalks, failed because he didn't seek enough consensus?

"She has got her beliefs," Pelosi's communications director, Brendan Daly, helpfully explained. "But we are here to win, and she understands that to do that you need to be in the middle." What was sad about this comment and the *Meet the Press* performance is that Pelosi, throughout her career, has been the exact opposite of a soulless, middle-of-the-road "leader." But the go-along-to-get-along mentality is the Democrats'

Achilles' heel. The minute they are given a chance to lead, all they want to do is follow the pack. Or worse, throw themselves on their own swords, as they did in the recall of California's governor in 2003.

THE FOOLS FACE A STACKED DECK IN CALIFORNIA

As the battle for California took shape, those opposing the recall faced a vexing dilemma: how best to deal with the unique nature of the recall ballot, which asked voters to make two decisions.

1) Shall Gray Davis be recalled (removed) from the office of governor?
2) Who should succeed Gray Davis if he is recalled?

The first half of the equation was easy for recall opponents: no. But what about part two? Should the Democratic Party offer up a fallback candidate "just in case" voters gave Davis the boot? Or would doing so weaken the already vulnerable governor? On the other hand, was gambling everything on Davis's political resurrection the ultimate sucker's bet?

The choice made by the Democratic leadership in Washington, Sacramento, and Hollywood is a perfect illustration of the foolishness that has dominated the party at the highest levels and enabled Bush to govern without real opposition.

STAND BY YOUR FOOL

I was in Ireland with my daughters, eating way too much homemade treacle pudding, when I read about the press conference in San Francisco at which Terry McAuliffe and Nancy Pelosi, standing shoulder to shoulder with Gray Davis, laid out the Democratic strategy to defend against the recall: they were going to stand by their man, consequences—and the people of California—be damned.

Pledging undying fealty and determination to defeat the right-wing recall power grab, McAuliffe summoned up visions of Florida when he said, "Once again, the Republicans are trying to steal an election from the Democrats." Pelosi stayed on message, agreeing that the recall was "part of a national Republican agenda to achieve what they cannot win at the polls." That should have been the beginning of the analysis, not the end of it. Yes, the recall had started as a right-wing power grab. But what the Democrats steadfastly refused to understand was that the recall had tapped into the mother lode of populist anger and frustration. Gray Davis had become a symbol of our broken political system. In endless conversations with my Democratic friends in Los Angeles, they could not get past their myopic obsession with the fact that Darryl Issa bought the recall. "What if the recall actually succeeds and there is no progressive alternative on offer in the second half of the ballot?" I asked an old friend with a long and admirable history of involvement in Democratic politics. "Well then, the Republicans will take over the state. Let them deal with the mess," he replied nonchalantly.

I was stunned. This was a man with a deep social conscience

who was nevertheless willing to countenance all that a Republican takeover would entail: more deregulation, more cuts to vital social programs, more pain for the millions already living on the edge. The term "party line" is often used as a metaphor but, in this case, the line was an impenetrable wall built not of conviction but of fiat.

The collective delusion of the liberal set was reinforced at dinner parties in Georgetown, Brentwood, and the Hamptons. At a *Fortune* magazine conference in Aspen at the end of July, however, I detected a glimmer of hope. Bill Clinton, answering a question from an audience member, mistakenly explained that anyone who voted no on the recall could not then cast a vote on the second part of the ballot—betraying a confusion which I thought might explain the Democrats' decision to eschew a second ballot strategy. "Oh," I thought, "maybe they don't realize how the rules of the recall work." So I explained them. "Really?" the former president responded.

I returned to California thinking that the Democrats' suicidal "Davis or bust" strategy would be radically revised after a call from Clinton to McAuliffe and a few other party bigwigs.

Instead, three days before the filing deadline, Lieutenant Governor Cruz Bustamante—the Democrat least likely to succeed against Arnold—broke ranks and declared himself a candidate. The original foolish strategy had now taken a new—and disastrous—turn. Bustamante would quickly emerge as another special-interest candidate, a wholly owned subsidiary of the state's Indian gaming interests. Compared to Davis and Bustamante, the two Democratic dogs in the fight, Arnold appeared even more appealing—a breath of fresh air and an agent of change.

GRAY DAVIS: THE DEMOCRATS CHOOSE DECISIVE INACTION

It should have been obvious to anyone that Gray Davis was so vulnerable that an offensive strategy was an immediate necessity. But in a defining moment of political foolishness, the Democratic establishment refused to face reality and simply and desperately circled the wagons to make a last-ditch stand in defense of Davis. It was the most heartbreaking and wasteful act since the Charge of the Light Brigade.

Stuck in the foolish paradigm of reaction over action, the Democratic leaders poutingly pledged to sit this one out. If we can't have Davis, we won't have anyone! That'll show 'em! Dianne Feinstein, Barbara Boxer, and Loretta Sanchez all passed. Ignoring the facts on the ground, and holding party loyalty above public service, the best the official wing of the party could come up with was a quasi-comical show of support: a succession of awkward campaign trail grip-and-grins between Davis and party stalwarts like Bill Clinton, Jesse Jackson, Al Gore, and the six major candidates then in the race to carry the Democrats' tattered flag in 2004. All nine candidates signed a letter opposing the recall while Gore recorded a telephone message that was played twice to a million voters one day before the election. Still, on October 7, 2003, all the king's horses and all the king's men couldn't put Humpty Davis together again.

Somehow the Democratic Party faithful were unable to hold two thoughts in their heads at the same time: being against the recall on democratic principle and recognizing that anger against Davis and the politics as usual that he represented were so palpable that the recall was more than likely to succeed.

This refusal to face reality has not only cost Democrats the governorship of California, it has brought pain to hundreds of thousands of Californians who are losing health care coverage and the opportunity to go to college because of the governor's budget cuts.

THE TRIVIAL PURSUIT OF THE WHITE HOUSE 2004

1. What is the relationship between George Bush's grandmother and Howard Dean's grandmother?

    A. They were briefly married to one another during a drunken weekend in Las Vegas.
    B. Bush's grandmother was a bridesmaid at Dean's grandmother's wedding.
    C. They were both condemned to die at the Salem witch trials.

(Answer: B. However, there is no truth to the rumor that either of them ever made an embarrassing videotape with Paris Hilton's grandmother.)

2. John Kerry's wife, Teresa Heinz Kerry, made which of the following lists in 2002?

    A. *People*'s 50 Most Beautiful People.
    B. *Forbes*' 400 Richest Americans.
    C. Mr. Blackwell's Worst Dressed List.
    D. *Roll Call*'s 10 Hottest Senate Wives.

(Answer: B. Mrs. Kerry is one of the heirs to the Heinz ketchup fortune and her net worth is estimated at $550 million.)

3. In the year 2000, which "honor" was bestowed on John Edwards?

   A. The Golden Globe for "Best Hair in a Political Performance."

   B. "Most likely to succeed" by his high school senior class.

   C. *People* Magazine's "Sexiest Politician."

   D. Soul Train's "Whitest Politician," tied with Dick Gephardt.

(Answer: C. Edwards was especially impressive during the swimsuit portion of the competition.)

4. Which of the following is NOT one of the *muy macho* alpha-male activities John Kerry is fond of?

   A. Piloting his own Cessna.

   B. Playing in pickup hockey games.

   C. Running with the bulls in Pamplona.

   D. Clearing brush from his property in a golf cart.

   E. Windsurfing.

   F. Kitesurfing.

   G. Shooting ducks with Justice Scalia on a game farm.

(Answer: G. That is one of Dick Cheney's alpha-male activities.)

5. In May 2001 the Bush administration gave $43 million to

   A. The Supreme Court as a thank-you gift.

   B. Monica Lewinsky as a thank-you gift.

   C. The Taliban, to suppress opium production.

D. CBS, to make a flattering TV biography of Ronald Reagan.

(Answer: C. In the White House's defense, though, they probably didn't realize the Taliban was also going to use the money to oppress women, buy illegal arms from the Chinese, and organize terrorist attacks on innocent civilians.)

6. Earlier in his life, General Wesley Clark had a cocker spaniel. What was the dog's name?

A. Kosovo.
B. Four Stars.
C. Veep.
D. Muffin.

(Answer: D.)

7. George Bush has never attended:

A. A cabinet meeting.
B. A funeral or memorial service for a soldier killed in Iraq.
C. A St. Patrick's Day Parade . . . sober.
D. A movie that didn't have explosions, car chases, and naked boobies.

(Answer: B.)

8. What did George W. Bush do for twenty-eight consecutive days in August of 2001?

A. Go on vacation.
B. Listen to Laura say, "George, it's *nu-klee-ur*, not *newk-u-lar.*"

   C. Run the country while Dick Cheney went on vacation.

   D. Nothing.

(Answer: A. Bush's August vacation was the second-longest in U.S. presidential history. The longest vacation was taken by Gerald Ford. It lasted two years.)

9. Finish this oft-repeated line from Howard Dean: "The flag of the United States doesn't belong to John Ashcroft and Rush Limbaugh and Jerry Falwell anymore,

   A. it belongs to anyone who wants to buy one at the local gun and liquor shop."

   B. it also belongs to presidential hopefuls, country singers, and anyone with a glitzy show in Las Vegas."

   C. it belongs to all of us."

   D. it belongs to anyone who can afford a $400 per hour lobbyist.

(Answer: C.)

10. What historical distinction does George Bush's sixteen-member cabinet hold?

   A. Each of them voted to support the war—the War of 1812.

   B. They are the wealthiest in history.

   C. They are the group of people most Americans would vote off first on *Survivor*.

D. In a beach contest, none of them would win the
swimsuit competition.

(Answer: B. The average net worth of Bush's cabinet
members is $10.9 million. By contrast, the net worth of
the average American family is just $71,600.)

11.   As governor of Texas, George W. Bush did what
152 times?

A. Used the phrase "Can I git s'more gravy?"
B. Accidentally walked into the ladies' room while
it was occupied.
C. Executed someone on death row.

(Answer: C. George W. Bush has the distinction of pre-
siding over the most executions of any governor in U.S.
history.)

12.   How many people who raised $100,000 for George
W. Bush's 2000 election campaign have since been
given government posts?

A. 31.
B. 41.
C. 51.
D. 61.

(Answer: D. Some would call this "just a coincidence";
others might call it "returning a favor" or "remember-
ing what side your bread is buttered on.")

13. George W. Bush owns 250 autographed

   A. Shot glasses.
   B. Baseballs.
   C. Photos of Elvis.
   D. WMD.

(Answer: B. Bush says the baseballs remind him of when he was a kid and he and his dad played football together.)

14. What did George W. Bush do moments before he signed the historic Treaty of Moscow with Vladimir Putin in 2002?

   A. Told Putin, "C'mon, pull my finger."
   B. Spit a wad of gum into his hand.
   C. Said to Putin, "G'head, turn the pen upside down, her clothes come off (*hee-hee-hee*)."

(Answer: B. I have to assume Bush spit out the gum because he can't chew and sign his name at the same time.)

15. While appearing on the *Late Show with David Letterman* in 2000, what did George W. Bush use to surreptitiously clean his glasses during a commercial break?

   A. A snotty tissue from his own pocket.
   B. Dave's tie.
   C. The jacket of Dave's producer as she bent over to give the host notes.
   D. The Top 10 List.

(Answer: C.)

16. While a student at Yale, Howard Dean took the classes History of the Soviet Union, Marxist Existentialism, Reason and Revolution, and Marxist Theory. Given this, a devious right-wing political operative might wrongly suggest what?

 A. "Dean's unfit for the presidency because he's secretly an anti-establishment radical."
 B. "Howard Dean got a broad-based liberal arts education."
 C. "Howard Dean is a closet sixties-era pinko liberal."
 D. "Howard Dean doesn't have the same values as ordinary Americans."

(Answer: A, C, and D. It should be noted that Dean also took the class President and Bureaucracy, among many others.)

17. In the October 2, 2003, *New Orleans Times-Picayune* obituary of eighty-one-year-old Gertrude Jones from Lebanon, Kentucky, where did family members say memorial gifts should be donated?

 A. "To a homeless shelter in the area."
 B. "To any organization that seeks the removal of President George Bush from office."
 C. "To her grandchildren's college fund."

(Answer: B. And if you would like to donate to an organization working to remove President Bush, you can contribute online at MoveOn.org.)

18. Barbara Bush once referred to her son the president as

    A. "Gayer than Liberace."
    B. "Drunk as a skunk."
    C. "Dumb as a fox."
    D. "Smart as a box of hammers."

(Answer: C.)

19. On two consecutive days in the fall of 2003, Senator John Kerry referred to himself as:

    A. "The Chili Man candidate for president" and "The Pancake Man."
    B. "The Hot Dog King" and "Captain Sauerkraut."
    C. "Señor Taco" and "El Burrito Grande por presidente."
    D. "The Lizard King" and "Mr. Mojo Risin'."

(Answer: A. In Kerry's defense, when you run for president, you have to do a lot of culinary pandering.)

20. Which of the following are actual quotes from President Bush?

    A. "The vast majority of Iraqis want to live in a peaceful, free world, and we will find these people and bring them to justice."
    B. "Poor people aren't necessarily killers. Just because you happen not to be rich doesn't mean you're willing to kill."
    C. "These people don't have tanks. They don't have ships. They hide in caves. They send suiciders out."

    D. "Well, I think if you say you're going to do something and don't do it, that's trustworthiness."

    E. "More and more of our imports come from overseas."

    F. "I'm a master of low expectations."

    G. "I promise you I will listen to what has been said here, even though I wasn't here."

(Answer: They are all quotes from President Bush.)

21. Despite growing up in New York City and the Hamptons, in his autobiography Howard Dean says of himself,

    A. "At heart . . . I feel like a citizen of the world."

    B. "At heart . . . I'm a country person."

    C. "At heart . . . I feel like I should say I'm from the country because voters traditionally like 'country boys.'"

    D. "At heart . . . I'm a city boy."

(Answer: B. Dean is a "country person" in the same way that Sean Hannity is a "fair and balanced" journalist.)

DEMOCRATS TUNE VIOLINS;
ROME SMOLDERS

With Terry McAuliffe as their standard bearer at the Democratic National Committee, the Democrats became stuck in a vicious cycle of victimization. They didn't act; they just were against stuff. Their wake-up call had been ringing off the hook for quite a while.

Before he blew himself up in Iowa, Howard Dean lit a long overdue wake-up firecracker under the party. And predictably, as soon as he showed that the way to turn on the electorate was to put an end to the party's endemic foolishness, he came under excoriating "friendly fire" attacks. "Howard Dean has climbed into his own spider hole of denial," sputtered Joe Lieberman after Dean said the capture of Saddam Hussein had not made America safer. The most disgraceful anti-Dean salvo was launched by Americans for Jobs, Health Care & Progressive Values, a shadowy group with ties to Gephardt's campaign, which ran a TV ad featuring a picture of Osama bin Laden and an announcer saying, "There are those who wake up every morning determined to destroy western civilization. Americans want a president who can face the dangers ahead. But Howard Dean has no military or foreign policy experience. And Howard Dean just cannot compete with George Bush on foreign policy."

Someone once said that the difference between Bush Republicans and Democrats is that Bush Republicans know they're right. The scintilla of self-doubt that was once a laudable aspect of the Democratic tradition of open-mindedness had become as burdensome as Sisyphus's boulder.

THE PHANTOM CANDIDATE

Al Gore said when he endorsed Howard Dean, "We need to remake the Democratic Party; we need to remake America; we need to take it back on behalf of the people of this country."

The more Democrats try to present themselves as Bush-lite Republicans, the more people will decide to stick with the original version. It happens in politics, just as it does in soft drinks.

And shortly after he announced his candidacy for president, John Kerry was even more graphic about the need to breathe new life into the Democratic party: "America doesn't need a Democratic Party that says 'yes but less' or 'yes but slower' to Republican policies that take us backward. It doesn't need a Democratic Party that is satisfied with defending our past achievements from Republican attack without also pursuing high ambitions for the future. I say to you: America doesn't need two Republican parties. America needs a Democratic Party resolved to make this nation safer, stronger, and more secure. And you and I are going to build it."

When a reporter asked Hillary Clinton if she, too, agreed that there was a need to remake her party, she tersely replied, "No." More than any primary season in recent Democratic memory, this one had a phantom candidate: Hillary and, by extension, the Clinton legacy. During his campaign Wesley Clark emerged as the candidate possessed by this phantom. Even before he announced, his Arkansas headquarters were swarming with Clinton loyalists including Mickey Kantor and Eli Segal. He was introduced to Hollywood's power brokers by Friends of Bill, Mary Steenburgen and Ted Danson. And he was heralded with a gauzy, seventeen-minute film bio produced by Linda Bloodworth-Thomason, the multimedia poet laureate of the Clinton years, who also produced the short film that introduced the soon-to-be forty-second president to America, "The Man from Hope."

But even as late as January, Steve Bing, the billionaire moviemaker and Wesley Clark supporter, and Ron Burkle, the billionaire supermarket magnate and Major Friend of Bill, flew to Las Vegas where Hillary was attending a fund-raiser. They all but got down on their knees to beg her to enter the presidential race, four years ahead of what most people believe is the Clintons' preferred schedule. Her answer was no. When Tim Russert asked her to say, "I will never accept the nomination in 2004," she responded in the present rather than the future tense. "I am not accepting the nomination," she said. It appears that the main reason the answer has remained no is that the Clintons believe that Bush isn't beatable in 2004—a version of the intrepid Colin Powell Doctrine: never start a war you're not already sure you can win. And if they don't think that their party needs to be remade, they will surely be proven right. Bush cannot be beaten with a Clinton-like strategy.

When Hillary spoke before the Council on Foreign Relations last December, she cited the president as one of the people "we owe a great debt of gratitude" for capturing Saddam. Whether you believe that the capture of Saddam has increased Americans' safety or not, it is hard to imagine a winning strategy for 2004 that includes putting the words "Bush" and "debt of gratitude" in any sort of proximity. You cannot defeat Bush unless you are willing to depict him as he is—a major danger to this country on both the foreign and domestic fronts.

In the Senate, Hillary cast votes supporting President Bush's positions 47 percent of the time in 2003, considerably more than John Kerry (30 percent.) Though she is still excoriated in the crackpot right-wing media as an archliberal, the truth is that, as a senator, Hillary Clinton has shown a tendency for triangulation that is downright, well, Clintonesque. For example, she sided with the current administration in supporting tougher bankruptcy laws on behalf of the financial industry and at the expense of small debtors and she sponsored a bill mandating stiffer work requirements for welfare recipients. "I have always tried to strike a balance," the former First Lady explained. "And to be someone who is a New Democrat, a third-way thinker . . . I think you have to view the world as it is, not as you would wish it to be."

That's a long, long way from the Bobby Kennedy tradition, summed up in the lyrical statement, "Some men see things as they are and ask, 'Why?' I dream of things that never were and ask, 'Why not?'"

On the campaign trail, John Kerry often quoted Kennedy's challenge. "That is the question at the heart of our campaign," he said at the California Democratic State Convention. "That is our cause. Why not have an economy where equal opportunity is a fact? Where people who work hard and do the right thing can not only make ends meet but can actually reach higher and hope for more? Why not give every working American access to high-quality, affordable health care? Why not have public schools where children set out on a lifetime of learning and possibility? Where 'no child left behind' is a promise kept, not broken and forgotten. Why not preserve our environment so our great-grandchildren can breathe clean air, drink clean water, and know that they too live in a land that can be called 'America the beautiful'? Why not have leadership committed to civil rights, equal rights, and affirmative action—a leadership committed to preserve and defend a woman's right to choose and a worker's right to organize? And why not have a foreign policy that strengthens our nation and our interests by advancing our values?"

So what is a New Democrat realist to do? Kiss and make nice with the party's idealistic swarm? Who knows, if all the planets are properly aligned, and the idealists prevail in November, Hillary may actually let her hair down, stop all the calculating and triangulating, and embrace the possibility that the party and the country can indeed be remade. Maybe you don't have to sell your soul to be elected.

GIVING THE FOOLS AN
EXTREME MAKEOVER

The administration of Bill Clinton has been both a blessing and a curse for the Democratic Party.

Clinton gave the Democrats the confidence that they could govern again. He rescued them, for a moment, from a twenty-year slide into backbiting chaos. To do so, he used a peerless talent for crafting broadly acceptable policies that appealed to swing voters by co-opting Republican themes.

In this respect, he was a virtuoso. But his governing philosophy of triangulation was not a solid foundation on which to build the future of the party. Clinton's political gifts are not transferable. In fact, he did more than leave the party without an heir; he left it rudderless. And completely unequipped to provide a coherent opposition to Bush, who came to power by stealing a page from the Democratic Leadership Council playbook and co-opting Democratic ideas and ideals. Bush outflanked the DLC brain trust by assuring swing voters he wasn't going to savage government and create a two-tiered society in the process—and then proceeded to do exactly that.

During the Clinton years, the Democrats in power were so focused on the CNBC version of prosperity that the White House was like a single-issue cable network: the 24-hour Boom Channel—All Prosperity, All the Time. The Clinton years were defined by pragmatism rather than by FDR's and

Bobby Kennedy's overarching vision. The state of the party's health was judged by contributions flowing from corporate America and Wall Street. These were considered vital nutrients, and the food supply could not be endangered by bold initiatives—particularly after the health care debacle. The decision was clear: From now on there would be only incremental improvements that wouldn't upset Wall Street. Instead of comprehensive health care for all Americans, a bill was passed to keep new mothers in the hospital for forty-eight hours after birth—another microscopic legislative initiative that made everyone feel warm and fuzzy, but left enormous health-care needs unaddressed.

The pragmatic argument had it that, with the country split, there was no appetite for grand visions, just for bits and pieces and odds and ends. In fact, half the country was tuned out, no longer voting or participating. (It still is. A bold vision can actually bring some of them back.) The other New Democratic illusion was that a pragmatic, incremental approach was the only way to gain power. We forget quite easily that in 1992 Bill Clinton won because of the effect of Ross Perot and because people liked him. In 1996 he won because his opponent was Bob Dole—an unelectable throwback to the past—and because people still liked him.

Based on Clinton's success, the fools in charge of the Democratic Party have come to believe that mimicry is invention. So triangulation remains the order of the day for the Clinton wanna-bes. But trying to reclaim Clinton's legacy won't lead Democrats to the Electoral Promised Land. Instead, they need to reanimate their traditional constituencies and draw new people into the fray. They need to stop dreaming of marginal swing voters and begin focusing on pulling together a new progressive majority.

The more the Democrats try to present themselves as Bush-lite Republicans, the more people decide that they will stick with the original version rather than a compromised competitor. It happens in politics, just as it does in soft drinks.

If there is a model for the 2004 Democratic nominee it is Robert F. Kennedy's tragically ended 1968 presidential campaign.

John Kerry was on board a ship, coming home from Vietnam the night Robert Kennedy was assassinated. Thirty-six years later, out on the campaign trail, he talks a lot about the legacy Bobby Kennedy left behind and about the need to move beyond politics as "the art of the probable–tinkering around the edges without any greater vision, without a sense of optimism and imagination."

At the time of his death, Kennedy was fighting not just to represent his party, but to transform it. And that's what Bush's opponent must do: bring an end to the prolonged identity crisis of the Democratic Party and its aimless drifting away from the toughest, but most important task ahead, the building of one indivisible nation. He must also make a decisive break with the spinelessness and pussyfooting that have become the hallmark of Democrats.

Kennedy was drawn into the '68 race by his indignation over the direction of American foreign policy. "This nation," he said, "must adopt a foreign policy which says, clearly and distinctly, 'no more Vietnams.'"

"This nation," the new Democratic leader will have to say, "must adopt a foreign policy which says, clearly and distinctly, 'no more Iraqs.'" It is suicidal to try and compete on the imperial playing field Bush and Karl Rove have laid out. No Democrat can win by playing "Whose swagger is swaggier?"

or "Whose flight suit is tighter?" Instead, he must unambigu-
ously make the case that we are in danger of losing the war on
terror by fighting it with the tactics of the past.

In the same way that Kennedy was able to take his outrage
over Vietnam and expand it to include the outrages perpetrated at home, the Democratic nominee will have to echo
Kennedy's appeal to the most noble traditions of the American
people: "With you I know we can keep faith with the American need and the American desire for peace and for justice."

And he will have to match Kennedy's passionate devotion
to finding solutions to the problems of "the excluded." In
1963, when RFK was Attorney General, he once called the entire Cabinet to his office at the Justice Department and then
locked the door, forcing them to stay there for four hours discussing how to best address the crisis of poverty in America.

It's not that the pragmatists and the idealists don't agree
on the kind of America they want to see. But ultimately, politics is about the means, and Clinton's incremental, school-
uniform approach will never get us where we need to go. In
the nineties, 15 million Americans lived in poverty despite
the fact that their homes were headed by full-time workers.
President Clinton couched the crisis in terms of monetary
policy rather than human misery: "Is there a noninflation-
ary way to add more workers?" he asked while embarking
on a four-day poverty tour in 1999. "Is there a noninfla-
tionary way to raise wages?" Clinton's tour had been meant
to echo the poverty tour Bobby Kennedy embarked on in
1967. But while Kennedy's tour shocked the nation's conscience with television pictures of hungry children in his
arms, Clinton's ninety-six-hour nod to suffering felt more
like a poverty pit stop by a drive-through dignitary. It was

like watching a Vegas lounge show with ersatz legends offering up feeble renditions of your all-time favorites. They've got the look, they've even got the moves; what's missing is the soul.

"When Robert F. Kennedy was assassinated, something died in America," said civil rights leader John Lewis. "Something died in all of us." If that something is to be reborn, the Democratic presidential candidate will have to lay out a bold, overarching vision of how to solve the real underlying crisis in America. The real crisis is one that we barely notice because we have grown so used to its effects. It's like a neighbor's car alarm that we don't hear anymore because it rings so often. America has become two nations divided by poverty, opportunity, and race. Every day brings more evidence of more people falling below the poverty line, more corporate leaders being fined for wrongdoing without having to admit wrongdoing, more rules—even laws—that the elite is permitted to disregard.

As John Kerry said in Iowa in the speech that marked the beginning of his remarkable campaign turnaround: "America, it's time to get real. Instead of George Bush's raw deal, we need a real deal that stands up to the powerful interests. That's built on people and products not privileges and perks . . . I'm running for president to take on the HMOs and drug companies and make health care affordable for all our people." And then he made the all-important connection between the problem and the solution: We all have to do our part. "So stand up if you have the courage to stand up to the polluters," he said. " Stand up if you have the courage to stand up to corporations that ship jobs overseas. Stand up if you have the courage to stand up for our civil rights, for civil liberties . . . Stand up if you have the courage to stand up for energy independence so young people in the Midwest never have to die for Mideast oil."

To embody an alternative vision and capture the heart of the electorate, the nominee will have to empower the people to stand up, put aside focus group–approved language and make demands on complacent consciences after years of pandering by leader after leader, Republican and Democrat. He will have to dredge up something too long forgotten in our politics: heart. He must appeal to the compassion and goodness of America and stir our souls to believe again in the possibility that our country can change—profoundly. Isn't that ultimately what presidential elections should be about? A collective reassessment of where we are and where we need to be. And a recognition that we'll never get there without the people's participation.

As renowned historian David McCullough put it, "The great presidents are people who caused those who follow them to do more than they thought they were capable of. . . . The great thing about JFK is that he did not say, 'I'm going to make it easier for you.' He said it is going to be harder, and he wasn't pandering to the less noble side of human nature— he was calling on us to give our best." Indeed, McCullough was one of those people—and there were thousands—who put successful or promising careers on hold to answer the call.

Likewise, the Democratic standard bearer in 2004 will have to convince the nation that fighting the war on terror has to go along with confronting the homegrown threats we are facing here today—the result of decades of neglect, even in the midst of our greatest prosperity, of those left out of the good times. At this time in our history, what we need more than displays of power are displays of wisdom. What we need more than preemptive action abroad is redemptive action at home, starting with the safety of our streets, especially the streets of our inner cities, which have become war zones. Since Bush took office, street violence has increased 33 percent. Over 215,000 people were assaulted near their homes in 2002, reversing a 32 percent decline in the two years prior. The heroes who are working to change this reality, whether it is Father Boyle in the barrios of Los Angeles or Geoff Canada in the mean streets of Harlem, know that, as Canada put it, "The only way we're going to make a difference is by placing well-trained and caring adults in the middle of what can only be called a free-fire zone in our poorest communities." Yet we hear more about random deaths on the streets of Baghdad and Mosul than on the streets of East New York and South Central L.A.

And gang violence is making a bloody comeback after plummeting during the 1990s: gang-related homicides have risen over 50 percent since 1999. Those suffering most from this increase are the members of the predominantly minority communities where these killings generally occur—innocent victims imprisoned in their own homes, afraid to venture onto the streets of their blighted neighborhoods.

"I watch my back every minute that I'm out there," said a young African American man living in south Los Angeles. "We know no one will protect us," said another. "We have to protect ourselves." In Los Angeles County alone there are roughly 100,000 gang members, 3,000 of whom L.A. Police Chief Bill Bratton considers "sociopathic." "They'll kill you in a second," he says grimly. Over the last 15 years, there have been more than 2,400 unsolved homicides in the low-income neighborhoods of south L.A.—seven taking place at just one intersection. Bratton calls this "domestic terrorism."

Why isn't this part of our Homeland Security debate? Just because it isn't taking place in Brentwood or on the Upper East Side?

Gangs are no longer concentrated in Los Angeles. The National Youth Gang Center estimates that nationwide there are 24,500 gangs with 772,500 members. In the last ten years, for example, the number of gang members in Denver has doubled—from 7,000 to 14,000—while state budget cuts have killed programs designed to discourage gang activity. In Salt Lake City, drive-by shootings were up 300 percent from 2001 to 2002, part of a 50 percent increase in gang-related crimes, while Portland, Oregon, has seen a 38 percent increase since 1999, and Tulsa, Oklahoma, saw a dramatic surge in homicides in 2003 as a war developed between two rival Crips gangs.

Not surprisingly, this rise in gang violence has coincided with a cutback in funding for gang prevention initiatives such as youth athletic leagues and after school programs. Bush Republicans are quick to talk tough on issues of law and order but are very slow to invest in the kinds of programs that help alleviate the social disorder that so often leads to criminal activity. There seems to be plenty of money for new cops to patrol Baghdad, but very little for those protecting America's inner cities. In fact, Bush's 2005 budget eliminates $1 billion in federal assistance for state and local law enforcement. It also drastically reduces funding—by 94 percent—for the Community Oriented Policing Services (COPS) program, which could result in as many as 88,000 fewer policemen patrolling our streets. And it cuts funding for programs to reduce violent crime and gang activity in high-crime neighborhoods by 30 percent.

As a result, homicides and violent crimes are going up for the first time in nearly a decade. If the Democratic nominee is smart, he'll make this into a major campaign issue. Crime going up under a Republican administration strikes at the core idea of Bush as the great protector. I can hear the TV spot now: "Are you really safer than you were four years ago?"

Those who doubt the need for a new kind of wisdom should read Arnold Toynbee's study of the rise and fall of civilizations. "Civilizations come to birth and proceed to grow by successfully responding to successive challenges," Toynbee wrote in 1948. "They break down and go to pieces if and when a challenge confronts them which they fail to meet."

Even though Americans remain as divided by class as the people of medieval Europe, they rarely heed the battle cries of class warfare. That's because being rewarded—even over-rewarded—for a job well done is as American as Elizabeth Smart's parents selling their story to CBS. We don't begrudge Russell Crowe his $20 million payday for *Master and Commander,* and we even smile indulgently at the $250 million A-Rod gets for playing baseball. It's the genius of the market, we tell ourselves, it's supply and demand. Indeed, most Americans, rather than resenting the wealthy, aspire to one day share their lofty status.

This is why this country's ever-widening division into two nations has so far had such little effect on our politics. But Americans also have a deeply ingrained sense of fairness. It's the injustice in our midst that is mobilizing a critical mass of people. The traditionally disenfranchised are being joined by small investors who see pensions and college funds disappearing, and by middle-class people who have either lost their jobs or have to supplement their incomes with visits to the local food bank.

BUILDING A CRITICAL MASS AGAINST SPECIAL INTEREST POLITICS

To build upon the growing outrage against this widespread economic injustice, we need to mobilize a critical mass against our pay-to-play political system. Most Americans already feel that big money is playing too dominant a role in our elections. Back in the summer of 1999, the *Wall Street Journal* asked voters if Bush's then-record-breaking haul of $37 million for his first campaign was "impressive and a sign of broad-based support" or "excessive and a sign of what's wrong with politics today." By 56 percent to 29 percent, the public said the latter. When Bush's fund-raising reached $70 million later in the campaign, a follow-up poll found that people were even more disgusted: 71 percent now found it excessive, and only 20 percent thought it was a sign of broad-based support. Of course, that was when John McCain was out on the stump railing against this obscene fund-raising.

Now the burden rests on Democratic shoulders. But many of the Democrats running for president were trolling for dollars in the exact same corporate watering holes as George W. Bush. Joe Lieberman is a case in point. Four of the top ten companies bundling thousands of dollars for Bush were also on the list of Lieberman's top ten contributors. According to the Center for Responsive Politics, a nonpartisan research organization that tracks individual contributions and codes them by employer and industry, as of the end of November 2003, Merrill Lynch, Credit Suisse First Boston, Goldman Sachs, and Lehman Brothers, four of the world's most powerful financial firms, had given $978,475 to Bush-Cheney '04, Inc. They had also delivered $128,050 to Senator Lieberman, who has been almost as good a friend of Wall Street in Washington as Bush. Goldman Sachs, the current employer of former Clinton Treasury Secretary Robert Rubin and former employer of New Jersey Democratic senator Jon Corzine, had not only bundled $198,725 to Bush and $31,000 to Lieberman; its executives had also hedged their bets by plunking down $76,000 on John Edwards and $62,500 on John Kerry.

When Howard Dean spoke in late September 2003 on the Boston Common, he struck a tone that resonated with the populist zeitgeist. "Two hundred and thirty years ago, right here in Boston, fifty dedicated patriots known as the Sons of Liberty boarded three ships in Boston Harbor to protest a government more concerned with moneyed interests than its own people. Those fifty patriots believed that they had the power and the duty to change their government."

Dean's use of America's revolutionary history struck a chord with me, having once stood at Boston Harbor with the good folks from Massachusetts Mass Voters for Clean Elections and dumped ballot boxes full of fake dollar bills into the water to protest the buying of our democracy by big money. "We stand at a critical moment in American history," Dean went on. "Either we come together and take action now to restore a politics of participation and a politics of the people, or we allow the Washington insiders and the special interests to continue to make the backroom deals that are destroying people's faith in our government. . . . The ideal of democracy is more powerful than money, yet today our democracy is threatened by a flood of special-interest money pouring into our nation's capital. Our founders understood that threat. James Madison and Thomas Jefferson spoke of the fear that economic power would one day seize political power. That fear has been realized with the Bush administration."

But the problem extends beyond this administration, as bad as it is. Today there are thirty-three lobbyists for every member of Congress. Only ordinary people, roused to action, by the tens, the thousands, and eventually the millions have the power to right these wrongs. Only they have the power to send those lobbyists home. If voter participation continues to steadily erode—turnout has dropped 10 percent in the last forty years—the special interests will continue to win.

Dean masterfully used the Internet to help average citizens empower themselves, to come together in new and old ways to do the hard, basic work of democratic self-government. So in early November, when Dean asked his supporters to decide whether he should opt out of the fund-raising and spending limits that come with participating in our nation's flawed but useful system of partial public financing for the presidential primaries, campaign finance reformers were inclined to give him the benefit of the doubt. Dean was, after all, the only candidate raising most of his campaign war chest from the little people.

This is a movement of voters just as interested in taking their party back from the moneyed interests as they are in taking the White House back from the Bush Republicans. And it is imperative that the people wing of the Democratic party is not crushed by the money wing after the nominee is chosen. Because if it is, the party will continue to be run—straight into the ground—by the fools and their financiers.

Someone once said that the difference between Bush Republicans and Democrats is that Bush Republicans know they're right. The scintilla of self-doubt that was once a laudable aspect of Democratic tradition of open-mindedness has now become as burdensome as Sisyphus's boulder.

THE FEAR FACTOR: WHY NASCAR DADS KEEP VOTING AGAINST THEIR OWN INTERESTS

It's a painful truth that the Bush Republicans have been able to exploit a deep reservoir of anxiety and resentment over the legacy of the progressive policies that began with the social reforms of the New Deal and crested in the 1960s and 1970s with civil rights, women's rights, and environmental protection measures—all of which were consistent with the GOP legacy of both Lincoln and Teddy Roosevelt. Nevertheless, many people saw these programs as the manifestation of an overly intrusive federal government that had lost its moorings. Ignorance, bigotry, and fear of losing newly realized economic status played a prominent role in stoking antipathy toward these reforms. In retrospect, it's clear that the nation would never have made the needed progress on civil rights, women's rights, and environmental protection without decisive action at the federal level. It's also clear, however, that we are still divided over both the means used to enact these changes and the ends they helped bring about.

This divide is most acutely reflected in people who logically—based on their economic standing—should align themselves with the Democratic Party. These are people who do not benefit from the economic policies championed by the Republican politicians they vote for. For example, the great majority of American families received less than $500 from Bush's famed tax cut, and this meager gain was offset by the collateral damage suffered by the states. Bush's fiscal policies will cost state and local governments about $185 billion between 2002 and 2005. State college tuition alone increased by an average of $579 in 2003. Working families suffer additionally as employment programs are slashed, environmental and health programs are dismantled, and public infrastructure is left to rot from lack of maintenance.

The Democratic candidate is going to have to offer an alternative to the Bush Republicans' resonant antitax position— one that makes it clear that in exchange for the taxes they pay, the American people (and especially NASCAR dads) will receive services of equal worth: good schools, a national health care system, a great mass transit system, and better access to state universities for their children. If the Democratic candidate can make this services-for-taxes connection clear—and deliver on giving taxpayers more bang for their buck—then the Bush Republicans will be far less able to exploit antitax frustration and build their governing philosophy on it. The truth—and progressives must not be afraid to say it—is that right now, ordinary people are paying too much for what they are getting.

The Democrats need to have a come-to-Jesus moment with the American people and explain why this is so. It's so because of the tax revenues we spend on the military—24.2 percent after three years of George W. Bush—and because of the decreasing proportion of taxes paid by corporations compared to individuals. In 1966, 23 percent of tax revenues came from corporations; in 2002 that portion was 8 percent. "President Bush has a war on work," John Edwards said again and again on the campaign trail. "He wants to eliminate every penny of tax on wealth and shift the whole burden to people who work for a living." On top of this, as a percentage of discretionary spending, what we spend on the military is now up to 51 percent, a crippling drain on our national wealth.

Right now the politics of pandering dictate that citizens be treated like hotel guests; candidates-cum-waiters offer us a choice of entrée without mentioning the bill. Grown-ups, and most voters qualify as such, understand that there is no free lunch. They're willing to pay a fair price if they get good value in return. Democrats need to address the electorate's antitax sentiments and explain that, by starving social investments and by diverting so many of our tax dollars to the military, Bush Republicans have helped create an economic reality in which resentment of paying taxes can flourish.

It's not an accident that Bush Republicans, who have made a religion out of tax cutting, have been loath to reduce the payroll tax—the most regressive, unfair tax of all, and the one that most acutely affects average Americans. In four out of five U.S. households, families pay more in payroll taxes than they do in federal income tax. The more the Bush administration cuts the taxes of its high-income backers, and the less corporations are being asked to pay, the greater the burden working Americans are asked to bear. When FDR and the New Deal established payroll taxation, it accounted for roughly 2 percent of federal revenue. Now, payroll taxes account for over 40 percent. There is also a potent connection between high payroll taxes and high unemployment, since a tax on work is, in essence, a tax on job creation. Economists estimate that lowering the payroll tax by as little as 10 percent, would, over the long term, increase the number of jobs available by 10 percent. That's why, in an effort to battle unemployment, a number of countries, including Australia, Canada, Germany, France, Denmark, and Belgium, are cutting their payroll tax rates. As former representative Jack Kemp, one of the few Republicans who has advocated shifting the tax burden away from payroll taxes, puts it, "It's not for Wall Street; it's for Main Street."

Over the last twenty years, the debate over taxes has been like political kabuki. The Democrats, when they have not simply gone along to get along, have been forced into what Howard Dean called damage control. "We must enter a new era for the Democratic Party," he said. "Not one where we join Republicans and aim simply to limit the damage they inflict on working families . . . I call now for a new era in which we rewrite our social contract. We need to provide certain base guarantees for all those who are working hard to fulfill the promise of America."

A campaign pitch based on a fair exchange of taxes for benefits will enable Democrats to reach across party lines and lure back to their side the blue-collar workers, the NASCAR dads, and the minority voters who are so fed up with the current system that they have either been voting Republican or not voting at all.

It will also bring an end to the prolonged identity crisis of the Democratic Party and its aimless drifting away from the toughest but most important task ahead, the building of one indivisible nation.

John Kennedy appealed to the highest American ideals, while his brother Bobby spoke to the urgency of so many unmet needs. Americans are ready for—and even eagerly awaiting—that double call once again.

The nominee will have to echo Bobby Kennedy's call to the most noble traditions of the American people. He will have to tell the Democrats of '04 what Kennedy told the Democrats of '68: "The forces arrayed against this position are so powerful . . . If we are divided then those who will benefit are those who wish to keep the policies of the past."

THE OTHER SIDE OF THE MOUNTAIN

TWO NATIONS AND THE
FOURTH INSTINCT

On November 24, 2003, President Bush spoke to a gathering of U.S. soldiers and their families in Fort Carson, Colorado: "Oftentimes, people measure the strength of America based on the number of tanks and airplanes we have, or the size of our wallets. No, the strength of America lies in the hearts and souls of our citizens. . . . The true strength of America is the American people, because we are a compassionate, decent, caring, loving people."

The rhetoric is no surprise. This is a vision of America that all our great leaders have held up as an ideal. What's startling is the source. That these words came out of the mouth of a man who has methodically done everything in his power to take us further and further away from that ideal. Every day brings new evidence that we are being encouraged to succumb to our most indifferent, narcissistic, and greedy impulses. The president spoke in the same speech about heeding "the universal call to love a neighbor just like they would like to be loved themselves." I found the soaring rhetoric offensive, juxtaposed as it is with the reality of growing suffering all across the country—suffering needlessly created by Bush's heeding of the call for "tax relief" at the expense of collective action aimed at helping those truly in need.

Now, many of us know that the Bush administration is fueled by high-octane hypocrisy. Pointing that out falls under the heading of necessary (even essential), but not sufficient. Playing counterspin the bottle only gets you so far. It's time to be proactive and work together on a nurturing, moral vision of the future, not based on questions of right or left but on questions of right or wrong. A vision that will reconnect us to those aspects of our history that exemplify the courage and generosity of our national character. It will challenge us to create a democracy where opportunity is truly available to all—built on our common values of compassion, fairness, and a commitment to *really* leave no child behind.

The kind of society we want is the one that citizens would construct if they adopted what philosopher John Rawls called a "veil of ignorance" and acted on the basis of fairness and justice, as opposed to their own self-interest. In other words, if you had no idea of your own status or prospects in life, and were asked to objectively decide who should be the beneficiary of George Bush's next round of tax cuts—a corporate CEO with a $25-million-a-year pay package or a single mother working two jobs and still not making ends meet—the vast majority of us would try to improve the lot of the mother. Not just because we might *be* that mother, or because of a sense of charity, but because we realize that even a small amount of assistance to a struggling family sends positive reverberations through a community. And tax cuts for the already rich do not. You can see the ripple effects when a parent can spend the time with her kids to help keep them engaged in their education and out of trouble. You can see them when these children grow up to be members of a productive workforce. You can see them in one less family needing to make use of the emergency room because they have no access to routine medical care. And you can see them in whole neighborhoods where sullen despair is replaced with hopeful optimism. So I ask you, which is the more practical investment? Which truly serves the interest of becoming a strong and prosperous country?

The heart of this vision is the fact that human beings are a mixture of self-interest and altruism (okay, with the possible exception of Karl Rove). In fact, in 1994 I wrote a whole book—*The Fourth Instinct*—about the instinct that compels us to go beyond our impulses for survival, sex, and power. While these three basic instincts link us to our past, the fourth links us to our future. It expands the boundaries of our caring beyond our solitary selves to include our families and friends, our communities, our world.

In a study on the roots of altruism, Dr. Ervin Staub, a psychology professor at the University of Massachusetts, analyzed men and women who had risked their lives during World War II to protect Jews hiding from the Nazis. "Goodness, like evil, often begins in small steps," Dr. Staub wrote. "Heroes evolve, they aren't born. Very often the rescuers made only a small commitment at the start—to hide someone for a day or two. But once they had taken that step, they began to see themselves differently, as someone who helps. What starts as mere willingness becomes intense involvement." What I called an instinct in 1994, modern science has since identified as a neurophysiological manifestation of empathy. Bottom line: our brain is hardwired for compassion.

The crisis in America that we barely notice anymore is that we've become two nations—divided by poverty, opportunity, and race. It's like a neighbor's car alarm that we don't hear anymore because it rings so often.

Yet beyond the occasional exhortation, we are not brought up to respond to our caring instincts as promptly as to our self-interest. That's where leadership comes in.

I once asked Senator Paul Wellstone what he thought made a great president. "A great president," he answered, "is one who successfully calls on all Americans to be their own best selves." Sadly, that hasn't happened much since John Kennedy asked us to "ask not." Since then, the prevailing model of leadership has been the leader as panderer, appealing to our most basic and most base instincts in a climate of fear—as if that's all we're capable of. And since September 11, to the garden-variety fears of losing one's job, losing one's health, or losing one's child to drugs, we've all been forced to add the fear of losing everything to terrorism. Fear has been mobilized to overcome our natural compassion.

The Bush administration has regularly and deliberately played up the fear of terrorism for political gain. "It will take one vial, one canister, one crate slipped into this country to bring a day of horror, like none we have ever known." That was the very first sentence of the very first political ad Bush ran for his reelection campaign. Clearly, Karl Rove has decided that control of the White House in 2004 will be determined by how successful Bush Republicans are between now and November at scaring the nation.

Since the Twin Towers fell, the White House has mastered the black art of frightening us for its own ends. Orange alerts are interspersed with constant reminders that we are at war—even when the topic under discussion is energy policy. Frank Luntz, the GOP's whiz kid spinmeister, recommended in a twenty-three-page communications memo that Republican candidates constantly remind Americans about the blackouts that rolled across the country last summer, calling it "the single strongest" argument for selling the GOP's antediluvian energy policy. A key Luntz talking point: "If we fail to act, Americans will face more and more widespread blackouts." So once again, "the single strongest" argument is made by playing the fear card—with Sheriff Bush, the gutsy Crawford cowboy, riding to the rescue to save our cowering nation.

Among FDR's "four essential human freedoms," freedom from fear was the fourth. The third was "freedom from want" and the fear that want produces—fear of facing another day without the certainty of food on the table or of facing another medical emergency without health care. But these are not fears our current president recognizes. He just increases them. There can be no two more starkly different American worldviews than Bush's and FDR's. Bush's presidency feeds on fear, while FDR famously asserted in his first inaugural address seventy years ago "that the only thing we have to fear is fear itself—nameless, unreasoning, unjustified terror which paralyzes." In January 1941 he contrasted a "moral order" with the "new order" of tyranny and fear: "A good society is able to face schemes of world domination and foreign revolution alike without fear." Bush's opponent will have to update the threats we face, but revive the spirit of FDR: "A good society is able to face schemes of world terrorism without fear."

There is a natural resistance to abandoning the politics of fear. The person who walks through the village telling people it's safe to come out runs the terrible risk of looking foolish—or worse. That's why those working to end the fear-mongering must paint a vivid picture of what life would be like on the other side of the mountain. By portraying a world at odds with the indifferent, frightened, and increasingly disengaged society we live in, we will be, in essence, reinventing the political wheel. And we will be excoriated for it. The fanatics on the right will warn that we will destroy the economy, kill jobs, and expose to our enemies our soft underbelly and our bleeding hearts.

But we must not respond in kind with our own apocalyptic scenarios. Instead we need people willing to say, "You know, those square wheels are really dumb. They don't work." And we also need people who will say, "I know this sounds crazy, but what if we built a round wheel?" Then we need people who will actually go out and build the round wheel, and people who will spread the word about these great, new round wheels.

Our national history is filled with examples of bold starts, new beginnings, and wrenching shifts in our national mind-set as our society evolved to curb its own worst excesses and to extend the reach of participation and opportunity to more and more people. But that process has come to a halt, and is, in fact, going backward. Let's reclaim that history before Grover Norquist and his friends can replace FDR on the dime with Ronald Reagan and irrevocably turn the New Deal into a raw deal.

OF RIGHTS AND WRONGS

Central to my interest in politics has been the application in our political lives of the biblical admonition that "to whom much is given, from him that much more shall be expected." That idea was at the core of the founding philosophy of this country.

Even before there was a United States of America, when John Winthrop landed in Massachusetts Bay in 1630, he stood on the deck of the *Arbella* and gave a speech that would reverberate through the ages, giving voice to the central American creed: "We must bear one another's burdens. . . . We must be knit together in this work as one man. We must entertain each other in brotherly affection; we must be willing to abridge ourselves of our superfluities, for the supply of others' necessities. . . . We must delight in each other, make others' conditions our own, rejoice together, mourn together, labor and suffer together: always having before our eyes our community as members of the same body."

The history of our country is studded with progressive breakthroughs—Lincoln, Teddy Roosevelt, FDR—followed by decades of consolidation, stagnation, and now regression. Martin Luther King Jr. and the civil rights movement provided the next breakthrough after FDR. "No individual or nation," said King, echoing the visionary leaders who preceded him, "can be great if it does not have a concern for 'the least of these.'" More specifically, "A nation that continues year after year to spend more money on military defense than on programs of social uplift is approaching spiritual death." The activists, the rebels, and the dissidents who challenge us to live up to our avowed principles of social justice are midwives of the next great collective breakthrough—ordinary people (and even sometimes public officials) who in simple or heroic acts of unrecorded generosity put into practice this American creed, so powerful that even politicians who undermine it feel compelled to pay lip service to it.

American democracy has evolved considerably over the past 228 years. At the founding of this remarkable republic, the rights and protections of women, blacks, Native Americans, and men without property were clearly not a priority. But over the centuries, as our society has matured, we have built on the values embedded in the Declaration of Independence and the Constitution and reinterpreted them so that they apply to all people regardless of race, faith, or economic status. The Emancipation Proclamation. The Nineteenth Amendment, giving women the right to vote. The New Deal, which put ordinary people back to work when the private sector couldn't. The Voting Rights Act of 1965. The Clean Air Act of 1970. The Clean Water Act of 1972. The Occupational Safety and Health Act of 1970. The Americans with Disabilities Act of 1990. These are all milestones in our journey toward a just society. They are also exemplars of the values held dear by most Americans, values that still—despite the best efforts of the Bush administration—make our nation a beacon of hope to the rest of the world.

It is now time to chart new milestones. There is so much work to be done—yet our path is being obscured by fear and the endless smoke and mirrors the current administration thrives on. All we're being asked to do is shop ourselves deeper and deeper into debt and keep a suspicious eye on our neighbors. Surely there is more to being an American than that.

REAL FAMILY VALUES

The values that gave rise to our great milestones, from the Bill of Rights to the Americans with Disabilities Act, are at the heart of what George Lakoff, a linguistics professor at Berkeley, identifies as the model of the "nurturing parent." This model has been the guiding force behind the most important social advances in our history, yet it stands in sharp contrast to the modern Republican model, which Lakoff describes as "the strict father."

The strict father sees the world as a dangerous place that rewards discipline. One must be disciplined to stand up to the evil that surrounds us, disciplined and self-reliant. Kids need to be tossed into the deep end at an early age. After all, it's sink or swim. The tough daddy world is competitive, and impediments to competition, like regulation, are immoral. The environment is simply a resource to be exploited. Wielding power—military, political, and economic—is always a good thing. As Lakoff puts it, "worldly success is an indicator of sufficient moral strength; lack of success suggests lack of sufficient discipline." Further, it is made clear at an early age that pursuit of self-interest is always in the common good: "If everybody pursues his own self-interest, the self-interest of all will be maximized."

Terms like "family values" and "tax relief" are examples of what cognitive linguists call "frames." These frames are the mental structures that we use to help us make sense of the world around us. "He who builds the frame," E. J. Dionne wrote, "almost always gets to choose the picture that's put inside."

The Republican frame has created a nice, neat dichotomy, that according to Lakoff, defines two types of children: "the mature, disciplined, self-reliant ones who should not be meddled with and the whining, undisciplined, dependent ones who should never be coddled." Using this simple frame, it is easy to see why the economic and regulatory policies of the Bush administration favor the wealthy (those being given credit for exhibiting self-discipline and a boundless energy for getting rich) at the expense of the poor (those who supposedly lack the self-discipline, motivation, and moral fiber to become rich). From this smug vantage point, social programs are viewed as immoral. By the same token, the avaricious among us are rewarded for their exemplary self-reliance by getting to keep an increasing percentage of their money, which means that they end up paying less to maintain the kind of society that made their wealth possible in the first place.

In theory we are all equal before the law. In practice, there are overwhelming privileges that come with winning the birth lottery. A perfect illustration of this? Our current president. If he had been born into a family in which the father had to make ends meet by working on the grounds-keeping staff of The Ballpark in Arlington, where the Texas Rangers play baseball, it's absurd to imagine that he would be in the Oval Office today. Instead, he had the good fortune to be born into a family whose public stature and private connections offset his notable lack of business acumen when it came time for a new owner-ship group to find a front man for the Texas Rangers. Bottom line, President Bush is in no position to lecture anyone about the virtues of hard work, discipline, and pulling yourself up by your bootstraps. Even by the internal logic of the Republicans' own framing, W doesn't cut it.

Nevertheless, and despite their rejection of Darwin's teachings on human evolution, the conservatives' socioeconomic model presumes a dog-eat-dog world, using terms like "tax relief" as an invitation to the communal howl. By couching their devastating tax cuts in terms that evoke fair-ness and responsibility, Bush, Rove, and the rest of the anti-tax kooks make their selfishness sound like a heroic rescue. Relief presupposes an affliction, an *unfair* affliction. And this deceitful appeal to fairness and the strict father fantasy may help explain why so many Americans support tax cuts even when it is not in their own self-interest to do so. "Taxes" and "spending" have taken on inescapable negative connotations that conceal the truth. The view of taxes as simply the membership fee for belonging to America is so out of fashion that the best most political leaders can muster is the notion that taxes are an unfortunate necessity, to be reduced whenever possible. This taxes-as-foul-tasting-medicine position is just as much a part of the strict father paradigm as the "tax relief" fraud. Come on, son, take your taxes like a man!

The central assumption of our economic policy is that "businesses create jobs"—and that this fact alone gives them complete absolution. Our whole political mind-set now is that, since businesses create jobs, we can never do enough for businesses. Business expenses, including business lunches and larger SUVs in the possession of small businesses, are worthy of tax credits. And even though businesses are supposed to be competitive, subsidies for businesses are considered—by Bush and Co.—the bulwark of a strong economy, not a handout like all that naughty social spending. It's no wonder that corporate profits have increased 75 percent in the last ten years. Yet the workers who have been instrumental in producing this increase in profits, and the dramatic increase in productivity, have only seen a 16 percent increase in jobs over the same ten years, and a minor uptick in wages.

Today 14 percent of personal income is going toward servicing personal indebtedness, while less than 2 percent is being saved. But, ironically, the strict father doesn't seem to be complaining. After all, debt fuels consumption. Consumption, even based on self-indulgent borrowing, is the basis of capitalism, and strict dad is all for that.

THE NEW RESPONSIBILITY VISION

Bush Republicans would like you to think that this is the only way to proceed. But, of course, it's not. In the world of the nurturing parent, this nasty and brutish perspective is replaced by the "ethics of care." We sink or swim together. And seeing it that way makes it much more likely that we'll still be swimming in the long run. This is the New Responsibility vision. Personal responsibility is essential, but so is developing a sense of responsibility for others. When responsibility extends beyond oneself and one's family to the larger community, government action and personal action are both part of our shared purpose.

The nurturing parent model relies on cooperation rather than aggression to accomplish goals. Strict dad may want to go it alone, but the nurturing parent sensibly suggests putting a team together instead. A *real* team—not a Coalition of the Willing Sycophants and Toadies.

To take a glass-half-full approach to George Bush, the strict father model can help explain why he might have believed in a greater good that justified his dishonesty in making the case for war in Iraq. The war is about punishing Saddam Hussein and, by extension, other tin-pot dictators for their insubordination. It's about imposing our will on weaker nations . . . because we can. It's about providing an instructive example for the child nations of the world: behave yourself or you'll be spanked. And it's about gaining control of a base of power in the Middle East in case more spankings are needed in the future. The strict father also takes the corporatist view that it's right and proper to use military force to open markets and exploit new labor resources. Military strength and corporate enrichment are always assumed to be in the national interest.

The Bush administration's philosophy draws heavily on such strict father neoconservative thinking. The neocons' troubadour was Leo Strauss, a professor of political philosophy at the University of Chicago. In a letter to Professor

Helmut Kuhn, Strauss provided a terrifying and all-too-familiar rationale for military action abroad: "I emphasize the relation to foreign enemies only because this is the most obvious and common case in which noble statesmen are not blamed for actions which under normal conditions would be unjust." And in case you didn't get it, in another letter, Strauss wrote to his close friend Carl Schmitt, the preeminent legal authority of the Third Reich, who drafted the key laws of National Socialism: "Because mankind is intrinsically wicked, it has to be governed. Such governance can only be established when men are united—and they can only be united against other people."

Strauss had a profound antipathy for both liberalism and democracy and a deep mistrust of the people. He placed all of his hope and trust in the elites. He would have been especially proud of Bush's Pioneers and Dick Cheney's secretive energy task force. Or indeed, of Cheney and Justice Scalia going duck hunting together just weeks after the Supreme Court agreed to hear Cheney's appeal of a U.S. District Court ruling ordering him to disclose who met with his task force.

In Lakoff's nurturing vision of the world, "the job of government is to care for, serve, and protect the population (especially those who are helpless), to guarantee democracy (the equal sharing of political power), to promote the well-being of all and ensure fairness for all. The economy should be a means to these moral ends. There should be openness in government. Nature is seen as a source of nurture to be respected and preserved. Empathy and responsibility are to be promoted in every area of life, public and private. Art and education are parts of self-fulfillment and therefore moral necessities."

I'd move to that planet tomorrow and, I suspect, so would many others. But there remains a substantial group of our fellow citizens that considers any resources spent on our less fortunate brothers and sisters to be wasted. According to strict dad, they just don't deserve it. Why don't they deserve it? Easy, the fact that they need it is proof they don't deserve it. And if we spend it on them, well, then there's less for the rest of us.

Strict dad favors those in positions of advantage. They are considered to have "succeeded" even if they have merely inherited their wealth or position. Being able to pass along this "success" by, say, repealing the so-called death tax is part of the creed. But because strict dad is so tough on the majority of the kids, a massive deception is needed in order to lure so many to submit to his rule. Hence the perversion of language to create a paranoid's nightmare world in which only an authoritarian father figure can rescue us.

Remember: he who controls the language defines the political debate. If we don't get the language right, we'll get nothing right. The Republicans' control of certain magical words, starting with "responsibility," has been a key to their success in recent years. We need to take these words back. So let's begin with responsibility, which is at the heart of the new vision, and reanimate it by coupling individual responsibility with social responsibility. We have to take care of ourselves in order to be able to take care of others. Why, you may ask, do we want to take care of others? After years of living without an inclusive moral vision for our country, we have to remind the American people that we are a republic built on responsibilities to each other, not just to ourselves. We must employ these principles of caring for each other not just in making public speeches but in formulating public policy.

Another magical word we have to take back is "family." Yet another is "values." Why is it that the term "family values" belongs only to those who find themselves in a traditional nuclear family? In a country that has enshrined the separation of church and state and in which many households are led by single parents or, in some cases, by two mommies or two daddies, can't the term "family values" belong to them too? Not according to Bush Republicans and especially not according to "family values" Republicans who don't believe Darwin had anything useful to offer.

They insist that "marriage is between a man and a woman." (I wonder if God told Pat Robertson this in the same conversation he told him that George Bush would "win in a walk.") In any case, the Pat Robertson crowd uniformly fails to mention that these days, marriage in America is quite often between a man who works eight hours a day in a factory and five hours a night as a security guard and then comes home to an empty bed because his wife is on the night shift, stocking shelves at Wal-Mart. And for all the talk about how much better off kids in unbroken homes are, there is very little said about how these barely-making-ends-meet parents are supposed to pull off the Ozzie and Harriet routine. God protect their kids if they need some help with their homework, a healthy home-cooked meal, or a little guidance through one of life's inevitable rough patches. Talk to your kids about drugs? When? In the waits at the emergency room, which you're using as your GP because you haven't got health insurance? But, hey, they're a "family," so all's right with the world.

Then we'll have to reclaim the word "taxes." Why has it become a synonym for "evil"? I understand that no one likes to pay good money for nothing. But fire and police protection aren't nothing. Just ask the residents of San Diego County who, despite repeated warnings over two decades, refused to

increase taxes, voting against twenty-one of thirty-two different fire protection ballot measures over the last eight years. In
the fall of 2003, sixteen people died and 2,469 homes were
destroyed in San Diego County during devastating wildfires.
Talk about penny-wise and pound-foolish. Roads, bridges, airports, and mass transit systems aren't nothing. National parks,
clean air, and clean water aren't nothing. A safe food supply,
functioning schools with well-trained teachers, and well-
equipped hospitals aren't vaporous apparitions either. So why
have we turned our back on the eloquent words of Supreme
Court Justice Oliver Wendell Holmes? "Taxes," he said, "are
what we pay for civilized society." Why have we forgotten
that? Because the conservatives have been preaching the
gospel of "tax relief" with such fervor that whenever we hear
it, we rise almost as one to say "amen" without thinking about
what we have just assented to.

This has got to change. As a society, we have to return to
the principle that public spending on education and health
care is a moral imperative—not a handout but an investment
in our future. And taxes are the only way to pay for them.
There can and should be a vigorous national discussion about
how our tax dollars are allocated, and about the relative effec-
tiveness of various social programs. But can we seriously argue
about the need for them?

Gary Hart, who has been seeking to reconnect the Democratic Party with Jeffersonian principles, wrote in his blog last
summer, "We used to define 'social' as the problems of our society—poverty, hunger, illiteracy, homelessness, joblessness,
the lonely aged, and on and on. If you use the word 'social' in
this sense, the sense in which it is traditionally used, you cannot be 'a fiscal conservative and a social liberal' for the very obvious reason that it costs some money to help those in need."

If an alternative moral vision is to prevail, ways to achieve the common good must become the central focus of a healthy democratic debate—not linguistic arguments over whether we are fiscally conservative, socially liberal, or trying to have it both ways.

FELIX UNGER FOR PRESIDENT!

Today the assumption is that you have to be an alpha male to win in politics. Or, if you're a woman, you must be a woman with alpha male qualities. The irony is that what our politics needs more than anything are the feminine values of nurturing and wisdom. These may have been considered luxuries when men were walking around in saber-toothed tiger pelts carrying clubs, but they have now become essential for our survival.

As Nancy Folbre explains in *The Invisible Heart,* a system that cared for children, the old, and the infirm, stopped functioning once millions of women—who were the system's caretakers—joined the workforce. And government programs have not been able to fill the vacuum. Indeed, if we don't strengthen the ethic of cooperation and reciprocity—if we don't have more responsible employers and a healthier civil society—there will never be enough money to fill the gaps.

Jonas Salk summed up this need at the end of his life when he wrote that modern society is now dependent not on the survival of the fittest but the "survival of the wisest: The evolutionary instinct compels us to bring out the best in ourselves and in others, to recognize our interconnectedness with everyone else."

To describe these distinctions in foreign-policy terms Joseph Nye, Dean of Harvard's Kennedy School of Government, uses the terms "soft vs. hard power." "One source of American soft power is our values. Others are attracted to follow our lead to the extent we're seen as a beacon of liberty, human rights and democracy. They're less willing to follow when we don't live up to our stated values. Nobody admires a hypocrite."

The Bush administration is all about hard power, military force, and a High Noon foreign policy, in which the sheriff acts alone. Even Condoleezza Rice brings no female principles to the foreign policy. On the contrary, she parrots the administration's line more faithfully than all the guys put together. She is the ultimate "team player"—and that's what a woman in politics is supposed to be, right?

In the heat of the 2000 election, author Naomi Wolf advised Al Gore how to project his alpha male. By imbibing a shotglass full of high-test testosterone, bookish, wonky, stiff-as-a-plank Al Gore could magically be reborn as . . . Alpha Gore, He-Man slayer of dragons and rescuer of damsels in distress. Wolf correctly noted that Gore was stuck in President Clinton's ample shadow—and wanted the Vice President to project leadership qualities, not his status as Number Two.

President Clinton was the alpha male, both literally and figuratively. Yes, he was the leader of the free world, but he was also commanding, good-looking, charismatic, and appealing to women. Gore on the other hand, has been faithfully married to the same woman for more than thirty years, he's a cultivator of ideas, and he's not a bit dangerous. He is the classic beta male. As veep he was Felix Unger, neat, fastidious, and anal retentive, while the President got to be Oscar Madison, a beer-drinking, cigar-smoking playboy. Audiences, and voters by extension, like Felix Unger. But they love, and by extension, vote for, Oscar Madison.

President John F. Kennedy was another alpha male. He was great-looking, rugged, he projected the air of a decision-maker, and was a war hero to boot. Plus, he was having sex with Marilyn Monroe. It makes perfect sense—in a high school-y way. The leader of the free world (captain of the football team) should be having sex with the most beautiful woman on the planet (head cheerleader), right?

Former presidential contender Paul Tsongas was another classic beta male. During his run for the White House, Tsongas told the electorate, "I'm not Santa Claus." And, no surprise here, he's also not president. That's because traditionally, Americans don't elect presidents who are soft spoken, thoughtful, and advertise the fact that they are not Santa Claus.

And they didn't elect Michael Dukakis either. Compounding Dukakis' troubles was the fact that he famously tried to impersonate an alpha-male—with horrendous results. Dukakis's campaign was nearly stopped dead in its tracks the day he put on an army helmet and rode atop a tank. The helmet was too big and dwarfed his head. He looked like a little boy playing war with his daddy's old army clothes. There will never be any historical sites that advertise "President Michael Dukakis slept here."

So if the voters don't want a classic beta male as their leader, what do they want? They want someone decisive, like Ronald Reagan. Someone with conviction, like FDR. Someone strong, like Teddy Roosevelt. Someone virile, like Arnold Schwarzenegger. They want a war hero like JFK, someone who fits the ever-changing description of "a real man." They will even settle for someone like Bush, who merely looks the part. But, if those were the only requirements, today we'd be singing "Hail to the Chief" to The

The goal of the Democratic nominee has to be not just to win the presidency, but to transform the Democratic Party and, in the process, American politics. Those are big dreams, but anything smaller guarantees the reelection of George Bush. And that would be a disaster.

Rock or Ollie North. (Hmmm, that gives me an idea for a totally crazy summer blockbuster comedy . . .)

Clearly there is something else going on in the 2004 zeitgeist: a craving for a candidate who speaks with moral authority that inspires and empowers. It is a long way from the alpha male leader as savior cliché—whether it is Bush projecting himself as the only reliable defense against the threats that surround us, or Schwarzenegger promising to terminate whatever ails us without asking anything of the voters.

Today we need someone strong, decisive and heroic . . . who's also nurturing, wise, and soulful—and who respects us enough to tell us the truth. Which is why a presidential contender like Howard Dean could say that he's not Santa Claus—that Americans are going to have to save themselves—and not get laughed out of politics altogether. At least not right away.

THE VISION PERSONIFIED

There are many different ways to reframe the political debate and create a new vision for the future. The up-from-the-streets civil rights movement is one model. But that kind of grass-roots effort takes years—or even decades—to reach a critical mass. A way to force a seismic shift in the political culture is for a presidential candidate to embrace a bold vision and make it the foundation of his—and therefore his party's—agenda.

It's as simple as this: if this year's Democratic nominee is to become the forty-fourth American president, he will have to offer more—much more—than a laundry list of better alternatives to George Bush's policies.

He will have to stay connected to the movement for real reform that is larger than any one candidate—and use the momentum and passion of the movement to put forward the new vision of the nurturing parent. To accomplish this, he must ask us to imagine a country where all people—not just the privileged ones—can send their children off to school in the morning confident that they will be safe and that they will learn.

He must ask us to imagine a country where everyone has comprehensive health care as a basic right. If your family doctor is the local emergency room, it's hard to enjoy life, liberty, or the pursuit of happiness.

He must ask Americans to imagine a country where the environment is an asset to be treasured, not a resource to be exploited, and where clean air and water are the norm, not the exception.

He must ask Americans to imagine a country where elected officials belong to the voters instead of being owned by special interests, and where policies are determined by what is in the public interest and not in the best interest of some corporation that eludes its tax obligations by opening a post office box in Bermuda.

And he has to paint a picture of a different kind of economy—one where productivity doesn't come at the cost of quality of life and where work is structured to allow parents to take care of their children.

This shouldn't be too much to ask for, yet in recent years our economy and society have been moving in the opposite direction: air and water quality are threatened; more families have been forced to have both parents working longer hours to make ends meet, if, that is, they can find jobs at all; our public education infrastructure is crumbling; disgracefully large numbers of people are homeless and millions are going without health insurance. This is the state of the union that Bush claimed in his 2002 address had "never been stronger." That would be true only if you measure the strength of our union by military might and the economic benefits that have accrued over the past twenty years to the wealthiest one percent of households.

Thirty-six years ago, Robert Kennedy stood in front of an audience at the University of Kansas and asked them to look at our economy in a radically different way. "Our gross national product is now over $800 billion a year," Kennedy said, "but that GNP—if we should judge America by that—counts air pollution and cigarette advertising, and ambulances to clear our highways of carnage. It counts special locks for our doors, and the jails for those who break them. It counts the destruction of our redwoods and the loss of our natural wonder in chaotic sprawl. It counts napalm and the cost of a nuclear warhead, and armored cars for police who fight riots in our streets."

The 2004 Democratic nominee will have to engage in a similar, soul-stirring questioning of many unquestioned assumptions.

He will have to display a concern for the poor people of this nation and the beleaguered middle class lacking among those currently in charge of public policy.

He will have to recapture the language of morality from the fundamentalists who have hijacked it and reduced it to sexual morality, and use it to spotlight the rampant immorality of the corporate sector instead.

He will have to force his own party to make a choice Democratic leaders have desperately been trying to avoid: between their corporate donors and the urgent need to articulate a powerful, populist case against the sordid actions of corporate America.

He will have to forge the kind of alliance that includes minorities and the dispossessed together with those among the influential, the affluent, and the powerful who are sick of the country we are becoming and of the grotesque parody of democracy we are being served.

He will have to provide an outlet for idealistic young people to be active in shaping our nation's future. And above all, he will have to appeal to what is best in us after years of politicians appealing to what is most selfish in us.

It's a tall order but that's what the times demand. Social movements are not sparked by subtle shifts in policy or new and improved versions of familiar proposals. Nor are they sparked by attacks alone, no matter how brilliant and justified. "Ronald Reagan," said Reagan speechwriter Peggy Noonan, "was a great communicator not because he said things in a big way but because he said big things. It wasn't the way he said it, it was what he said." The Democratic nominee, too, has to speak of big things, and if he does, I have faith that we can make the journey to the other side of the proverbial mountain. It will take vision, faith, and perseverance, but it can be done. I know because I've covered comparable ground in my own journey of political transformation.

NOT ALL CHARITY IS CREATED EQUAL

I have no greater heroes than the men and women who are working up close and personal—sometimes wrenchingly so—to turn lives around. But they will be the first to tell you that even if they never slept, they would never on their own be able to turn around the tragic realities that surround us— including the fact that America has more homeless children today than at any time since the Great Depression. The bottom line is that the task of overcoming poverty is too monumental to be achieved without the raw power of government appropriations.

Yet programs that help the poor are all too often the first to be scaled back when self-styled "compassionate conservatives" take office—whether in George Bush's America, where the House passed a bill requiring working mothers on welfare to work forty rather than thirty hours a week to qualify for assistance, or in Arnold Schwarzenegger's California, where the very first spending cut announced by the new governor was a freeze on cost-of-living adjustments for welfare recipients.

During the recall campaign, Schwarzenegger was asked if he trusted the private sector. "Oh, absolutely," he replied. Although my faith was never that unwavering, I too once believed that the private sector—especially Republican multimillionaires who talk incessantly about less government—would rise to the occasion and provide the funding needed to replicate and sustain on a large scale the many private social programs that have proven successful. But I found out firsthand that it's much easier to raise money for fashionable cultural causes and prestigious educational institutions than for homeless shelters and mentoring programs for at-risk children. The annual $3,500-a-plate, black-tie ball for the Costume Institute of the Metropolitan Museum of Art raises enough money to buy plenty of warm winter coats for children in New York City. But instead the funds go to preserving and displaying the evening gowns of the social elite.

And there is, of course, no consistency in charitable giving. It fluctuates depending on the economy, the stock market, and the philanthropists' mood. Donations by the country's top sixty philanthropists, for example, totaled $4.6 billion in 2002, down from $12.7 billion in 2001. These drastic fluctuations are not the only problem. If the private sector is to play a serious part in addressing social crises in America, we need to stop defining charitable giving as any tax-deductible contribution to any old 501(c)3—a classifica-

tion that lumps together a struggling soup kitchen and a university with an endowment larger than the GDP of the poorest one hundred countries. There's a compelling reason for
the government to not reward these donations equally. Just
take a look at the Slate 60, the online magazine's answer to
the Forbes 400. It's an annual list of America's top charitable
givers. Year in and year out the list is dominated by those giving to already flush universities and museums—often to fund
buildings bearing the giver's name.

After I wrote about my objections to the buck-is-a-buck-is-
a-buck standard of the Slate rankings, its then editor, Michael
Kinsley, suggested I come up with a formula for adjusting the
list—correcting for true philanthropic spirit as one might correct for inflation. So in 2000 I devised a compassion index, or
as Slate dubbed it, "the Slate 60 Huffington Virtue Remix."
The Slate 60 is based on the principle of praise, but those on
the uncorrected list got plenty of that. I thought it was time
for a little humiliation.

The virtue remix awarded minus points for self-aggrandiz-
ing gifts that only serve to make the world of the superrich
just a little nicer, and plus points for gifts that help overcome
poverty, alleviate suffering, and turn lives around. For example: minus 10 percent for investing in buildings instead of
people (with another 15 percent deduction if the gift goes to
a building named after the donor); 20 percent off for "self-
referential giving" directly connected to the donor's business
interests; and a sliding scale of demerits based on the age of
the donor at the time of giving—a.k.a. the "What took you so
long?" factor. A 10 percent bonus, on the other hand, was
awarded for giving to K-12 education, where the crisis is,
rather than to Ivy League colleges, where the prestige and the
big bucks are. And there was a 15 percent bonus if giving
time went along with the gift of money.

The effect of the index on that year's list was telling: Forty-three donors had more points taken away than added, while only four gained points. A few donors dropped more than twenty places, and one moved up thirteen. The biggest hit was taken by William Porter, founder of the Internet brokerage E*Trade, and his wife, Joan. Their $25 million gift to MIT had placed them in a tie for the twenty-seventh spot on the original Slate 60, but they dropped thirty spots for donating a) to a building at b) an already well-endowed institution that c) is related to Mr. Porter's business and d) was named after himself.

Also feeling the sting of the index was Robert G. Mondavi, chairman of Robert Mondavi Winery, who was docked 30 percent for his self-referential gift of $20 million to the American Center for Wine, Food, and the Arts in his hometown of Napa, California. After sniffing and sipping (and yes, spitting), I found the donation cheeky and vainglorious, with strong notes of venality, and a hint of disingenuousness. Then there was Elmer E. Rasmuson, the former chairman of the National Bank of Alaska, who was penalized 20 percent for waiting until his ninetieth birthday party to announce a $50 million gift to the Anchorage Museum of History and Art. Did Elmer hit eighty and think, I'd better wait, there might be a $50 million emergency just around the bend? On the brighter side of the remix, cell phone mogul Craig Mc-Caw and his wife, Susan, moved up thirteen places for their $15 million to the Foundation for Community Development and the Nelson Mandela Foundation, striving to bring health care, economic development, and peace to Africa.

The original catalyst for the Slate 60 was Ted Turner's warning that the "superrich won't loosen up their wads because they're afraid they'll reduce their net worth and go down on the Forbes list." His corrective was "to honor the generous

and shame the stingy." The next step is for us all to acknowledge the obvious: Not all generosity is created equal, and so
we need to honor those among the generous whose sights extend beyond their own enclaves. Compassion and philanthropy can't fix America's problems on their own. But they fill
an even smaller portion of the gap between rich and poor
when they are directed where they are not urgently needed.

COMPASSIONATE CONSERVATISM IN THE HEADLINES

"Low-wage workers can't count on pay boost from new
overtime rules" *Associated Press*, January 6, 2004 •
"Prosperity Eludes Much Of Southeast" *Tampa Tribune*, November 9, 2003 • "Disappointing Gains; Only
1,000 new jobs in December" *Newsday*, January 10,
2004 • "Where are all the jobs? Expected surge in employment failed to materialize last month" *San Francisco
Chronicle*, January 10, 2004 • "The State of the Dream:
Unfulfilled; New Report: Black-White Gap Still Huge"
U.S. Newswire, January 7, 2004 • "Jobless Count Skips
Millions; The rate hits 9.7% when the underemployed
and those who have quit looking are added" *Los Angeles
Times*, December 29, 2003 • "Tennessee's jobless rate
increases in November" *Tennessean*, December 19,
2003 • "46% of schools 'left behind'; State test scores
show poor progress under controversial Bush law"
Hartford Courant, December 18, 2003 • "School dis-
tricts fall short; 99 systems in state put on warning list,
but many educators question federal standards" *Hartford Courant*, December 4, 2003 • "Budget Ax Would

Fall Heavily on the Poor, Ill" *Los Angeles Times*, January 10, 2004 • "Poverty in Michigan balloons by 25%; Recession drives number of poor to 1 million in '02" *Detroit News*, December 28, 2003 • "Fort Bend food pantry faces a growing need" *Houston Chronicle*, January 8, 2004 • "Changes to plan for kids criticized; Some services in Head Start would be cut under proposal" *Columbus Dispatch*, January 1, 2004, • "Extra benefits end, put jobless on edge" *The Kansas City Star*, December 31, 2003 • "Charity pantries are running low; Big demand outpaces supply of holiday food baskets in Bay Area" *San Francisco Chronicle*, December 21, 2003 • "For pickets, a growing sentiment of pessimism; Reduction in benefits takes mounting toll" *San Diego Union-Tribune*, December 20, 2003 • "State budget belt-tightening squeezes health care for kids" *USA Today*, December 19, 2003, • "Public, private employees feeling pinch of rising healthcare costs" *Los Angeles Times*, December 14, 2003 • "No rest for the needy; With hunger at record levels in Niagara County, food pantries are scrambling to meet the need" *Buffalo News*, December 7, 2003 • "Child-care center at risk; Money shortages could force cutbacks in infant programs" *Fort Lauderdale Sun-Sentinel*, November 28, 2003 • "Hunger has a new face; Ranks of those needing assistance increasingly include people with jobs" *Chicago Tribune*, September 1, 2003 • "Single mom learns hard lesson as budget woes KO'ed program" *Boston Herald*, February 25, 2003 • "For children of the incarcerated, Father's Day is just another day without Dad" *Austin American-Statesman*, June 15, 2003 • "When Time Runs Out; Welfare reform of 1996 pushes some people off rolls before they can sustain themselves, U. study finds; Welfare Reform: Families Falling Through Cracks" *Salt Lake Tribune,* January 5, 2003 • "Day care cuts strap poor; State plan may jeopardize welfare-to-work effort" *Detroit News,* July 18, 2003 • "Disconnected in metro Detroit: Residents who can't afford phones are cut off from basic necessities" *Detroit Free Press,* July 10, 2003 • "Los Angeles Study Says Welfare-to-Work Reforms Leave Recipients Below Poverty Line; Findings criticize L.A. County's emphasis on fast employment rather than training. Welfare officials dispute report." *Los Angeles Times,* July 23, 2003 • "State's poor losing gains made in '90s; Since 2000, signs of poverty on rise, report says" *Milwaukee Journal Sentinel,* October 15, 2003 • "Daily Choice Turned Deadly: Children Left on Their Own" *New York Times,* October 19, 2003 • "Laid-off take survival jobs to pay the bills" *USA Today,* October 23, 2003 • "Lean Times Strain Agencies: As their budgets dwindle, nonprofit groups struggle to help people who have lost jobs" *Columbus Dispatch,* OH, September 22, 2003 • "Underemployment up as degrees gather dust; Graduates settle for less in harsh market" *Houston Chronicle,* August 10, 2003 • "Downwardly Mobile: Thousands scrape by after losing good jobs" *New York Daily News,* July 20 2003 • "Underemployed search, cling to what they have" *Chicago Tribune,* April 4, 2003 • "Poverty comes even to those who work hard" *The Oregonian,* November 26, 2003 • "City's Working Poor A Study In Despair" *New York Daily News,* November 21, 2003 • "For Middle Class, Health Insurance Becomes a Luxury" *New York Times,* November 16, 2003 • "You have to feed your family; Working But Hungry: Having a job no longer means there's food on the table" *Patriot Ledger*, Quincy, MA, September 26, 2003 • "Poor Working Parents Losing Health Benefits" *Columbus Dispatch*, May 25, 2003 • "Poor but working: Families struggle" *Herald Times Reporter*, Manitowoc, WI, March 2, 2003 • "Working parents struggle with transportation" *South Bend Tribune*, IN, February 26, 2003 • "Working poor face social service cuts" *Bellingham Herald*, WA, December 27, 2002 • "From Middle Class to the Shelter Door; In a Trend, New Yorkers Face Poverty After Last Unemployment Check" *New York Times*, November 17, 2002 • "Aid Clock Ticks Down: County's first recipients of benefits in a five-year welfare-to-work program near limit, but many say they need more time" *San Diego Union-Tribune*, September 23, 2002 • "Persistent, quiet poverty belies image of suburban affluence" *Philadelphia Inquirer*, August 25, 2002 • "Welfare clock running out; As 5-year limit on benefits approaches, poor parents need financial help despite finding new jobs" *San Francisco Chronicle*, July 7, 2002 • "Living with a hefty rent burden; Low incomes put ceiling on options when looking for a roof to live under" *South Bend Tribune*, IN, July 1, 2002 • "Low-wage full-time workers still struggling, says study" *Associated Press*, May 27, 2002 • "Low-wage earners need help to become self-sufficient" *Capital Times*, Madison, WI, May 20, 2002 • "Former welfare recipients live in poverty, study says; The study also says that they continue to use some government assistance such as food stamps" *Des Moines Register*, April 26, 2002 • "After Welfare, Working Poor Still Struggle, Report Finds" *New York Times*,

April 25, 2002 • "Welfare-to-work mothers face array of new problems" *Kansas City Star*, April 16, 2002 • "Poverty Outlasts Welfare Reform; Recipients Landing Jobs, Staying Poor, Study Finds" *Hartford Courant*, February 19, 2002 • "The poorly paid; How do near-minimum wage workers in Alaska survive?" *Anchorage Daily News*, December 16, 2002 • "Scraping by: Getting by is getting harder and harder for working poor" *Connecticut Post*, November 18, 2002 • "Butte, Mont., Working Poor Spend Lives Juggling Time, Money to Make Ends Meet" *Montana Standard*, October 5, 2003 • "Welfare changes could leave many in cold" *Fort Collins Coloradoan*, October 6, 2003 • "Soup Kitchens See Signs Hunger Is On The Rise" *Journal News*, Westchester County, NY, August 18, 2003 • "1 in 3 Workers in Ventura County Can't Pay Basic Costs, Study Finds; Those earning less than $10 an hour are found to be struggling to make ends meet, let alone advance." *Los Angeles Times*, June 17, 2003 • "Farmworkers going hungry" *News & Observer*, Raleigh, NC, May 13, 2003 • "Numbers don't add up for the underemployed: Best efforts, followed rules yield less success" *Contra Costa Times*, October 19, 2003 • "Life on the edge: Getting off welfare is just the start for families trying to make ends meet" *Orange County Register*, September 22, 2003 • "More working households turn to food pantries to get by" *Associated Press*, August 31, 2003 • "Child care cuts hit bone; Thousands of working parents who were receiving state aid for child care will get less or none, as revised eligibility standards go into effect" *Star Tribune*, Minneapolis, MN, July 27, 2003 • "More turn to pantries to feed a family: First-

time users, including workers who are considered underemployed, drive up demand" *Omaha World Herald,* December 15, 2002 • "Working poor aren't making ends
meet; They earn too much to qualify for assistance" *Fort
Wayne News Sentinel,* November 21, 2002 • "Welfare
rules fail activists' reality check: Bush's latest plan adds
work hours, shortens training" *Boston Globe,* October
10, 2002 • "Retirement crisis looms as many come up
short" *USA Today,* July 19, 2002

PORTRAITS OF STRUGGLE

In the months following September 11, as the immediate shock of the attacks wore off, to be replaced with a
deep sense of grief, Americans struggled for an appropriate way to mourn the dead. The death toll was so
large that, for those of us fortunate enough not to have
had friends or family in the towers, the Pentagon, or on
one of the doomed planes, it was difficult not to see the
3,000 lost lives as a faceless mass of people. Trying to
come to grips with the tragedy in a new way, one that
acknowledged the dead as real people, the *New York
Times* began running a series of short biographical
sketches of the victims of 9/11 called "Portraits of
Grief." Because the process of identifying the bodies
and confirming the dead proceeded in fits and starts,
some days there would be dozens of portraits; other
days there would be just a few. Unlike the traditional
full-blown obituary of the great, the good, and the infamous, "Portraits of Grief" made the indelible point
that the dead of 9/11 were people just like us.

Inspired by "Portraits of Grief," the following are sketches of a handful of the legions of Americans currently falling through the tremendous tears in our social safety net.

Marzs Mata

Detroit, Michigan. Just getting to and from her $11-an-hour job as a Comcast customer service rep is a Herculean task for the fifty-year-old Marzs. Unable to afford a car and suffering with rheumatoid arthritis, she gets up every morning at 4:00 so she has enough time to shower, get dressed, make her lunch, and wait for her morning pain medication to kick in before she catches a 5:30 bus to get to work on time. The commute home is even more grueling, involving three different buses and taking as long as four hours to complete. Besides bouts of bad weather, Marzs has to deal with bus stops without benches, long waits on high-crime corners, a lack of public bathrooms, and hours of boredom, especially since she no longer has a way to listen to the music she loves. "My Walkman died about a year ago," she says. "That had been my salvation." So she sits, and rides, and dreams of someday being able to afford a car.

Armando Sandoval, Rayshawn Ward, Roger Myres

San Leandro, California; Tar Heel, North Carolina; Bellaire, Ohio. Armando Sandoval, Rayshawn Ward, and Roger Myres are among the millions of American workers who are increasingly finding themselves under fire on a variety of fronts, facing rampant job insecurity, poverty-level wages, rising health insurance costs, and unsafe working conditions. Call it the Wal-Martization of the working class. Following in a great and proud American tradition, all three tried to improve their lot in life by forming a union at their respective workplaces—only to find themselves harassed, intimidated, and eventually fired for their union activity.

Before being terminated, Armando Sandoval was a 19-year-old worker at the San Leandro plant of Cintas, the largest provider and industrial launderer of rental uniforms in North America. He earned $7.50 an hour loading and unloading uniform delivery trucks. Although Cintas has enjoyed 34 consecutive years of growth, with profits of $234 million in 2002, it still pays many of its workers wages that leave them below the federal poverty line. Workers are also being asked to bear the brunt of rising health insurance costs—making it impossible for many, including Armando, to afford it. Plus, Cintas workers must endure unsafe working conditions—the company has been cited over one hundred times by OSHA for violating federal health and safety laws. In an effort to change this, Armando became a visible supporter of his coworkers' attempts to unionize, and was fired in June 2003.

Rayshawn Ward, 28, is the father of an eight-year-old son with another child on the way. For two-and-a-half years he worked for Smithfield Foods in Tar Heel, North Carolina, the largest hog processing facility in the world. Workers there, primarily African Americans and Latino immigrants, kill and process thousands of hogs a day. In his time with the company,

Rayshawn worked in a number of departments, including the cut floor, box room, and kill floor. Troubled by the company's low wages, job insecurity, and racial discrimination, Rayshawn became a union activist. Following an unsuccessful union election, he was beaten by the company's private security guards and fired.

Roger Myres was born in 1961 and raised in Bellaire, Ohio. Like many of his family members before him, Roger went to work in the area's coal mines, where he worked for over twenty-eight years. In February 2002, Roger and his co-workers at Ohio Coal's Nelms mine decided to form a union because of increasingly unsafe working conditions and mandatory 12-hour shifts. A leader in the organizing campaign, Roger was threatened with the loss of his job by Ohio Coal management. After months of being involved in the organizing effort, he was discharged, along with thirty-two of his co-workers. At the time of his termination, Roger was the only certified mason working at the mine.

Frank and Claire Bentivegna

Yonkers, New York. Frank, 72, and his wife, Claire, 71, are two of the growing number of seniors who find themselves having to make the choice between paying their bills and buying medicine. The couple's $1,200-a-month retirement income doesn't allow Frank to receive benefits that would help cover the costs of the nine medications he has to take every day. So sometimes he has to choose: his health or his rent.

Rosa Rosario

Roslindale, Massachusetts. If there's an opposite of a mooch, a freeloader, a welfare-grubber looking for a handout, then Rosa Rosario is it. Rosa, 20, works the night shift as a nursing assistant and attends nursing school during the day. Her biggest challenge as a working mom on the bottom rung of the socioeconomic ladder is obtaining child care for her asthmatic daughter during the hours when she is working or in school. In order to get the necessary voucher for her daughter's day care, Rosa has to navigate an exhausting maze of red tape and indifference. When she gets to the end, she has to start all over again. The time-consuming process of keeping her daughter enrolled inevitably comes at the expense of work or school, yet another illustration of the impossible Hobson's choice forced upon poor working parents. Recently Rosa aged out of the Massachusetts free dental-care plan for children; she cannot afford to pay for routine dental care on her $434-per-month salary. Still, she is philosophical. "I guess I'll be toothless," she jokes.

Jo-Ann Nelson

Dorchester, Massachusetts. Jo-Ann Nelson is the sort of homeless person the fanatical right likes to pretend doesn't exist. Moving among shelters and friends' houses in the Boston area, Jo-Ann rises at 4:30 in the morning in order to begin a daylong journey to get her five children to their schools or school bus pickup spots. Although the school district is required by law to transport Jo-Ann's children from wherever they are staying,

Three million jobs have been lost in the last three years. Let's try for three million and one— George Bush's.

in practice the schools simply ignore the law. Jo-Ann's problem is that she earns slightly too much from extremely unreliable child support payments to qualify for welfare. She's just above the cutoff point, the official national poverty level of $15,260 per year. A more realistic independent study determined that a family of Jo-Ann's size in the Boston area needs about $50,000 per year to be self-sufficient. Recently settled in an apartment subsidized by the Office of Transitional Assistance, Jo-Ann is receiving only emergency aid, which she understandably fears could evaporate at any moment. But with an apartment of her own, one fear, at least, has been removed—the fear of her daughters being raped, as two of them were last year when they had no place of their own.

Orlando Fonseca

Harlem, New York. Although he may be too proud to accept the characterization, forty-four-year-old Orlando Fonseca is a classic example of an American who, despite a lifetime of hard work, remains locked in poverty. A high school dropout who subsequently earned his GED—with little effect on his salary—Orlando now works at an advertising agency, where he makes $25,000 a year. Still, he is grateful for what he has. "It's getting harder to find a job," Orlando says, "and I'm just happy to be working. Manhattan is very expensive. I have three grown kids and we live in public housing. We all kind of pitch in together. That's the only way we are able to make it work." Medical insurance is a particular problem for Orlando and his family. Because he is not destitute, he is ineligible for the sort of low-cost coverage that he needs. Clearly, there is something very wrong with a system in which Orlando has a clear incentive to quit his job or work fewer hours in order to earn less money so that he can qualify for health care. Between a bureaucratic rock and a policy hard place, he muses, "You think you are making extra money, and it turns out you are making just enough to get you by. There are still a lot of things, opportunities that you are not able to have."

Lisa Brown

Fresno, California. Don't talk to Lisa Brown about family values. Lisa, a single mother, is the victim of a brutal irony: because she looks after her eleven-year-old son, Alexander, who suffers from Down syndrome and needs full-time care, she is ineligible for social security, unemployment, workers' comp, and health care. The state of California pays Lisa $7.50 an hour to care for Alexander. Because she has a bacteriology degree from UC Berkeley, Lisa would theoretically be able to get a much higher-paying job if she gave up taking care of her son herself, but high turnover and scarce supply among home-care workers make this impossible. The reason there are so few reliable in-home caretakers is obvious to Lisa since she is one: low pay and no benefits. Yet even the inadequate program that Lisa relies on to pay for her care of Alexander, called Protective Supervision, is on the chopping block under the Schwarzenegger budget cut. Of her plight, Lisa says, "I don't want Alex left in the hands of someone who can take advantage of him, and I don't want to place him in an institution. It's just such a struggle. I don't care about being poor, I'll deal with it, but I can't live on nothing."

Cynthia Jackson

Seattle, Washington. A measure of our collective humanity as a society is whether we give our fellow citizens the sort of second chances we would give them if they were our own brothers, sisters, husbands, wives, or children. Cynthia Jackson embarked on adulthood with a great deal of promise. A star athlete, she had to drop out of college after scholarship money and student loans ran out. Still, she was able to land and hold a good job with the Federal Reserve in Seattle until she became ill from a severe allergic reaction caused by an asbestos abatement project in her office. Chronically ill ever since, Cynthia descended down a spiral of self-destructive behavior that led from occasional marijuana use to crack cocaine addiction and a series of abusive relationships. Cynthia has waged battles with both the state and a hopeless financial situation to continue to be able to care for her two kids, who themselves have severe health problems. Thanks to her own desire to change her situation for the better and to be a good mom to her kids, and aided by a publicly funded mental health program, Cynthia has not used crack in four years. She has begun to turn her life around. A caring society, especially a rich one, must find a way to offer a helping hand to people like Cynthia, who have turned away from the brink and are trying to return to a productive life.

Bernadette Cisneros

St. Paul, Minnesota. Bernadette Cisneros, a thirty-year-old mother of two, was born on the Pine Ridge Indian Reservation in South Dakota. An Oglala Sioux, she now lives in St. Paul, Minnesota, where she is struggling to raise her kids and complete her training so that she can fulfill her life's dream to work as a medical assistant. In trying to support her kids Bernadette makes use of state aid programs like the local Ramsey Action Program, which helps pay her heating and electric bill, and the Minnesota Family Investment Program, which offers assistance with her rent. Still, it hasn't been easy. While her work situation continues to be uncertain, she must also struggle with her daughter's asthma. As of this writing, she is trying, with limited success, to both care for her kids and work at a job to support them.

Dagmar Baker

Santa Rosa, California. Dagmar Baker, a fifty-nine-year-old divorced mother of two grown children, contracted polio when she was seven days old. Over the course of her life, she has had twenty-two operations to treat the effects of the disease. Confined to a wheelchair since a botched operation in 2002 damaged her sciatic nerve, Dagmar is no longer able to get the physical therapy that her doctor says could enable her to walk again because her Medicare benefits expired in September of 2003. As she explains, "I was at a point where I was just getting the strength to walk, and now I'm set back because I have used up my physical therapy benefits." Although she longs to be fully independent, walking again and working as she did in the 1970s, Dagmar faces instead a very gloomy prognosis: an increasingly homebound, sedentary lifestyle in a home that she may not be able to afford for much longer.

Jennifer Borel

Nacogdoches, Texas. "Just because I receive assistance from the state does not make my family different from others. My family (especially my children) still has the same needs and wants as any other families. My family is a very normal family; we eat dinner together, go to the park together, go to church together, and do many things that other families do together. The only difference is in my family there is only one parent and we receive assistance. I do not like being on assistance. It isn't one of the things that I am proudest of, but at this point in time it is something I do need."

That's Jennifer Borel, a thirty-year-old divorced mother of two, writing about her struggle to raise her kids, to get her daughter to choir practice or her son to a soccer game, while studying full-time for her college degree and working part-time for minimum wage as a cashier and waitress. For Jennifer college was, oddly enough, a last resort, though, as she puts it, "not a bad resort." Lacking any job skills and abandoned financially by the fathers of her kids, without friends or family capable of sharing her burden, Jennifer faced the stark choice of either joining the military or getting the education she needed to find a decent job. Unwilling to leave her kids in unreliable hands if she were deployed overseas, she embarked upon the latter course, despite the grueling schedule it imposed upon her life. For now, were it not for the government assistance she receives, Jennifer would be forced into the impossible situation of having to work harder and harder to provide less and less for her kids, who would end up spending much of their childhoods without her care and supervision.

Dolores Alcantar

Los Angeles, California. If you think that, at the very least, you can always find a job at the post office, think again. Forty-two-year-old Dolores Alcantar, a single mother of four, has been working for the postal service in the City of Industry, California. She endures long morning and evening commutes, six-day-work weeks, and long hours, but the hardest part of her job is that it is about to end. After less than a year, Dolores's temporary job is being phased out. Dolores saves on rent by living at her mother's house, another temporary arrangement that adds uncertainty and anxiety to her life. Neither Dolores nor her kids (ages two to twenty) have health care. The saddest thing about her situation is that not only does Dolores need to work, she wants to work, and she's willing to do the sort of jobs that many people would turn down. In the past five years, she's worked as a maid, at a factory that makes backpacks, and at a recycling plant—never for more than minimum wage. Her primary obstacle is her limited English, which she is able to improve only very gradually because she has no time or money to attend class. To her new governor, she says, "From children to the elderly, provide health insurance for all, rather than taking it away from the poor."

Tony R.

Los Angeles, California. Some 30,000 abused and neglected children in Los Angeles County are put in foster care, with the court placing 40 percent of them with relatives. That's what happened to troubled teen, Tony R. (Since he's a minor, I've withheld his last name.) With his mother in jail, he was living in foster care with his grandmother and three siblings. When he got into trouble with the law and was put in a probation camp, his grandmother lost the monthly federal foster care payment of $597. When Tony was released from camp, his probation officer gave a report to the court asking the judge to "suitably place" Tony with his grandmother—a legal distinction that would reinstate the federal payment. Instead the judge refused to "suitably place" Tony but still chose to release him to his grandmother, who could not afford to care for him without the federal assistance. The judge also ordered Tony to attend a "continuation school" that required school uniforms. Not having enough money to buy one, and facing incarceration if he didn't show up for school, Tony solved the problem by stealing the uniform. He was caught and reincarcerated for ten months. Thus, the system successfully turned yet another struggling child on the brink into a delinquent one. And all at great human and financial cost.

Lisa Rodriguez

Fairfield, California. Lisa Rodriguez makes $11 per hour working as a janitor at Travis Air Force Base. Lisa's immediate peril—and that of her family—is a simple matter of mathematics. A widow for the last eleven years, Lisa cares not only for her own two kids but also for her late husband's three children from a prior marriage. In addition she helps support her own parents, who have been impoverished by their living expenses, especially health insurance, for which her mother pays $600 per month. Social Security, mercifully politically sacrosanct—at least for now—helps out with $160 monthly payments for each child, but in the last year, Lisa has been disqualified from both Medi-Cal and a food stamp program because at $440 per week before taxes, she supposedly earns too much. Lisa currently relies on California's Healthy Families program for limited health care for her kids. Capping Healthy Families, as has been proposed, will leave families like Lisa's that are not yet enrolled with nowhere to turn. In hope of helping others, Lisa has been something of a spokesperson for the program, testifying before the California State Senate in December 2003. Describing her experience, she says, "I've learned that you have to pick your battles in life. I lost ninety-two dollars, what I make in a day, when I missed work on December 10, 2003, to speak about Healthy Families before the California Senate. In the long run, if I can keep kids on Healthy Families, it's worth losing a day's pay."

Maria Perez

Los Angeles, California. The terrible toll of the Bush administration's policy of neglect of the working poor is easy to ignore, not because Americans are innately callous or selfish, but because so many of the effects are invisible. Maria Perez is a forty-nine-year-old single mom with four kids, two of whom are still at home. Maria works as a certified nursing assistant at a convalescent home where she earns $9.35 per hour for the difficult work of tending to full-care geriatric patients—changing diapers, giving them showers, and keeping them occupied with activities. As a team leader at her workplace, Maria also supervises other workers, a task she describes as more onerous than satisfying, responsibility without reward. The result is that Maria lives, day in and day out, with the sort of stress that comes with negotiating the minefield of her daily existence. "Work is very stressful for a job that gets paid very little," she says. Besides her job, Maria must also cope with the innumerable burdens that come with poverty, including the death of her son in a random drive-by shooting in their crime-ridden neighborhood. Like so many of the hardworking poor, Maria sees an obvious and simple solution for her problems: job skills training. But how she could ever find time to work, take care of her kids, and attend class is another matter. After living in this country for twenty-five years, Maria has become utterly disillusioned with her government. "I live confused," she says. "I can't believe in any single politician or piece of legislation. I can only believe in God."

SACRIFICE IS FOR SUCKERS

"And all our military families that mourn can know this: our nation will never forget the sacrifice their loved one made." That was the president speaking to assembled military families at Fort Carson last November. I wish a member of a mourning military family had asked Mr. Bush why soldiers and their families are the only ones being asked to sacrifice. What about the rest of the country?

The truth is that in speech after speech since September 11, the president has been asking very little of us. During one speech he recommended we "be a Boy Scout leader or a Girl Scout leader." At another he suggested that Americans "put their arm around somebody who hurts and say, 'I love you. What can I do to help you? How can I make a difference in your life?'" Unfortunately, he failed to mention what to do when the answer comes back: "Take your arm off me and get me some affordable health insurance!"

Now, I'm not saying that there is anything wrong with being a Boy Scout leader or telling people that you love them (even when you don't; by the way, Mr. President, I love you). Indeed, I'm all in favor of these things. But there is a world of difference between urging easy, spare-change charity and championing a cause that will transform our society. It's the difference between patronizing us with flaccid, stump-speech rhetoric and invoking patriotism to rally us as a nation to a common cause. Imagine how different our country would be if President Bush had used his political capital after 9/11 to call on the American people to commit themselves to a large, collective purpose.

So here is a new bargain that the Democratic nominee should strike with the American people: "Let's put an end to the tyranny of low expectations," he should say. "You can expect a lot more of me, and I will ask a lot more of you."

President Bush claims to believe in our country. So why doesn't he believe in us enough to ask us to make a collective commitment to confront both the horrors wrought by terrorists and the horrors wrought by random violence in our inner cities and by woefully inadequate health care, education, and housing? Why doesn't he believe in us enough to ask us to share in the sacrifices necessary to build a country of real opportunity for all, and a sturdy social safety net? I believe the country was ready to do that after September 11, and I believe it's still ready.

Far from asking us to share in the sacrifice, since September 11 all the president has asked us to do is return to our normal lives. His opponent should ask, "But why stop there? Why not commit ourselves to larger goals and a greater purpose? To living not merely normal but better lives?" George Bush urged us to "get down to Disney World in Florida," and Arnold Schwarzenegger urged us to "Buy cars! Buy new cars! Buy used cars!" But spending a wad of cash cannot be all our leaders ask of us. The truest expression of American character has always been not our will to amuse ourselves but our choice to give of ourselves.

While campaigning for the nomination, John Kerry spoke about ushering in a new era of national service: "We have seen before," he said, "what happens when we appeal to the best instincts of America. Confined to his wheelchair, Franklin Roosevelt summoned Americans to stand tall against the tide of depression. Sixty years ago, his Civilian Conservation Corps sent millions of the young out to rebuild the nation even as they built a better life for themselves. John Kennedy called my generation to the Peace Corps—and Lyndon Johnson's VISTA opened up the chance to serve in the most forgotten places in our own land, valleys of deprivation and despair so often unseen and unheard."

Remember September 12, 2001? On that day blood banks overflowed, tens of millions of dollars poured into charities, and such a throng of people showed up to help at

The truest expression of American character is not our will to amuse ourselves but our choice to give of ourselves.

Ground Zero that most had to be turned away. It was the worst of times, yet it was the best of times. It was in the middle of that horrible crisis that the best aspects of the American character—generosity, selflessness, courage—came to the fore and reminded us of those intangible qualities that make our nation great.

Despite the passage of time, the values and spirit that emerged that day are still very much part of who we are, and can still be harnessed, if the right leader issues the challenge. In this spirit, the Democratic nominee will have to talk straight to the American people, because this president certainly won't. Instead he is telling the nation that we can carry the burden of a worldwide war on terror and the Iraqi occupation while giving ourselves a multitrillion-dollar tax cut and a huge new prescription drug benefit without cost containment. We can't, of course. But he assumes that he will be safely reelected before enough Americans realize it.

Further evidence of Republican hypocrisy can be found in Bush's empty promises for programs that encourage service. Take his promise to increase funding for AmeriCorps, a network of national service programs that provides stipends and college grants to young people who commit to working in local communities. Reiterating a pledge from his State of the Union address, Bush promised graduating Ohio State University students in 2002 to "increase AmeriCorps by 50 percent." Apparently the Republican Congressional delegation didn't get the memo; it instead killed $100 million in emergency funding for AmeriCorps before the 2003 summer recess. Bush continues to pay lip service to AmeriCorps but does nothing to stop the hemorrhaging caused by poor management and reduced funding. The promise of increasing AmeriCorps by 50 percent is hanging out there unfulfilled.

Equally egregious is the president's say-one-thing-do-an-

other touting of Teach for America, a remarkable program
that has placed 10,000 new college graduates in inner city and
rural community schools. Teach for America founder Wendy
Kopp sat next to the first lady at the State of the Union address
in January 2002. A year earlier she had received the president's
accolade at a school in Atlanta: "I am proud to stand up and
talk about the best of America and Wendy Kopp. . . . I hope
young Americans all across the country think about joining
Teach for America." Cut to July 2003, when Teach for America lost its entire $14 million in AmeriCorps funding, and
3,200 teachers lost their grants. Around that time I found myself sitting next to Wendy Kopp on a shuttle flight from
Boston to New York. She was, not surprisingly, stunned by the
reversal and desperately looking elsewhere to make up for the
cut in funding.

Nor is AmeriCorps the only example of the Bush bait and
switch. We also have Citizen Corps and the USA Freedom
Corps and the Peace Corps. In 2002 the president created
the Citizen Corps program as a way for average citizens "to
join in the war against terror." "This is a way where you can
help America," the president said in Knoxville, Tennessee, in
April 2002. "The government will help, as well. I put in my
budget $203 million to help on the Citizen Corps pro-
grams." Well, not really. In 2002, Citizen Corps received
only $25 million, in 2003 it received nothing, and in 2004 it
received $40 million.

The same with the USA Freedom Corps. In June 2002 the
president announced what he called "an historic partnership.
We are bringing together the broadest group of service organizations ever assembled to create the USA Freedom Corps
Network." Historic partnership? It's more like a job search en-
gine for volunteers. And the director of the USA Freedom
Corps, John Bridgeland, resigned at the end of last year.

So did Peace Corps Director Gaddi Vasquez. The president had pledged in June 2002 that we would be "doubling the size of the Peace Corps." But Vasquez explained that this was not going to be possible, because of lower-than-expected funding. The president still trots out his commitment to great service initiatives like the Peace Corps or Ameri-Corps. Or, with great fanfare, he announces new initiatives like the USA Freedom Corps. But the sad fact is that these are little more than rhetorical commitments, lacking any serious presidential backing.

This Grand Canyon–sized gulf between stated beliefs and actions or, more accurately, inactions was pointed out recently by the Reverend Joseph C. Hough, president of the faculty of the Union Theological Seminary, when he took to task those in the administration who consider themselves to be devoutly religious and yet have no problem ignoring the poorest segments of American society. "If Tom DeLay," he explained, "is acting out of his born-again Christian convictions in pushing legislation that disadvantages the poor every time he opens his mouth, I'm not saying he's not a born-again Christian, but as the Lord's humble fruit inspector, it sure looks suspicious to me. . . . There is no justification under heaven for some corporate executives to make one thousand times as much as their average worker."

AMERICORPS AND ME

Ask any supporter of AmeriCorps and he'll tell you that AmeriCorps acts like a magnet, drawing in volunteers to communities where they are desperately needed.

But during my Republican years, when I believed that many of our social problems could be solved with lots of charity, I scoffed at the notion of offering financial support to volunteers. After all, isn't "paid volunteer" an oxymoron? In fact, on October 17, 1995, I testified against AmeriCorps in Congress, convinced that young people should volunteer out of the noble impulses of their hearts, not because they are getting a few dollars in return. "Helping those in need is a moral imperative," I testified back then. "It is our responsibility—our obligation—and in a completely different realm from getting loans to go to school or money to live on. The people I most admire in this world are volunteering their time every day without the benefit of any fancy, bureaucratically run programs."

That's still true. What's different is that I've come to realize what a vital role programs like AmeriCorps can play in supporting the charitable efforts of those working in the trenches.

My conversion began roughly two seconds after I finished my testimony. Harris Wofford, the former senator from Pennsylvania who was then running Ameri-Corps, came rushing up to me. I was expecting him to read me the riot act, but instead he asked me to lunch. I was taken aback but intrigued, and off we went for some grilled chicken, a green salad, and a side order of crow.

I must admit I'm a sucker for passion, and Wofford—who had been instrumental in setting up the Peace Corps and had worked closely with Robert Kennedy—had more passion than an entire season of *Sex and the City.* And now he was bringing it all to bear on the AmeriCorps mission of fostering national service by training 50,000 Americans a year to, among other things, tutor at-risk kids, build homes, help seniors, clean up trails and rivers, and assist the victims of natural disasters. "My dream," Wofford explained, "is to make service of a substantial kind a common expectation of young people."

It was a masterful seduction. I don't think I'll ever forget the moment when we first locked eyes and he said to me, "Together we can crack the atom of civic power." I soon witnessed firsthand how, far from undermining the spirit of giving, as I had feared, AmeriCorps members actually draw in other volunteers. Indeed, Wofford estimates that "every AmeriCorps member generates and makes possible the work of about twelve occasional volunteers."

As it turned out, the list of erstwhile AmeriCorps foes converted by Wofford is long and impressive and includes many lawmakers not noted for flapping in the wind of legislative fashion, like Senators John McCain and Rick Santorum, and former Rep. John Kasich. In fact, McCain and Santorum—who once mocked AmeriCorps as a place "for hippie kids to stand around a campfire holding hands and singing 'Kumbaya' at taxpayer expense"—each ended up introducing legislation to expand the program. Kasich was adamantly opposed to AmeriCorps until he started researching a book on leadership and compassion and discovered that the program he admired most, the Harlem Peacemakers, would not have been possible without the participation of fifty AmeriCorps members.

Still deeply committed to mobilizing the country's young people, Wofford took over as chairman of America's Promise—a post first held by Colin Powell. Of course, charm and enthusiasm can only get you so far. In the end it was confrontation with reality that transformed the thinking of so many influential Republicans. While, in theory, the private sector can rise to the occasion and provide the time and money needed to solve social problems, in the real world—of which conservatives pride themselves on being the only true inhabitants—it simply doesn't. It is sad but true that the task of overcoming our social problems is too monumental to be accomplished without government and all the incentives we can muster to urge Americans—especially young ones—to make service a part of their lives.

CIVIL SOCIETY:
HANGING IN THE BALANCE

For our society and economy to work, there must be balance and partnership between the public and private sectors. Once again, Bobby Kennedy points the way. According to Peter Edelman, who served as Kennedy's legislative assistant (and who later resigned in protest as assistant secretary of Health and Human Services when Bill Clinton signed the Welfare Reform Act), RFK's vision straddles the partisan squabbling pitting the Great Society against the Rising Tide. "Robert Kennedy," writes Edelman in *Searching for America's Heart,* "was the first to espouse values of grassroots empowerment and express doubts about big bureaucratic approaches, the first to call for partnerships between the private and public sectors and insist that what we now call civic renewal is essential, the first to put particular emphasis on personal responsibility."

The moral vision that America needs must be similarly balanced, and should not be seen in left-right terms, which conceal more than they reveal. Unlike policies identified with the left, this moral vision is decidedly not antibusiness. Instead, it is probusiness so long as business is ethically conducted, and so long as the rule of law applies no less to corporations than it does to ordinary citizens. In the same way, this vision for America is not against free markets. It's against the current system of unfair markets where the rules are bent for those who can afford to buy influence and politicians. Subsidies, tax credits and lax enforcement of accounting and securities laws are all obstacles to a truly free market, and benefit only those who can afford to play the game. Those without adequate access and power are relegated to the sidelines.

Currently, businesses do not have to account for the costs they inflict on the community. Imagine, for example, if we imposed "dumping fees" on companies that sell fossil fuels to compensate the community for the pollution these fuels create. Not only would the community be reimbursed for some of the health care cost of the pollution, but businesses would have an incentive to switch to cleaner fuels in order to reduce their fees. The result would be a classic win/win situation. Instead of the win/lose game we're playing now.

What we have at the moment, however, is anything but a balanced relationship between the public and the private sectors. If there were ever an era in which the fox was incontrovertibly in control of the henhouse, this is it. Want to drill for oil on previously protected public lands? Go right ahead! Want to avoid installing pollution control mechanisms while you modernize your power plant? By all means! Need permission to increase logging on public lands? How about a subsidy to ranch cattle on environmentally sensitive rangelands? Want to own all the radio stations, newspapers, and television stations in any given town? What about a whole state? Afraid that a modest increase in fuel economy standards will ruin your plans to sell more giant SUVs? Come on down! A free pass is offered to all. In the long run, however, if government is unwilling to safeguard people's health and manage a prudent, sustainable use of our natural resources, we are all at risk.

Obviously, government is not the sole answer to all these problems. But the unfettered free market is clearly not the answer either. If it had been left to the market, child labor would likely still be a part of the American economy. The fact is that the free market does not discriminate between those economic activities that are beneficial and those that are damaging. By traditional economic measures, a forest can only be valued when it is cut down for paper or timber. Yet as Michael Gelobter, director of Redefining Progress, a think tank devoted to promoting sustainability, points out, "In the case of clear-cutting, the GDP counts that sale of wood as growth. But cutting down a 30-year-old tree is a liquidation of a 30-year-old capital item. To count that as cash income is an accounting error. It's a depreciating error."

As John F. Kennedy said in 1963, "Our most basic common link is that we all inhabit this planet. We all cherish our children's future. And we are all mortal." There are many examples of government playing an instrumental role in harnessing the market to achieve positive change for our children's future. The debate should not be about big versus small government, but about leadership that protects the status quo versus leadership that can see around the corner and provide incentives for the future waiting to be built.

I believe more fervently than ever that government dollars, however many trillions of them, will never mend broken lives without citizen engagement. What I have found, whether in South Central L.A. or in downtown Washington,

D.C., is the truth of what the Reverend Henry Delaney, who has been transforming boarded-up crack houses in Savannah, Georgia, once told me: "I want to get people involved in what we're doing. It's like putting a poker in the fire. After a while, the fire gets in the poker too."

THE NEW CONTRACT FOR A BETTER AMERICA

For government to do its part in turning this moral vision into reality, the Democratic nominee must flesh it out with a comprehensive agenda that resets the country's priorities.

Here's my suggestion: Let's take a page from the GOP playbook of 1994 and offer up not a "Contract with America" but a "New Contract for a Better America."

Here's a draft:

1. ACHIEVE ENERGY INDEPENDENCE

America must have a sane energy policy that protects the environment, stresses fuel efficiency, and invests in clean and renewable energy. Forty-two years ago, President John F. Kennedy challenged America to realize its greatness, calling for the Apollo Project to put a man on the moon in a decade. Eight years later, Neil Armstrong bounced across the lunar surface. The Democratic nominee must promise that, as president, he will use the unique bully pulpit of his office to call on all Americans to commit themselves to the goal of achieving energy independence in a decade—with no more environmentally destructive drilling and no more unsafe nuclear waste.

At the Massachusetts State Convention in July 2003, John Kerry was unequivocal about the importance of this: "Now we must engage in the greatest challenge of all. We must decide that just as President Kennedy challenged us to go to the moon in the 1960s, we will 'go to the moon' right here on earth by declaring that never again will young American soldiers, men and women, be held hostage to our dependency on Middle East oil. We need a president who will boldly set America on the path to energy independence. God only gave us 3 percent of the world's oil reserves. There is no metaphysical or miraculous way for us to drill our way out of a 60 percent foreign oil dependency. We have to invent our way out of it and I want American jobs and American ingenuity leading the way."

We can do this by investing in energy efficiency, modern electric infrastructure, and renewables like solar and wind, and by putting an end to the corporate welfare that subsidizes obsolete technologies. A great model is the new Apollo Project, a $300 billion program proposed by unions and environmental groups to create 3 million new jobs while reducing America's foreign oil dependence over the next ten years. We can do it by investing in technologies that bring us closer to realizing the hydrogen future, the next generation of hybrid cars, mass transit options that are clean, fast, and more convenient, and "green buildings"—energy-efficient homes and offices. We should also make LEED (the environmental standard by which green buildings are designed) the standard for all new buildings, which would result in huge energy savings and an enormous improvement in urban environments.

It surely does not make any sense that China's fuel economy standards exceed our own, or that Congress has actually undone energy efficiency standards, leaving us more firmly than ever in the clutches of imported oil. The Democratic nominee must promise not only to make us oil-independent from foreign countries harboring terrorists, but also to make our government independent of the interests of Big Oil and the outmoded policies crafted to serve it.

AN ENERGY SPEECH FOR THE DEMOCRATIC NOMINEE

My fellow Americans, I come before you today to announce that, if elected, I will call on the American people to put an end to our destructive and shortsighted dependence on oil.

During World War II, President Roosevelt created the Manhattan Project—the remarkable wartime effort that enlisted the greatest scientific and technical minds in the country to help defeat the tyranny of fascism. Today, as we fight the war on terrorism, we must commit the same all-out effort to freeing ourselves from the nations and terrorists holding us hostage through our addiction to oil.

With this in mind, I will call upon Congress to immediately enact legislation to raise the mileage standards for cars and SUVs to forty miles per gallon—a move that will save American car owners $45 billion each and every year on their gasoline bill, money that can be used to stimulate our economy.

I will also direct Congress to close the senseless loophole that allows the biggest gas-guzzlers to get the biggest tax breaks, starting with the ludicrous tax credit signed into law by the current president that increased by 400 percent the already substantial write-off available to buyers of the least efficient SUVs. People buying fully loaded Hummers, Navigators, and Land Cruisers should not be able to immediately deduct from their tax bill the entire purchase price of their vehicles. Instead I will call upon Congress to transfer those incentives to hybrid cars that get sixty miles to the gallon as opposed to ten.

As was made refreshingly clear by the National Highway Safety Administrator, Dr. Jeffrey Runge, when it comes to SUVs, size doesn't equal safety. The rollover death rate is three times higher in SUVs than in cars. So our current policies aren't fair, they aren't smart, and they aren't safe.

But Washington can't solve this crisis on its own. That's why I will challenge the American auto industry to use hybrid technology already available to produce a full line of socially responsible vehicles—including hybrid SUVs. More than ever, we need the talent and entrepreneurial spirit Detroit has exhibited in the past. We must also mobilize the resources at our disposal to develop the hydrogen fuel cell technology that will set us free from our dependence on oil. We can't simply drill our way to energy freedom. It can only be achieved through conservation and innovation. And rest assured, if American industry doesn't rise to this mission, its competitors will.

President Bush has asked Americans to do their part in the war on terror by shopping and traveling. It isn't enough. Look into your children's eyes and imagine telling them that because of our greed and thoughtlessness they will be inheriting a more dangerous world.

I'm calling on you to commit yourselves to this large, collective purpose of security and oil independence—and to the shared sacrifice needed to meet this monumental challenge. I'm asking each of you out there to do your part by making your next car a more fuel-efficient one. An increase of just three miles per gallon would save us from having to import 1 million barrels of oil a day—and from having to go begging for it, hat in hand, to countries that harbor terrorists, like Saudi Arabia.

And I will call on governors around the country to follow the lead set by Gov. Mitt Romney of Massachusetts, who has proposed trading in his state's fleet of SUVs for cars that cost less, pollute less, and get better mileage.

My friends, we have everything we need to win the war on terrorism. We just have to summon the strength, the spirit, and the drive that have defined every turning point of this great nation.

We can do better. We must do better. We will do better.

2. PRESCRIBE A CURE FOR THE HEALTH CARE EPIDEMIC

America is on the brink of a health care disaster. We have 43 million Americans uninsured and millions more facing a black hole of inadequate coverage as increasing numbers of employers scale back on the benefits, if any, they offer workers. In order to address the crisis, the Democratic nominee has to establish three bedrock principles: 1) Health coverage has to be universal. 2) It has to include preventive care. 3) It has to put an end to the economic tyranny of the pharmaceutical industry, which, with its massive lobbying and campaign contributions, has succeeded again and again—including in the latest Medicare bill—in buying protection from sensible cost-cutting measures.

Of all the Democratic candidates, Wesley Clark laid out the clearest rationale for a health care safety net—one based on the military model. Over the course of thirty-four years in the military, he learned firsthand that those who don't receive adequate medical attention don't live up to their abilities. As Clark put it on the campaign trail, "We should be doing much more with preventive and diagnostic care. We need a comprehensive preventive medicine program for this country. We call it 'executive fitness' in the army. It's an executive wellness program. Why isn't there an American wellness program?"

If an ounce of prevention is worth a pound of cure, then a few pennies of prevention could save some of the $1.55 trillion that Americans are currently spending on health care. Studies by the Preventive Medicine Research Institute show that simple lifestyle changes like a healthier diet and moderate exercise can reduce the need for expensive treatments like heart bypass surgery and angioplasty by up to 80 percent, with immediate cost savings per patient of approximately $30,000. But the seemingly obvious strategy of improving the health of Americans by preventing them from becoming ill in the first place remains largely untried. Public education to encourage people to reduce their cholesterol level by making simple lifestyle changes rather than taking a pill could save a large portion of the $15 billion spent every year on cholesterol-reducing drugs, not to mention the cost of the ailments caused by high cholesterol. Sure, the makers of Lipitor won't like it—disease is their business—but a healthier America means providing our citizens with the information and the encouragement they need to increase their chances of staying out of the hospital—and the disease economy—in the first place.

This is not bleeding-heart liberalism, it's pragmatic leadership that ultimately saves money as well as lives.

A popular definition of insanity is doing the same thing over and over again while expecting a different result. Well, that seems to be the White House theory on the power of tax cuts to produce new jobs: it didn't work before; let's try it again.

3. TREAT LOST JOBS AS A SOCIAL CALAMITY, NOT A LAGGING ECONOMIC INDICATOR

Three million jobs have been lost in the last three years. Let's try for three million and one—George Bush's. Instead of celebrating every tiny percentage increase in the GDP, even when there is no real increase in jobs to go with it, we need to redefine our idea of national economic health. And it should start with recognizing that when a great number of Americans are out of work the economy cannot be called "healthy." The crippling effects of unemployment extend well beyond unemployed workers' dwindling bank accounts. Child abuse and neglect, divorce, crime, poor health and drug addiction are often the devastating side effects of lost jobs.

If the Democratic nominee is to return the country to an era of job creation, he must initiate a threefold plan.

First, he must propose, as Wesley Clark did, a $100 billion "Restore America" plan. Some of the money will be used to improve homeland security by hiring and training first responders, public health personnel, and security providers for critical installations and ports. Other funds will be paid out to states and cities to finance the hiring of workers to repair and rebuild crucial civic infrastructure like roads and schools.

The second job creation measure has to be a comprehensive package to plug the drain of jobs overseas. It must include tax credits for companies that keep and create jobs for American workers and must close loopholes that encourage employers to ship jobs abroad. It is estimated that at least 15 percent of the jobs lost since the Bush recession began have been lost due to corporations outsourcing jobs to lower-paid foreign workers. And these are not just blue-collar manufacturing jobs; experts predict that by the end of 2004, one in ten U.S. technology jobs will have been shipped overseas.

Finally, in keeping with a forward-looking energy policy, investing in renewables will not only be good for the environment and for oil independence but it will also tap into a multibillion-dollar world market, creating an explosion of well-paying high-tech jobs and nurturing the next generation of job-creating entrepreneurs.

4. TRULY LEAVE NO CHILD BEHIND

The Democratic nominee must put children at the top of his agenda. Not merely to leave no child behind but to put every child first.

Our nation's children continue to get the short end of the policy stick because they have no powerful lobby to make sure they are not always the first to be targeted by budget cuts. After all, they can neither vote nor contribute. Maybe the answer is for poor, uninsured kids to organize and create a junior version of the AARP—the FVA (Future Voters of America).

The president made his No Child Left Behind Act the heart of his domestic agenda. It turned out to be another broken promise, this time to our children. During the Bush years we have moved further and further away from the fundamental principle that every child should begin life on an equal footing when it comes to the basics: a good school, access to health care, and clean air and water.

Indeed, the supreme irony is that we are now willing to invest tens of thousands of dollars a year on a child who goes wrong and winds up in the criminal justice system but are begrudging the far smaller amount it would cost to help these kids lead the kind of productive lives that would keep them out of jail in the first place. We can pay now, or pay later. The problem is, later is much more expensive—and not just in dollars. "What genuinely Judeo-Christian society," asks Jonathan Kozol, who has written extensively about children growing up in poverty, "would ever spend more than ten times as much to incarcerate a child as it would to educate him?" Yet New York City now spends as much as $130,000 a year per child in a secure juvenile detention center. In California things have gotten so bad that a class-action lawsuit has been filed on behalf of one million poor children forced to attend crumbling schools with no books, no chalk, no working bathrooms—but plenty of rats and roaches.

To make this case, and reverse this inequity, the Democratic candidate will have to use not just specific policy proposals but powerful imagery and compelling language to capture the public's imagination about the tragic circumstances that millions of children find themselves in. There is no excuse for the richest nation in the world to have one million homeless children. Or three million reported cases of abuse and neglect. Every year we hear the horror stories that touch our hearts and prick our conscience for a few moments: children chained to bedposts, foster kids starved by greedy parents, a little boy burned every day with an iron. But by calling these things "abuse," we begin to see them as an inevitable aberration in society. Little by little, we become inured to the reports. So instead of "neglect and abuse," I suggest we call them "torture." And that we refuse to accept it.

George Bush told us again and again that we invaded Iraq

to stop Saddam Hussein from torturing his own people. Well, a million children are tortured in this country every year. Do we need satellite photos and intelligence reports before we stop leaving them in imminent danger of being tortured again? George Bush spent billions of dollars to stop torture in Iraq. But he hasn't done anything to stop the suffering here. His opponent must.

5. BREAK DOWN BARRIERS AND CREATE NEW OPPORTUNITIES IN EDUCATION

John Edwards has said, "At the heart of the American dream there's a simple bargain: if you work hard and play by the rules, America will give you the chance to build a better future for you and your children. Now as never before, education is the key to that opportunity." The greatest betrayal of the Bush years is that this promise has been broken; government is not holding up its end of the bargain.

Bush's opponent must make a full frontal assault on the deeply fraudulent No Child Left Behind Act. The problem is not, as some have said, that the act needs more funding to be properly implemented, although the administration's scheme to take credit for the bill without providing the funds to pay for it is another example of the classic Bush bait and switch. The problem is that the No Child Left Behind Act is rotten at its core because it is based on false assumptions.

The bill requires that all children attending schools that have been failing for two years be given the chance to move to a better school. But good public schools are bursting at the seams. And even before the president underfunded the act by $9.4 billion, there were no provisions in the legislation to fulfill the promise of parental choice that was at the heart of the bill. Parents have been given a choice but nothing to choose from.

The fallback is itself another false promise. After a student has been in a failing school for three years, the act makes federal money available to the child's parents for "supplemental education services" such as private tutoring. The idea, I guess, is "If our schools can't teach your kids, maybe you can find somebody who can." But with the resources the bill provides the student would only be able to see a tutor less than once a week—hardly enough to offset the flaws and weaknesses of a failing school. Yet the bill does demand that schools spend their resources to test students again and again and again so that each year both the child and the parents will be painfully reminded just how badly the child is failing—and being failed.

That's pretty much the extent of the impact the No Child Left Behind Act will have on the lives of millions of children. But at least the Washington establishment can move on, satisfied that they've "done" education.

We must reverse the slide of resources away from the areas of greatest need, both in K-12 schools and college education. In his 2005 budget, Bush freezes Pell Grants for our nation's poorest college students and completely eliminates funding for thirty-eight education programs. This administration has been punitive toward afterschool programs for low-income children, Even Start (a program that provides literacy help to at-risk children), mentorship programs, the Dropout Prevention Program, and programs providing rehabilitation for juvenile offenders. Even though the president has been stressing the goal of closing the achievement gap between low- and high-income children, his administration has cut programs intended to improve teacher quality in low-income neighborhoods. The bitter irony here is that federal money invested in teacher education pays enormous dividends in the near and the long term. The government should pay the entire tuition of any student who will train to be a teacher and then commit to working for five years in a community with a teacher shortage. It will be worth every penny.

While the oxygen of the reform debate is being absorbed by the flashy sideshow of the controversial issue of vouchers, almost 600,000 students nationwide are taking part in an education innovation that is flourishing across the land: public charter schools. The nominee needs to make the expansion of these schools central to his education agenda, especially since they are proving particularly successful in helping low-income, at-risk students and bringing much-needed innovation to a calcified public education system.

Part of the ongoing War on the Poor (did I mention that the rich are winning?) is the dispiriting fact that cuts in higher education are much deeper in community colleges—which primarily serve lower-income Americans—than they are in the wealthiest private colleges. Ivy League schools, for instance, receive between five and eight times the national average in public funds to pay for work/study programs—ridiculous when you consider how many fewer members of the Yale student body need work/study aid than students at a two-year college serving low-income communities.

In California, students at Stanford, one of the most richly endowed universities in the country, receive almost one hundred times as much federal money to help them through college as students at the California State University at Fresno, many of whom are children of local farmworkers. This kind of disparity too often makes a community college degree—the only opportunity for higher education for millions of Americans—prohibitively expensive.

There's certainly no shortage of talk about education. Politicians and bureaucrats seem willing to endlessly tinker with our education system, making small, incremental changes. But parents and their kids have a vastly different timetable. Rochelle Mackabee, a mother who moved her son to View Park Preparatory Charter School in Los Angeles, put it this way: "I was sitting in a school meeting, listening to teachers and the principal talk about how they weren't going to be able to improve reading and math scores until years down the road. And I turned to a friend of mine and said, 'Our kids will be in high school before they turn things around. We have to get out of here.' And we did."

The American Dream tarnishes when the most basic tool for advancement is effectively out of reach. While education is primarily a state issue, the Democratic nominee must use his bully pulpit to set priorities and commit to fighting any cuts in spending that disproportionately affect poorer Americans.

6. CALL A TRUCE IN THE DRUG WAR

The question of how to handle the racial and economic injustice of our government's failed war on drugs has become an electrified third rail of American politics—a subject neither party is willing to touch for fear of being incinerated on contact. Meanwhile, the drug war's distorted priorities are playing a major role in the division of America into two nations: one getting away with so-called youthful indiscretions, the other locked away, disenfranchised for life. One primarily white, the other largely black and brown. One affluent, the other shut down and shut out from living the American Dream.

The consequences of a drug policy driven by fear and denial are alarming: America now has more people living behind bars than any other country—over 2 million crowd our nation's jails and prisons (an additional 4 million are under some form of correctional supervision, including probation and parole). A disproportionate number of these Americans are people of color. Despite the fact that the same percentage of whites use drugs as blacks, black men are jailed ten times more often than white men. As a result, one out of seven black males in their late twenties is sitting in jail right now. This sorry state of affairs will never change until our political leaders stop trying to score easy PR points off the drug war—at the expense of the poor and minorities—desperately vying to be seen by voters as the toughest on crime.

The Democratic nominee must take the lead on this issue. He must promise to put an end to America's crippling addiction to the war on drugs and to put those resources to work where they're desperately needed—in protecting our inner-city streets from random violence. By doing so he will show that the Democratic Party has finally come of age, and he will put President Bush squarely on his heels—forced to defend the drug war's hypocrisy, its far-reaching injustice, and its disgraceful waste of time, talent, and treasure.

A DRUG WAR SPEECH FOR THE DEMOCRATIC NOMINEE

My fellow Americans, I want to talk to you about matters of war and peace. But not about the war in Iraq. No, today I want to talk to you about another destructive war—this one being waged here at home. I want to talk to you about our government's war on drugs—a $40 billion-a-year disaster whose victims can be found scattered across the American landscape.

This war on drugs has turned into a war on people of color—with mandatory minimum sentences, unfair powder and crack cocaine differentials, and 46 percent more black young people incarcerated on drug charges than white ones. Yet President Bush, John Ashcroft, and their drug czar steadfastly refuse to admit that the drug war has failed to stem the tide of drug use in America and that it's driving our country into an ever-tightening state of lockdown—with two million people behind bars.

The truth is that despite the hundreds of billions of dollars spent since Richard Nixon first declared war on drugs in 1971, drug use is soaring among our nation's young. Over 10 percent of children twelve to seventeen were using drugs in 2002, more than double the number ten years earlier.

And what has been this administration's most notable response? TV ads painting millions of American kids as terrorists. In the world according to Bush and Ashcroft, the kid smoking a joint at a party is the moral equivalent of Osama bin Laden.

It's time to admit the obvious: not only has the drug war failed, it's wildly illogical. Just think: even though drug treatment has been proven over and over again to be a far more cost-effective way of fighting drug use, the Bush administration continues to pour most of its resources into wasteful drug raids and interdiction.

Not only doesn't this make sense, it doesn't make dollars and cents. The average cost of maintaining a prison inmate is about $30,000 a year. The average cost of a drug treatment program is about $4,000. But we're still putting only 20 percent of our federal drug-fighting resources toward treatment. As a result, almost 4 million addicts are not receiving the treatment they desperately need. And it's not as if the American people have to be convinced about what's more effective. An overwhelming majority of Americans say they favor treatment over prison for those convicted of drug possession. This pathological prioritization of the drug war has crowded out far more pressing concerns—including even the war on terror.

Before September 11, more than twice as many FBI agents were assigned to fighting drugs as to fighting terrorists, and a far greater amount of the FBI's resources was dedicated to the war on drugs. But beyond the allocation of money and manpower, counterterrorism units were treated like the bureau's ugly stepchildren, looked down upon by FBI management because they weren't making the kind of high-profile arrests that spruce up a supervisor's résumé and make the evening news. Let's face it, canvassing flight schools in search of suspicious students is nowhere near as sexy as one of those big drug busts with the bags of coke or bales of pot piled high for the cameras.

It's now painfully clear that there were terror warning signs aplenty before September 11, but they were disregarded by distracted FBI officials who had their eyes on a very different prize. And it isn't just the FBI. This drug warrior mind-set infects the entire law enforcement community, starting at the top. As soon as he was confirmed as attorney general, John Ashcroft jumped right in. "I want to escalate the war on drugs," he said. "I want to renew it. I want to refresh it." He has been true to his word, waging a crusade against medical marijuana clubs in California, even though it is one of twelve states that have decriminalized the use of pot for medical purposes.

And even after the FBI's highly touted reorganization in 2002, which included the reassignment of four hundred narcotics agents to counterterrorism, there are still over two thousand agents spending their valuable time and energy fighting a fruitless drug war.

Another tragic consequence of this war is the way it has been used to perpetuate the divisions in our country. Look at Rush Limbaugh, who serviced his drug habit with illegally procured prescription drugs, went into rehab for six weeks, and now is back on his radio show as though nothing has happened. Or take Noelle Bush. While as a parent I can empathize with what her family went through, it cannot be denied that she has been given every break in the book—and then some. On the other hand, as governor of Florida, her father has made it harder for others in her position to get the help they need by cutting the budgets of drug treatment and drug court programs in his state. He has also actively opposed a ballot initiative that would send nonviolent drug offenders into treatment instead of jail. I guess what's good for the goose gets the gander locked away. The lesson is, if you're gonna get caught doing drugs, make sure your father is the governor.

Of course, Jeb Bush's wildly inconsistent attitude on the issue—treatment and privacy for his daughter, incarceration and public humiliation for everyone else—

is part and parcel of the galling hypocrisy that infects America's insane drug war on every level. And so is Rush Limbaugh's case. A glaring double standard has been a hallmark of our nation's drug policy for decades. It's why African Americans make up only 13 percent of the country's drug users but 55 percent of those convicted of drug possession and 74 percent of those sent to jail on possession charges.

If America's drug laws were applied consistently, Jeb Bush and his family would be evicted from their publicly funded digs, just as people living in public housing can be thrown out of their homes if any household member or guest is found using drugs—even if the drug use happened someplace other than in the housing project. And Noelle could find herself joining the tens of thousands of young people unable to get a college education because of a provision in the Higher Education Act that denies financial aid to students convicted of possessing illegal drugs.

It's not surprising that poor kids are routinely sent to jail while rich kids are given a slap on the wrist and a ticket to rehab, or that poor parents are thrown out of their houses while powerful parents are given our sympathy and understanding. But it's unjust. Unfortunately, despite these two cases hitting very close to the White House, neither Noelle Bush's nor Rush Limbaugh's experiences have opened President Bush's mind and heart enough to force him to rethink his ruinous drug policy.

So we've got to do it for him—by voting him out of office.

If elected, my administration will no longer continue leading this country down a path clearly heading in the

> wrong direction. We know what works—treatment. And we know what doesn't work—incarceration. We just need the political will to turn what we know to be true into public policy. That's the kind of leadership I intend to provide.
>
> The government's war on drugs has become a war on its own people. It's well past time for the American people to sue for peace.

7. SECURE THE HOMELAND FIRST

Homeland Security has become the Bush administration's ugly stepchild compared with favored son Iraq. The White House has put the safety of all Americans at risk while claiming to hold our security as its highest priority. It seems elementary that, after September 11, security measures would have been instituted to create a safety cordon around vulnerable ports, airports, and nuclear facilities. Instead, a muckraking college student was able to plant box cutters, modeling clay, bleach, and matches on two airliners in September 2003.

Meanwhile some intrepid *ABC News* reporters were able to ship fifteen pounds of depleted uranium (the fact that they were able to obtain depleted uranium is alarming in and of itself) to Los Angeles from Al Qaeda–infested Indonesia without detection. The response of the Homeland Security Department was to threaten ABC with smuggling charges.

And experts from the Department of Energy report that sensitive nuclear facilities like the Los Alamos National Laboratory have repeatedly proven vulnerable to mock terrorist attacks, despite having received advance warning of the im-

Crime going up under a Republican administration strikes at the core idea of Bush as the great protector. I can hear the TV spot: "Are you really safer now than you were four years ago?"

pending assaults. "In more than 50 percent of our tests at the Los Alamos facility," Rich Lavernier, a Department of Energy security specialist, reported, "we got in, captured the plutonium, got out again, and, in some cases, didn't fire a shot, because we didn't encounter any guards." Some of the homeland security gaps verge on the comical—at least for those with a morbid sense of humor. Keys, not metaphorical ones, but actual keys, to sensitive facilities across the country are missing or lost and no one seems to know if they have fallen into the hands of Al Qaeda or just between the couch cushions. Among the lost keys are those that open doors at Lawrence Livermore Laboratory, the Sandia National Labs in New Mexico, and the secret installation in Tennessee known as "Y-12" where bomb-grade uranium is processed. The managers of "Y-12," the "Fort Knox of highly enriched uranium," have reported that more than 200 keys are missing.

Seaports and commercial ships continue to remain wide open to terrorists along with the millions of tons of cargo that pass through them daily. By the deadline of December 31, 2003, only half of the ships and a quarter of the ports required by the Coast Guard to submit security plans had done so. To implement these plans when and if they are ever finalized, will cost, according to the Coast Guard, more than $7 billion. But, up through the end of 2003, the Bush administration had spent less than $400 million on port security.

The Environmental Protection Agency has listed 123 chemical manufacturers, users, and storage sites that, if attacked, could produce a death toll of over 1 million people. There are another 700 sites with the potential to cause a death toll of more than 100,000. All of these are woefully undersecured. John DePasquale, the former head of security for Georgia Pacific, offers this pungent analysis, "Security at a 7-Eleven after midnight is better than at a plant with a 90-ton vessel of chlorine. A guy with a suitcase full of explosives can kill tens of thousands of people and we're not doing anything about it."

These failures have to be contrasted with a homeland security strategy that really protects the homeland, starting with a multibillion-dollar homeland security trust fund to provide state and local governments with the resources they need to keep our people safe.

First, the ridiculous color-coded defense alert system must be drastically overhauled so that it does something more than efficiently terrify the public. People need to be told what they can do when the alert status changes so that our ever-growing sense of anxiety does not afford the terrorists even a small victory. (Shared intelligence, improved by rebuilding our relationships with new and old allies, is another key to our security, lost like those at Lawrence Livermore.)

Equally important to our security is stopping the ongoing civil war being waged in the streets of our inner cities. Homeland security must be more than just an antiterrorist grab bag. It must also acknowledge the mayhem being perpetrated by evildoers here at home. We need more funding for neighborhood watch groups to increase their number and improve their training. And we need to recognize that gang violence is a byproduct of our failed drug policy and our failing criminal justice system, which returns prisoners to the streets more calloused and dangerous than when they were incarcerated.

While the macho view of leadership takes us on distracting and destructive adventures abroad, the Democratic nominee must put forward a different vision that starts with our safety here at home.

8. BE A LEADER, NOT A BULLY

Wesley Clark described our current foreign policy low this
way: "The Bush administration has squandered in two years
the moral authority America spent generations building. It
started when President Bush said to the world, 'You're either
with us or against us.' As a result, even some of those who
were with us are now against us. And those, like Tony Blair,
who are still with us pay a political price for it. America is
hurt as well. We are less secure when our friends suffer for
standing by our side. With fewer partners, we are left to meet
dangers alone."

But it's not just the opposition party that's questioning the
president's prosecution of the war on terror. A report pub-
lished by the Army War College in January should be required
reading for every voter who is still under the illusion that Bush
is the answer to our national security concerns: "The global
war on terrorism as presently defined and conducted is strate-
gically unfocused, promises much more than it can deliver,
and threatens to dissipate U.S. military and other resources in
an endless and hopeless search for absolute security. . . . The
United States may be able to defeat, even destroy, Al Qaeda,
but it cannot rid the world of terrorism, much less evil."

To counter the Bush administration's unilateralism and
preemptive defense strategy, the Democratic standard-bearer
will have to strengthen old alliances and build new ones by
consulting and acting in concert with other countries and the
United Nations. He must promise to honor and abide by international laws and treaties. And, in the hope of being respected in return, must respect other nations and cultures.

While this may sound like an invitation to share an international group hug, it is, in fact, the smartest way to fight terrorism when the most potent weapon we have against it is information. And nothing shuts down channels of information more quickly than the hostility toward America that is festering around the world. As Secretary of Offense Rumsfeld has acknowledged, the danger at the moment is that for every terrorist we eliminate, we create ten more to take his place alongside those minted afresh every day by the madrassa schools. We don't need to give the sponsors any unnecessary recruiting help. We must lead the world, not bully it, and part of our leadership must be honoring international treaties, like Kyoto and the international trade agreements that determine behavior for nations the same way laws do for individuals. America's word must be good.

A truly strong America can afford to recognize the value of allies. It's only the blustering America of George Bush that, as Dick Gephardt put it, treats "our own allies like so many flies on the American windshield" and tries to convince the world we can go it alone.

9. RESTORE INTEGRITY TO THE POLITICAL PROCESS

The American political system has turned clinically dysfunctional. Both parties are in deep—but very well funded—denial about the state of modern America. Their addiction to ever-greater doses of campaign cash clouds their ability to discern the true crises in the society they claim to lead. And while both Republicans and Democrats pay focus group–tested lip service to campaign finance reform, they collude and conspire not only to defend the corrupt status quo but to break new records in gobbling up money and undermining our democracy.

Even as less than one percent of the population, the wealthiest among us, now provides most campaign contributions, our mainstream politicians continue to deny that a leveraged buyout of our political system is well under way. The truth is that our representative republic has been supplanted by a permanent and unaccountable government of powerful special interests.

The only tool we have to fix the problems of this country—the democratic process—is itself broken. Which is why nothing will fundamentally change until we solve the problem of money in politics. We must break the grip of what campaign finance reform champion John McCain has called the "iron triangle" of lobbyists, big money, and legislation, and the only way to do that is to overhaul the way we finance our campaigns. The most effective means for restoring the integrity of our electoral process, and repairing the public's tattered faith in its elected representatives, is through the full public financing of political campaigns. It's the mother of all reforms: the one reform that makes all other reforms possible. After all, he who pays the piper calls the tune. If someone's going to own the politicians, it might as well be the American people.

There are three recurring complaints you hear about our political system: campaigns cost too much; special interests have too much influence; and far too many good people choose not to run simply because they don't want to spend hours each day begging for money. Full public financing of elections addresses every one of these core problems: it lowers campaign spending, it breaks the direct link between special interest donors and elected officials, it levels the playing field so that good people have a viable chance of winning, and it ends the money chase for those running and those already in office. Think of it: No hard money, no soft money, no endless dialing for dollars, no quid pro dough deals. No more lobbyists sitting in House and Senate offices literally writing their own loopholes into law. No more hidden corporate welfare surprises buried in huge spending bills. No more dangerous relaxation in safety and regulatory standards that can be—but rarely are—traced to campaign donations. Just candidates and elected officials beholden to no one but the voters. The good news is, the Clean Money/Clean Elections concept is not some pie-in-the-sky fantasy. It's already the law in five states, and in the two states where it's fully implemented, Maine and Arizona, the results have been inspiring: more people running for office, more competition, more contested races, more women and minorities running, and a more independent pool of legislators elected.

In Maine, 55 percent of the state house and 77 percent of the state senate were publicly financed candidates. As a result, the people of that state are getting more independent leadership: Maine was the first state to pass universal health care and the first to win a major victory over the drug companies on the issue of bringing down exorbitant prescription drug prices. In Arizona, nine out of the top eleven statewide officials, including Janet Napolitano, America's first-ever Clean Money governor, were elected in 2002 without a single special interest donation. It's time to unprivatize our public policy. Especially now that the relationship between those in power and those seeking to influence them is becoming cozier by the day as more and more public servants pass through the revolving door connecting Capitol Hill and K Street. Howard Dean laid out a detailed menu of political reforms, including a promise to fix the presidential public financing system by increasing the amount in public funds candidates can qualify for and raising the spending limits for primary candidates, who often need more resources to introduce themselves and their positions to voters. He also proposed a public financing option for all federal campaigns, not just presidential elections.

In addition, TV and radio stations must be required to offer free air time to candidates and the toothless Federal Election Commission must be made more muscular and more independent. Instant runoff voting, Internet voting and nonpartisan redistricting legislation are all essential reforms if we are to put our democracy back in the hands of the people.

If the Democratic nominee really wants to show that he is on the side of the people—not the moneyed interests that currently dominate our politics—he must remind our nation that if you have a lot of money, you should be able to buy a shiny new car, a cool flat-screen TV, or a vacation home in Aspen. But you shouldn't be able to buy political power. Democracy should be a marketplace of ideas, but it should not be for sale.

10. PUT PEOPLE ABOVE CORPORATE PROFITS

Despite a tidal wave of corporate scandals, trillions of dollars in market value lost on Wall Street, and hundreds of thousands of jobs shipped overseas never to return, the corporate-financed fanatics of the GOP have somehow managed to convince the nation that whatever is good for business is good for America because—all together now—businesses create jobs. That's why, the reasoning goes, we can't afford to upset corporate America by closing tax loopholes, putting an end to outrageous offshore tax shelters, or even punishing those found guilty of fraud and abuse. Instead, we've been terrified into timorously accepting that the road to prosperity must, inevitably, be paved with craven concessions to companies that too often reward us with nothing more than rapacious greed and corruption. On top of it, as we've learned, especially in the Bush years, not all jobs are created equal and not all jobs are created here.

The Democratic nominee has got to stand up and say, "Enough is enough." This is exactly what John Kerry did in his stump speech: "I have a message for the influence peddlers, for the polluters, the HMOs, the drug companies, big oil, and all the special interests who now call the White House home. We're coming. You're going. And don't let the door hit you on the way out." And he went on to be specific about building a prosperity "where we shut down every tax loophole, every benefit, and every reward for any Benedict Arnold CEO or company that sends jobs and profits overseas." Putting an end to offshore tax havens is a perfect issue for Kerry to spotlight and use to capture the backing of the largest possible body of supporters, namely taxpayers.

In this time of soaring deficits, corporations use shelters to continue to cheat the government and the public out of $70 billion a year, while hardworking Americans are forced to dig deeper and deeper into their own pockets to make up the difference. It's the kind of issue that so epitomizes the unfairness of the current system, it sticks in people's throats. You want to talk to people about being unpatriotic, Mr. President? This is it.

The Democratic nominee should make an unequivocal pledge: "It will be a hard and fast rule of my administration that any company that reincorporates offshore or makes use of offshore tax shelters in order to avoid paying its fair share will not be able to do business with the U.S. government. Period." You want to move your "headquarters" to Bermuda? Fine. Enjoy the trip. But don't continue to use our tax dollars and infrastructure to pad your bottom line.

That means that a company like Halliburton, which has forty-four subsidiaries in offshore tax havens, would not have been eligible to receive those multibillion-dollar, no-bid contracts to rebuild Iraq. Putting this issue on the front burner would certainly make for a wonderful talking point during the upcoming vice-presidential debates with Dick Cheney.

A SPEECH ON CORPORATE RESPONSIBILITY FOR THE DEMOCRATIC NOMINEE

My fellow Americans, when he could no longer ignore the tidal wave of corporate scandals that washed up on the front lawn of the White House, President Bush fell back on his tried-and-true formula of PR politics: have a big photo op, declare victory, move on, and hope the public will consider the problem solved. And so he smiled for the cameras, signed the ironically named Corporate Responsibility Act into law, vowed "No more easy money for corporate criminals, just hard time," and acted as if the Enron, WorldCom, and Global Crossing scandals were now a thing of the past. Corporate reform was another "mission accomplished."

But a quick survey of the news since that day in July 2002 reveals that it's actually been monkey business as usual on Wall Street: Freddie Mac is under investigation for accounting irregularities, yet its chairman and CEO walked away with a severance package worth millions; Boeing is the subject of Pentagon and Justice Department probes of a $21 billion deal negotiated by a Pentagon employee while she was also negotiating her next job with Boeing; and Guidant admits it lied to the government and hid thousands of serious health problems, including twelve deaths, caused by one of its products. Is this America or a banana republic?

You'd think this country's CEOs would have gotten the message. They have, after all, in the course of the last few years gone from American Idols to America's Most Wanted. But no matter how battered their reputations, they still appear determined to rescue themselves instead of their sinking ships. For today's captains of industry, the maxim in a crisis seems to be "To hell with the women and children, save the lifeboats for us!" In the clubby confines of America's boardrooms, the sky is the limit. Compensation committees are working overtime coming up with ever more creative—and devious—ways to boost the earnings of top executives. From 1990 to 2002, according to the *Los Angeles Times*, Michael Eisner, CEO of Disney, made over $800 million while Disney's shareholders made less than if they had invested in treasury bonds.

The picture is even bleaker for those down on the factory floor or crammed inside an office cubicle, where ordinary workers are seeing their pension plans slashed or eliminated altogether. Less than half of those currently employed in the private sector have any kind of pension coverage. And 40 percent of companies that do offer pension plans are exploring ways to reduce them. Companies are also cutting back on matching contributions to their employees' 401(k) accounts. Some, like Ford, Goodyear Tire, and Charles Schwab, have decided to completely do away with matching contributions. Even those workers who are able to hang on to their matching contributions can't rest easy: it turns out that the vast majority of corporate pension funds are critically underfunded. In fact, close to 90 percent of the S&P 500 companies that offer traditional pension plans are running a deficit.

In just a few short years, the nest eggs of American workers have gone from sunny side up to seriously scrambled. Even as our country has taken steps to abolish welfare for those at the bottom, we've allowed the high-end corporate class to weave a giant safety net for its members. Is this corporate welfare really any different or less costly than the kind Republicans inveigh against? To use the familiar argument of the GOP: how are we ever going to get corporations to act responsibly when we keep rewarding them for irresponsibility? To say nothing of criminality. They give the "free market" a lot of lip service. But, in the end, it's the business class they really serve.

Last year, corporate welfare cost taxpayers $175 billion, leading to the lowest level in corporate income tax as a percentage of GDP since the early 1980s—only 1.2 percent. Even at a time of soaring deficits, we continue to allow over a million corporations and wealthy individuals to cheat the public out of billions of dollars a year by hiding their profits in offshore subsidiaries.

This accounting sleight-of-hand is no small matter: it's depriving the U.S. Treasury of billions of dollars a year.

Even more galling, after ripping off taxpayers, many of these companies are being rewarded with massive federal contracts. Scandal-tainted Tyco, for instance, pocketed $1 billion in public money in 2001 while evading $400 million in taxes by opening up a P.O. box "headquarters" in sunny Bermuda.

Taxpayers are also taking it in the wallet on the local level where, all across the country, local governments, facing the biggest budget crisis since the Great Depression, are being forced to slash programs and cut services. Do you think there might be a connection between these cuts and the fact that corporations are currently turning over 30 percent less of their profits to the taxman than they did twenty years ago? You can bet your vanishing afterschool care, prenatal health program, and local law enforcement service there is.

Corporate tax shelters robbed states of $12.4 billion in desperately needed revenues in 2001. In order to really understand the devastating impact these lost revenues are having, let's put some flesh and bone on the numbers. In Florida, for instance, just $7.7 million would have saved a program that provided glasses and hearing aids for low-income people. In Oregon, $14.5 million would have saved the Hillsboro school district from having to shut its doors seventeen days early last year. In Kentucky, $2.6 million would have allowed Governor Patton to leave behind bars the 883 prison inmates he released early in a desperate effort to balance the state's budget. There can be no doubt that the twenty-five-year-old woman who was raped by one of these freed inmates just three days after his release would consider that $2.6 million money very well spent.

The list goes on and on. Vital programs and services cut or eliminated that could have been saved had corporate America just done the right thing and paid what it owed.

Market forces have no intrinsically moral direction, which is why, before he wrote *The Wealth of Nations,* Adam Smith wrote *The Theory of Moral Sentiments.* Ethics should take precedence over economics. But it often doesn't. We know this because we've seen the results of capitalism without conscience: the pollution of the air we breathe, the water we drink, and the food we eat; the endangerment of workers; and the sale of dangerous products, from cars to toys to drugs—all in pursuit of ever-greater profits. The public good is auctioned off to the highest bidder.

A magnetic compass should always point north; a moral compass should always point out that cheating and fraud are dead wrong. But our country's self-appointed morality czars have been deafeningly silent on this kind of economic indecency. How screwed up are the priorities of our business leaders? Well, Adelphia's John Rigas considered himself so moral that he refused to carry the Playboy Channel on his cable systems, but thought nothing of looting $3.1 billion from his company's coffers. Or look at Wal-Mart, pulling three men's magazines off the shelf at the same time that it treats women like second-class citizens, fires workers who try to unionize, and is being sued in thirty states for refusing to pay overtime.

Are scantily-clad girls more immoral than cheating your workers? It's time for our business and political leaders to expand morality beyond sex and drugs to include lying, hypocrisy, and callous indifference to those

Do you want to live in a country where our leaders respect us enough to tell us the truth?

Do you want to create a country where hard-working Americans are put first—and 'trickle-up' not 'trickle-down' is the economic order of the day?

Do you want to create a country where the rules are the same for the rich as for the poor?

in need. That is the kind of leadership we must have if
we're ever going to eradicate the culture of greed, corruption, and unethical behavior that has come to dominate both Wall Street and Washington. If you give me
the chance, that is precisely the kind of leadership I in-
tend to provide.

Good night, and God bless America.

RALLYING CALL

Just after Christmas, I was having dinner at a noisy Japanese
restaurant in New York with one of my daughters and some
close friends from Washington. Their eleven-year-old son is
passionately committed to George Bush's reelection. Constantine engaged me in debate with an enthusiasm I could
only admire.

"Arianna," he said with the enchanting optimism of a
Greek-American eleven-year-old, "I'm going to convince you
that you should support Bush in November. Here are two
questions you have to answer. The first question is: Are you
for more or less taxes? The second question is: Do you want
to fight the war on terrorism?"

My first thought was, hats off to George Bush. He and his
team have done such a masterful job in framing the 2004
election that even an eleven-year-old can be perfectly on message. The Democrats cannot win in November if that remains
the framework for the election.

There are many rational answers to Constantine's questions.
As far as taxes are concerned:

"There is no free lunch. When the federal government

cuts taxes, state and local governments increase them or cut services to make up the shortfall."

"Nobody likes taxes, but everyone likes what they pay for: police protection, schools, hospitals, roads."

"We Americans consider ourselves a fair people, and yet George Bush is shifting the tax burden from wealthy people, who are now being taxed less, to working people, who are now being taxed more."

And as for the war on terror:

"I'm all for fighting the war on terror. But I can't for the life of me figure out why the war on terror is being fought in Iraq."

"To win the war on terror we need friends and partners, not a growing list of enemies."

"President Bush has been paying a lot of lip service to the war on terror, but I'm not feeling safer yet. Are you?"

But that's still accepting the Bush framework. And that's not enough. We need to change the questions, not just give the correct answers. And the questions have to be about what kind of America we want to live in.

So, this is what I would ask Constantine—and Americans of all ages:

"Do you want to create an America where your taxes guarantee you a safe neighborhood, a good school, health care, and a safety net if you stumble?"

"Do you want to be safe in your own country or do you want to waste precious lives and resources on military adventurism?"

Up to now, the Democratic Party framing has been, "We too can be as good as the president at fighting terrorism." The new Democratic leader has to make clear that the war in Iraq has distracted America from fighting the war on terrorism and made anti-Americanism much more intense, especially among young Arabs, from whom so many terrorists are drawn.

We are at a watershed moment in American politics. On the one hand we have the Cheshire cats—smiling, well-funded marquee men like George Bush and Arnold Schwarzenegger. The Republican figureheads have become more finely chiseled, and harder to beat. Which is why Bush's opponent must have as a goal not just to be president but to transform the Democratic Party and, in the process, American politics. Those are big dreams, but anything smaller guarantees the reelection of George Bush. And that would spell not just deterioration but disaster for decades to come.

If the Democrats want to reclaim the White House, they must first reclaim the language of patriotism and the language of responsibility. They have to wrestle the flag from the hands of the Republicans who have desecrated it by using it to advance their own tribal interests. And they have to take back "responsibility" from the grossly irresponsible GOP that has saddled our children with a national debt that will reach $12 trillion over the next ten years.

United behind their new leader, the Democrats can be a party for all Americans, and help restore sanity and soul to our political life. The vision of New Responsibility challenges us to live by the values that we saw at work in this country after September 11—accepting responsibility not just for ourselves and our immediate family but for everyone who needs care in our community.

"In every dark hour of our national life," Franklin Roosevelt said, "a leadership of frankness and vigor has met with that understanding and support of the people themselves which is essential to victory." And now it is the people who need to take the lead, and ask themselves, each other, and the man who would be president some tough questions—and not accept commencement speech answers:

"Do you want to create a country where opportunity is real for everyone—and not just the economic elite?"

"Do you want to live in a country where our leaders respect us enough to tell us the truth?"

"Do you want to create a country where programs for the most vulnerable are not the first to be cut when times are tough?"

"Do you want to live in a country that not only produces over $10 trillion of wealth a year, but makes the kind of investments in health and education that leave us all stronger?"

"Do you want to live in a country where the number of poor people is getting smaller rather than larger?"

"Do you want to create a country where hard-working Americans are put first—and 'trickle-up' not 'trickle-down' is the economic order of the day?"

"Do you want to live in a country where huge industrial companies can't buy the right to pollute our air and water?"

"Do you want to create a country where the rules are the same for the rich as for the poor?"

It is time for everyone who has not already done so to answer the call to action. And to say "enough" to both the fanatics and the fools.

ACKNOWLEDGMENTS

Maybe it's because I've finally learned something about book writing—this is, after all, my tenth book—or maybe it's because this is the best support team I've ever been blessed with, but the writing of this book has been remarkably angst-free. Even though the deadline was the toughest I've ever had—thanks to spending seven weeks of the time I was given to write it running for governor. There are, I can tell you, easier ways to put off writing.

On the other hand, there was something wonderfully liberating about going from 4 AM make-up calls for early morning TV shows during the campaign to writing at my desk in sweats and no make-up, a fire burning in the study, and my kids dashing in and out after school.

But I couldn't have done it without such a great team. It was fabulous and far-flung—from Brazil, where Billy Kimball continued to offer his brilliant editorial and creative guidance even as he was trying to make a good impression on his future wife's Brazilian family; to Wilmington, North Carolina, where I found crack researcher Roey Rosenblith when I spoke at his university; to Harvard, where I drafted Andy Barr and Ryan Cunningham, two members of TeamFranken (Al Franken's research squad), to sift through FDR speeches and Roman history; to New York, where Bess McKinney and Emily Lodish burned the midnight oil and ran up my Lexis-Nexis account; to assorted parts of California, where Farrah Hassen, Drew Mendelson, and Chris Kyle gathered facts on everything from offshoring American jobs to "The Grapes of Wrath" (attentive readers will note that Steinbeck's classic ended up on the cutting room floor), and Jim Gilliam showed he could sniff out just about any fact and solve any technological crisis (including the time my 14-year-old daughter's iPod went on the fritz).

Masterminding this motley crew was my 22-year-old research director, Colin Sterling, who, as well as being a dead ringer for Harry Potter, turned out to be an unflappable and extremely organized manager.

Which brings me to my office, where Nicole Hastings and Noah Helpern, key members of the team, worked through long nights and even longer days, right up until—and, to be perfectly honest, past—the Sunday night deadline when the Miramax courier arrived at my door to pry the book out of my hands and take it to New York. And my thanks to Julie Ross, who kept my personal and professional lives going with aplomb—right down to distracting that courier for an extra few minutes so I could add one last sentence. Speaking of the courier, thank you, José Lopez, for being so patient!

To Roy Sekoff, the Wicked Wit of the West, my great friend and creative sounding board, my deepest gratitude.

Many thanks also to Stephen Sherrill and Jon Hotchkiss for all their editorial contributions, Micah Sifry for all his help navigating the vagaries of modern campaign finance laws, and Mark Valentine, who lent his important insights to the last section of the book. And to George Lakoff, my profound thanks for being such an inspiration and so generous with his time and his ideas.

For helping me pull together the Portraits of Struggle, I'm very grateful to Carol Biondi, Lisa Smithline, Karen Bass, Betty Reid Mandell, Tom Lengyel of "Faces of Change" at the Alliance for Children and Families, Madeline Janis-Aparicio and Danny Feingold of the Living Wage Campaign, Karen

Klestzick and Richard Murphy of the Community Food Re-
source Center, Eleiza Braun and Bernard Pollack of the AFL-
CIO, Sandra Bryant and Leticia Ortiz of All People's
Christian Center, Kathleen Miller and Dana Simon of SEIU
250, Barbara Clifton Zarate of Community Action in Marin,
Jacque McLaughlin of the Solano Kids Insurance Program at
the Solano Coalition for Better Health, Torie Osborn and
Margarita Ramirez of the Liberty Hill Foundation, Judith
Lichtman and Jodi Grant of the National Partnership for
Women and Families, LaDon James of the Center for Com-
munity Change, Nicole Russo-Okamato of United Way,
Kuliema Blueford of the Urban League, Karina Moreno of the
Children's Defense Fund, Jenny Kattlove of the Children's
Partnership, Jesse White of the National Coalition for the
Homeless, Gloria Martin of the Family Refuge Center, Aaron
Hecht of ACORN, and Kim Schaffer of the National Low In-
come Housing Coalition.

I can't say enough about my wonderful editor, Peter Guz-
zardi who, having edited Stephen Hawking, brought a serene
and time-bending quality to the urgency of getting rid of Bush
in 2004. Or about my amazing literary agent Richard Pine—
this is our fourth book together and it gets better and better.

To my speaking agent Carlton Sedgeley, and everyone at
Royce Carlton, thank you for your creative input on everything.

To all my friends who read different versions of the manu-
script and vastly improved it, I'll be forever grateful: Mary
Arno, Eli Attie, Lawrence Bender, Bob Borosage, Gary Bost-
wick, Robert Brody, Kimberly Brooks, Marc Cooper, Scott
Frank, Don Hazen, Alex Keyssar, Terrence McNally, John
Masius, Sara Nichols, Rob Reiner, Lynda Resnick, Stuart
Sender, Ralph Smith, Lynn Sweet, and especially Robert
Greenwald, who gave me invaluable feedback every step of

the way—even when he was almost e-mailless in Mexico, yet still found a way to get back to me

Thanks also to the team at ArnoldWatch.org—especially Jamie Court—for answering all my questions about our new governor's initiatives and contributors. To Tony Newman for answering all my drug war questions, Josh Bivens at the Economic Policy Institute for answering all my budgetary questions, Karen Marsh for answering all my questions about Citizen Corps, Charlie Cray for answering all my corporate corruption questions, Chief William Bratton for answering all my crime-related questions, and Arthur Schlesinger for—when everybody and everything else failed—answering a vexing question about Catholic theology. Thanks to Taryn Gaffney for the many ways she helped the manuscript see the light of day, and to Florie Brizel, Mary Daily, Kimberly Edds, and Sharon Suri for their exacting copy editing.

To the magical Miramax team, thank you, thank you, thank you! To Jonathan Burnham, whose brilliant insights shaped the book; to JillEllyn Riley and Kristin Powers for near-magically turning my words into the book you are now holding in record time; to Chuck Robertson and Daniel Adel for their impeccable design and art work; to Kathy Schneider, Hilary Bass, Bruce Mason, and Bumble Ward for all the imagination and energy they brought to the book's promotion; to Dev Chatillon for making sure all the legal "t"s and "i"s were crossed and dotted. And to Harvey Weinstein for telling me every time he saw me during the writing process: "What the hell are you doing here—you should be writing my book!"

To my incredible sister, always such a source of love and support, my love and gratitude.

The book is dedicated to my daughters, Christina and Isabella. I love you more than I can say, and I'm so proud of you.